BERNARD MALAMUD

A Study of the Short Fiction

Also available in Twayne's Studies in Short Fiction Series

Twayne's Studies in Short Fiction

Gordon Weaver, General Editor
Oklahoma State University

BERNARD MALAMUD
Photo by Janna Malamud

BERNARD
MALAMUD

A Study of the Short Fiction

Robert Solotaroff
University of Minnesota

TWAYNE PUBLISHERS • BOSTON
A Division of G. K. Hall & Co.

Copyright © 1989 by G. K. Hall & Co,
All rights reserved.
Published by Twayne Publishers
A Division of G. K. Hall & Co.
70 Lincoln Street, Boston, Massachusetts 02111

Twayne's Studies in Short Fiction Series, No. 8

Copyediting supervised by Barbara Sutton.
Book design by Janet Z. Reynolds.
Book production by Gabrielle B. McDonald.
Typeset in 10/12 Caslon by Compset, Inc.

Printed on permanent/durable acid-free paper
and bound in the United States of America.

Library of Congress Cataloging-in-Publication Data

Solotaroff, Robert.
    Bernard Malamud : a study of the short fiction / Robert
Solotaroff.
      p.   cm.—(Twayne's studies in short fiction ; no. 8)
    Bibliography: p.
    Includes index.
    ISBN 0-8057-8316-4
    1. Malamud, Bernard—Criticism and interpretation.   I. Title.
II. Series.
PS3563.A4Z89   1989   89-34183
813'.54—dc20   CIP

For TC and my children

From the crooked timbers of humanity,
no straight thing is made.

—Kant

Contents

Preface

Some of the best American short story writers of the twentieth century turned away from the form in the later stages of their careers to concentrate upon the novel. Hemingway published two stories—and embarrassing ones at that—in the last twenty-two years of his life. Only nine of the eighty-five stories that Faulkner published in his life came out in his last two decades. Even that apparently tireless generator of fine short stories, John Cheever, occupied himself much more with novels than with stories in his last two decades.

This was not the case with Bernard Malamud. Having started writing stories in the early 1920s, when he was eight or nine, he continued to write them until shortly before his death in 1986. By the time Philip Roth met Malamud, in February 1961, the older man had collected in *The Magic Barrel* (1958)—"four or five of the best American short stories I'd ever read (or ever will). The other stories weren't bad either."[1]

By early 1961 Malamud had published seventeen stories; twenty-eight[2] more were to appear before his death. About five of these— "Idiots First," "The Maid's Shoes," "Talking Horse," "The German Refugee" and "The Silver Crown"—also belong to the first tier of the American short story, and, as a body, the remainder are also a good deal better than "not bad." When, as a part of his career-long rhythm, Malamud completed a novel and turned again to writing stories, he brought impressive ingredients to the enterprise: an ear capable of capturing the most subtle dissonances of the troubled self—and occasionally the euphoric self; a strong sense of which characters belong in the same story; a powerful sense of compression; interpenetrating capacities for sympathy and for ferocity; an imagination which could—in a novel like *The Fixer*—convincingly create an early–twentieth-century Russia he had never seen but which, in his most characteristic stories, mixed the fantastic and the commonplace to produce a blend that was all his own.

More often than not, the locale for stories of this kind was *his* New York, a quasi-placeless, quasi-timeless blend of Manhattan and Eastern European ghettos and *shtetls* (villages or small towns largely inhabited by Jews). Here Malamud could successfully weld his ethical bent, his gift for fantasy, his modernist temperament, his sense of history, and his linguistic origins as a member of a largely Yiddish-speaking family. But continual or even consistent use of this terrain would have finally served to imprison Malamud's imagination, not to liberate it.

Consequently, I have paid particular attention to the other narrative efforts that accompanied and then succeeded the strategies that created the tales of what some readers, myself among them, call the folk ghetto: the locale of such great stories as "The First Seven Years," "Take Pity," "The Loan," "The Bill," "The Magic Barrel," "The Death of Me," "The Cost of Living," and "Idiots First." In other words, I have tried to trace the technical continuities, variations, and experiments in the stories as well as the thematic ones. And though my essay is not primarily a biographical one, I have tried in it and in part 2 to offer some sense of the life that created stories that, in Robert Alter's words, "will be read as long as anyone continues to care about American fiction written in the twentieth century."[3]

Since my space was limited and since I wanted to say something about each of the forty-five stories, I have had to scant my discussions of some of them. This is particularly the case with the stories that came out after *Idiots First* (1963) and that were not collected in *Pictures of Fidelman* (1969). I chose to devote more space to the stories of the first three collections (*The Magic Barrel* [1958], *Idiots First*, and *Pictures of Fidelman*) than to the uncollected ones or those in *Rembrandt's Hat* (1973) because I feel that the earlier stories are as a whole richer, more arresting. In fact, I feel that Malamud's talent was so relatively often at full flood in the first three collections that all aspects of these works are of unusual interest, as they always are if they are composed during a period when a gifted writer is at, or close to, the peak of his or her powers. Even issues like the reasons for a particular story's falling short take on some of this heightened importance.

But I have been skating too easily over *Pictures of Fidelman* by calling it a collection—though Malamud also used that designation on one occasion. More frequently he referred to *Pictures* as a novel, and though this is not the place to attempt conclusive definitions of such slippery words as *short story* and *novel*, *Pictures* has enough continuities for me to consider it a novel. But it is a novel composed of six stories, not six chapters. Since I feel that the first Fidelman story, "The Last Mohican" (collected first in *The Magic Barrel* and later in *Pictures of Fidel-*

man), is a *Magic Barrel* story in ways that the remaining five are not, I discuss it in the second chapter, which addresses the other stories of the first collection. Though the next two Fidelman stories ("Naked Nude" and "Still Life") were collected in *Idiots First*, I felt that they could be best handled if I considered them with the final three Fidelman stories in a separate chapter.

Robert Solotaroff

University of Minnesota

1. Philip Roth, "Pictures of Malamud," *New York Times Book Review*, 20 April 1986, 1.

2. My total does not include "A Long Ticket for Isaac," an early version of what became "Idiots First." See the Bibliography.

3. Robert Alter, "Ordinary Anguish," *New York Times Book Review*, 16 October 1983, 36.

Acknowledgments

The following are reprinted by permission of Farrar, Straus & Giroux, Inc.: Excerpts from *The Magic Barrel* by Bernard Malamud, copyright 1950, © 1959, 1961, 1962, 1963 by Bernard Malamud. Excerpts from *Idiots First* by Bernard Malamud, copyright 1950, © 1959, 1961, 1962, 1963 by Bernard Malamud. Excerpts from *Pictures of Fidelman* by Bernard Malamud, © 1958, 1962, 1963, 1968, 1969 by Bernard Malamud. Excerpts from *Rembrandt's Hat* by Bernard Malamud, © 1968, 1972, 1973 by Bernard Malamud. Excerpts from *The Stories of Bernard Malamud*, copyright 1950, 1951, 1952, 1954, © 1955, 1956, 1958, 1959, 1961, 1968, 1972, 1973, 1983 by Bernard Malamud; copyright renewed © 1977, 1979, 1980, 1982, 1983 by Bernard Malamud.

"Not Horror but 'Sadness'" by Joseph Wershba reprinted by permission of The New York Post Co., Inc., © 1988.

"The Writer's Task" by Bernard Malamud reprinted from *Writing in America* by John Fischer and Robert B. Silvers, © 1960 by Rutgers, the State University. Reprinted by permission of Rutgers University Press.

The following are reprinted by permission of the New York Times Co.: "Pictures of Malamud" by Philip Roth, © 1986; "Interview with Bernard Malamud" (13 October 1963), © 1963; "Theme, Content and the 'New Novel'" by Bernard Malamud, © 1967; "For Malamud It's Story" by Israel Shenker, © 1971; and "A Talk with the Novelist" by Ralph Tyler, © 1979.

"An Interview with Bernard Malamud" by Leslie Field and Joyce Field in *Bernard Malamud: A Collection of Critical Essays* reprinted by permission of the publisher, Prentice-Hall, Inc., Englewood Cliffs, N.J.

"Bernard Malamud: 'My Characters are God-Haunted'" by Curt Leviant (*Haddassah Magazine*, June 1974) reprinted by permission of *Haddassah Magazine* and the author.

"The Art of Fiction: Bernard Malamud" by Daniel Stern from *Writers at Work*, Sixth Series, ed. George Plimpton, © 1984 by The Paris Review, Inc. All rights reserved. Reprinted by permission of Viking Penguin, Inc.

Acknowledgments

"Long Work, Short Life" and "In Kew Gardens" by Bernard Malamud reprinted by permission of Russell & Volkening, Inc., as agents for the author; © 1987 by the Estate of Bernard Malamud, © 1985 by Bernard Malamud.

"Bernard Malamud's Fiction: The Old Life and the New" by Theodore Solotaroff reprinted from *Commentary* (March 1962) by permission of *Commentary* and the author. All rights reserved.

"The Bread of Tears: Malamud's 'The Loan'" by Charles E. May and "Myth on Myth: Bernard Malamud's 'The Talking Horse'" by Beth Burch and Paul W. Burch (both in *Studies in Short Fiction*) reprinted by permission of the president and fellows of Newberry College.

"Jewish Writers" by Mark Shechner in *Harvard Guide to Contemporary American Literature* reprinted by permission of Harvard University Press, © 1979 by the president and fellows of Harvard College.

"Remembrances: Bernard Malamud" by Cynthia Ozick reprinted by permission of the author.

Some of the paragraphs in part 1 appeared earlier in "Bernard Malamud" by Robert Solotaroff, adapted by permission of Charles Scribner's Sons, an imprint of Macmillan Publishing Company, from *American Writers*; © 1983 by Charles Scribner's Sons.

I would also like to thank Ann Malamud, Burt Rush, Miriam Lang, Doris Milman, and Tim Seldes both for their assistance and their permission to quote from letters and telephone conversations; Lawrence Lustig and Harry Schwartz for putting me in touch with Mr. Rush, Mrs. Lang, and Dr. Milman; Dan Flory, Arthur Geffen, Gordon Weaver, and Liz Traynor for editorial suggestions; and the Department of English of the University of Minnesota for the quarter leave that provided much of the time for the writing and editing of the book. Most of all I thank my wife, Claudia, for her patience and encouragement during the project.

Part 1

THE SHORT FICTION: AN ESSAY

Beginnings

In 1980 the sixty-six-year-old Bernard Malamud explained in this way why so much of his work has an unhappy cast to it: "People say I write so much about misery, but you write about what you write best[;] . . . As you are grooved, so you are grieved. One is conditioned early in family life to an interpretation of the world. And the grieving is that no matter how much happiness or success you collect, you cannot obliterate your early experience—diminished perhaps, it stays with you."[1]

His primary interpreters of the external world's resisting force, Max Malamud and Bertha Fidelman Malamud, met in America, though they both grew up in the Ukraine. They fled czarist Russia between 1905 and 1910, but the benign possibilities of the New World largely eluded them. By the time Bernard was five, in 1919, Max had managed to rise from his initial American job—driving a cart filled with dairy products—to becoming a partner in a "fancy grocery" in the pleasant part of the Borough Park section of Brooklyn, to which he had just moved with his family. But as was the case with Morris Bober, the doomed grocer in Malamud's second novel, *The Assistant*, Max was cheated by the partner and the store folded.

After a brief sojourn in Flatbush the family moved to a primarily gentile Brooklyn neighborhood: the northwestern part of the Gravesend section. Here Max opened a German-style delicatessen that, like the dying grocery of the novel, declined into a poor store, and here the family remained. Bernard moved out when he was twenty-five, but his father and mother went from the store to the grave and his younger brother Eugene went from the store to "a hard and lonely life"[2] that ended when he was still in his fifties. When Bernard and his brother were in grammar school, his mother began helping her husband in the store, particularly nights, when Bernard was left to run the streets.

To an extraordinary degree, Malamud's characters are often prisoners who are driven to sharp apprehension of the metaphorical or literal walls that enclose them. It is likely that the original, powerful prison-image grooved in the author's sensibility was the store in which his parents usually worked seven days a week, sixteen hours a day, closing only for occasional Jewish holidays. In spite of the 112-hour work week, the store usually offered only a marginal living: the times when business was good were brief, and there were stretches of months or years when business was very bad indeed.

Understandably, both parents were "worriers, with other faults I wasn't much conscious of until I recognized them in myself."[3] The primary source of *The Assistant,* Malamud's most impressively sustained performance, was "mostly my father's life as a grocer, though not necessarily my father."[4] To be an immigrant grocer in the novel was to give one's life to perhaps the most overwhelming symbol Malamud ever created. The grocery is what it is, so convincingly a dying store that the reader can feel in his or her bones the enervation of entering such a place to face its desperate but resigned proprietor. Described as a tomb, an open grave, the "bloodsucking store"[5] is also more than what it is: an emblem of the burdens of the past and of our present existence; an emblem of the palpable weight of our bodies, of the nearness of the deaths of these bodies.

If the actual store was not quite this overwhelming, and if Max Malamud did not respond to the circumstances of his life with quite the pain and pathos of Morris Bober, he "harbored few expectations of something better."[6] Of his mother, Malamud said that "she had been disappointed in life,"[7] and that she would have understood *Dubin's Lives,* his study of mid-life crisis, because "she also had some kind of unhappiness of middle age."[8] Bertha Malamud had little chance to overcome her sorrows: after a long illness she died while still in her forties. Bernard was fifteen at the time. Several years later, Max remarried, and because Bernard did not take to his stepmother, this was another source of sorrow to him. According to Dr. Doris H. Milman, a friend of the author's during his late teens and early twenties, his unhappiness with the situation at home precluded his ever referring to his family: "It was as though he had no life other than that of school and friends and the feelings and emotions and reactions attached thereto."[9] When he considered Bertha's early death, Max's poverty and added "the handicapped brother whose lamentable fate had become Bern's responsibility," Philip Roth imagined that "he'd had no choice but to forego youth and accept adulthood at a very early age."[10]

Children in difficult circumstances are often impressively resourceful as they go about growing up as best they can. Those with siblings usually gain nourishment from their interactions but Malamud has never suggested that this occurred in his case. Outside the home were the possibilities of the different neighborhoods the Malamuds inhabited, and the author several times expressed his gratitude for all he found there: "I played all over the neighborhood, helped build huts, cooked mickies, carried on long running games, stole tomatoes from the Italian vegetable farmers, and once in a while gypped the El to Coney Island, where I spent long hours on the Midway, on rides, and watching the ocean. Some nights I rode the El the other way and wandered in Times Square."[11] Elsewhere he listed the running games with an obvious reverence—"Chase the White Horse, Ringolevio, Buck-Buck, punchball and one 'o'cat"[12]—and added to the pleasures of his childhood smoking in cellars, playing blackjack, and wearing sneakers every summer. In his earliest published comments about his youth he said that he and his friends "skated, sledded, climbed trees[;] . . . the ocean [after the gypped rides to Coney Island] especially at night moved me. But we were good boys. All we wanted was a little honest fun. . . . There was adventure and a sense that one was a boy. One got to know people all over the neighborhood. This is important."[13] Malamud did not have to forego his boyhood at all that early an age.

The neighborhood also offered grammar school, which in large part enabled Malamud to write in 1975, "My childhood was comparatively happy, school making up somehow for a meager family life."[14] Appropriately enough for a writer who taught during most of the last forty-six years of his life, his first written fiction was his way of responding to an assignment he fulfilled when he was eight or nine. Asked to write something about Roger Williams, Malamud produced a story about Williams's encounter with a bear. His teacher was encouraging, and other assignments were met with stories by the young Malamud, already "feeling the glow"[15] as he told his friend and interviewer, Daniel Stern, more than a half century later.

By the time he was ten he expanded his narrative terrain by giving friends "long, minutely detailed, probably boring descriptions of the plots [of movies he was seeing]. I soon became aware I was a storyteller. I've always been one."[16] When he was in the eighth grade he created a one-issue "newspaper," with his own lead story supplemented by other students' contributions. His sense that he might have some worth and future as a writer was deepened by his tenure as an editor of the Erasmus Hall High School literary magazine and by the encouragement his teachers gave his essays. In his high school years, Malamud would sometimes stay in the back room of the store and try to write stories. But his first successful marketing of his clerking in his parents' store was an essay, "Life Behind the Counter," which he wrote in his senior year in high school and which won him a medal.

The possibilities of education continued to excite Malamud during his years at City College, from 1932 to 1936. For example, when one professor compared his work with that of two illustrious former students, the cultural historian Lewis Mumford and the philosopher Irwin Edman, Malamud "couldn't walk home that night. I was up in the air."[17] But he commented in a brief 1975 memoir that he found the long hours of commuting on the subway tiring, and he must have found the financial pressures of these years frustrating, if not embittering. In response to a query about Malamud's jobs during his undergraduate years, Miriam Lang, a good friend throughout the thirties, wrote, "In the depths of the Depression Bernie's family suffered severe financial hardship (as portrayed in *The Assistant*), and he had to help out any way he could. He was very sensitive about having to work his way through City College while his more privileged friends attended private colleges. Therefore, while I knew he worked, I never asked the specifics, nor did he volunteer them. I always assumed he helped his father in the store, but in addition I seem to recall he was earning money at odd jobs after classes. One Christmas vacation, he told me he had worked overtime so that he could afford to take me to the theater."[18]

In fact, Malamud never fully lost the sense of the unfairness of his having, like so many of his characters, to struggle mightily to make up for a late start. He was thirty-six and had been writing steadily for ten years before he was paid for a story. Two years later he published his first novel, *The Natural,* and he clearly identified more with the Roy Hobbs (his protagonist) who enters the major leagues at the age of thirty-five than the eighteen-year-old rookie we first see. At the age of sixty Malamud—who never learned the Hebrew alphabet because he was never sent to Hebrew school—still regretted that, as a consequence, he couldn't read the Yiddish books in his childhood home: "In a way I feel I was gypped, just as I was when I didn't have the opportunity of learning music."[19]

But Malamud's home gave him more than cultural privation and unhappy models. As he told Curt Supplee in 1982, "he was the beneficiary 'not of having happy parents but of having *good* parents,' who instilled in him the necessity of 'doing well by others.'"[20] If there was no comforting home library there was *The Book of Knowledge,* which the grateful grocer bought Bernard when the nine-year-old was recovering from pneumonia: "twenty volumes where there had been none[;] . . .

considering the circumstances an act of great generosity." Both parents consistently encouraged his educational aspirations, both "were gentle, honest, kindly people, and who they were and their affection for me to some degree made up for the cultural deprivation I felt as a child. They weren't educated but their values were stable. Though . . . comparatively poor, especially in the Depression, . . . I never heard a word in praise of the buck."[21] Marcus Klein titled his fine essay on Malamud's fiction "The Sadness of Goodness." We can easily guess the source of Malamud's habit of blending decency and melancholy.

The Malamuds also gave their son what would prove to be the invaluable cultural resource of the languages they spoke: Yiddish, and "Yinglish"—American English as spoken or written by an Eastern European immigrant whose native language is Yiddish. What Malamud eventually made of the earliest speech patterns imprinted in his memory was no less than his greatest fiction. Miriam Lang's comments on some of his earlier linguistic accommodations are valuable: "according to what he told me, Yiddish and not English was his first language and thus, when he entered kindergarten . . . he realized that he'd better learn to speak like 'the other kids.' As a matter of self-preservation, he—and other children like him who had to function without the prop of bilingual education—managed to learn English quickly. However, to my ears, there was always a slight intonation in his voice." Lang reasonably proceeded to conjecture that undiluted Yiddish and combinations of Yiddish and American English

> lay within him, ready to be summoned deliberately or subconsciously whenever it was required.
>
> Thus, Bernie spoke in more than one tongue. An early example of this might be from our high school years when, after a date, he'd walk me home in the quiet, upper-middle-class neighborhood where I lived. In his teenage way of showing off, he would ad-lib, switching back and forth from a Hebrew or Yiddish chant to Shakespearean iambic pentameter. Torn between laughter and worry over what the neighbors would think, I'd try to hush him. How could I know that this was an early manifestation of the tongues in which he would write?[22]

Malamud's parents offered him access to more formal examples of Yiddish culture. Since his mother had several relatives who worked in the Yiddish theater, Malamud had an early introduction to the works of two playwrights who are better known as the first masters of Yiddish

fiction, Sholem Aleichem and I. L. Peretz. Sometimes, on Jewish holidays, the Malamud family would cross over to Manhattan and take in
a play by Aleichem, Peretz, or another Yiddish playwright. In 1958
Malamud said that he wrote about Jews because "I know them. But
more important, I write about them because the Jews are absolutely
the very *stuff* of drama."[23] He first confronted this penchant for drama
lifted to aesthetic form at the Yiddish theaters of Second Avenue. In
the summer between his junior and senior years at City College he
tried out his own dramatic forms in the less polished Jewish ambiences
of the Catskills as "an entertainer (writing and acting in what he called
skits)."[24]

During the next academic year, he acted in a group largely made up
of former Erasmus students and they put on two comedies in Brooklyn:
George S. Kaufman's and Edna Ferber's *The Royal Family* and *Goodbye
Again*, by Allen Scott and George Haight. According to Burt Rush, a
member of the group, he and the other members felt that Malamud
had as much future in the theater as he did as a writer of fiction.[25]
Another member, Dr. Milman, suggested that Malamud controlled his
personae as carefully in life as he did on the stage: "It was characteristic
of him that he presented himself differently to different people. Thus
we all knew different things about him and had different views of him.
Even in his correspondence, he wrote differently to different people,
told them different things. I am not suggesting that he was in any sense
a dissembler, merely that he was an enormously complex individual,
many-faceted."[26]

Malamud graduated from City College in 1936, when he was twenty-
two. He sporadically wrote stories in college and in the remaining years
of the thirties, but it was not until 1940 that he committed himself to
"sit down . . . in a rooming house in Brooklyn and . . . write, write,
write and write."[27] The remorseful sense of wasting of one's youth and
opportunities, as well as the struggle to gain discipline, are such recurrent themes in his later fiction that the drama of these years is particularly interesting.

Malamud felt that a regular writing schedule would only come to
him when he was securely lodged in a tolerable job, but these were
hard to come by during the depression. One possible employer was the
public school system of New York City, which paid a beginning regular
teacher $2,500 a year, financial security at that time. But the require-
ments were rigorous: an M.A., a year as a teacher-in-training, passing

first the substitute's, then the regular teacher's exam—all the time struggling against the ferocious competition the depression years provided. Malamud got a government loan and began the M.A. coursework at Columbia in the fall of 1936; he didn't complete the degree until 1942. After working at a series of short-term jobs—he's mentioned a yarn factory and department stores—he took "several civil service examinations, including those leading to jobs of postal clerk and letter carrier. This is mad, I thought, or I am."[28] From February 1939 to January 1940 Malamud was a teacher-in-training at Lafayette High School in Brooklyn where "the $22.50 a week earned by a teacher-in-training outclassed the $12–15 a week paid to secretaries."[29]

During the late thirties and early forties, Malamud also tutored English, usually to Jewish refugees—including such relatively famous ones as the actor Sig Rumann and Friedrich Pinner, the former financial editor of the Berlin *Tageblatt*. When World War II made it impossible for Pinner to distribute his financial newsletter in Europe, he, like Oskar Gassner of "The German Refugee," took gas.[30]

During these years, Malamud was a great deal more burdened than Martin Goldberg, the breezy narrator of the 1962 story. The author's laconic summary, offered more than forty years later, was "It was now four years after my graduation from college, but the four felt like fifty when I was counting."[31] Miriam Lang's response to a query about this stage of Malamud's life helpfully places it in a larger context:

> There were indeed two sides to Bernie's nature, one private, the other public. From the time I met him, in 1930, he was basically melancholy, partly because of tragic circumstances in his family life, partly because of some inchoate sadness in his makeup, and partly because of his high aspirations. While still in high school, and certainly by the time he reached college, his aim was to be an author (not a mere writer), but the prospect of fulfillment seemed frustratingly remote. At the same time, he strained at lightheartedness in the manner of Pagliacci, with an undertone of what was to become in his writing the characteristic Malamud irony.
>
> During those years after college, he was in fact brooding and dissatisfied because his goals exceeded his grasp. It wasn't the *angst* of a young man asking, "Where am I going?" but rather "When am I going to get there, if ever?" Still, he was always good lively company with a great sense of the ridiculous and he managed to keep his downside hidden from everyone except those closest to him.[32]

The Short Fiction: An Essay

During the spring of 1940 Malamud was offered a job in the census section of the Department of Agriculture in Washington. He was able to check enough estimates of drainage ditch statistics during the morning to work on his own writing at his desk during the afternoon. During this time he wrote some sketches, two or three of which he published for five dollars each in *The Washington Post*. (See his reminiscence of this period in part 2.) Though he was promoted "to receive a salary of $1,800 per annum[,] . . . in those times . . . 'good money,'"[33] a position as a "permanent substitute" ("at what was then deemed the princely sum of $42.50 a week"[34]) opened up for him, teaching English at night at Erasmus Hall, mostly to immigrants.

Malamud moved back to Brooklyn in 1940, began teaching and, most important, began his ten-year apprenticeship as a writer. In 1945 he married Ann de Chiara, whom he had met three years earlier, and the couple moved into a small apartment in a brownstone building in Greenwich Village. His regimen of devoting at least five mornings and afternoons to his writing was broken when his wife gave birth to their first child in 1947. To compensate for her lost salary, Malamud had to add daytime teaching to his evening load, and it was his attempt to find time to write while he supported his family that led him to apply for and gain the position of composition instructor at Oregon State College in Corvallis, where he began teaching in 1949.

By this time the discipline that Malamud exercised in the practice of his craft had become—and would remain—overwhelming. During his twelve years at Oregon State he wrote three novels and at least fourteen publishable stories while teaching, as Richard Astro tells us, "four sections of English Composition in a rigid and closely supervised program" for ten of those years. (Grants largely freed him from teaching for two years.) Because "there was a department policy stating that only members of the faculty with Ph.D.'s might teach literature classes[,] . . . Malamud was annually given large doses of composition with only an occasional section of an introductory literature course and a short-story writing class to break the monotony."[35] His Mondays, Wednesdays, and Fridays were for classes, office hours, and paper grading; Tuesdays, Thursdays, Saturdays, "and I sneak parts of Sundays,"[36] for novels and short stories.

When, in 1961, he found more benign working conditions at Bennington College, teaching only one day a week, he was able to raise the number of weekly writing days to five. In 1971 Malamud said of his creative tenacity, "I have a terrifying will that way."[37] In the memoir that he published a month after Malamud's death, Philip Roth described that will as "the molten obstinacy at the core"[38] of the man and its heat helped to fill every day. Four years before his death, Malamud's son Paul spoke of the example his father set of "'incredible and absolutely consistent discipline,' reading every night in his slow, methodical way, underlining frequently. When shaving he would suddenly think of a sentence and 'then he'd call out of the bathroom and ask me to write it down in the notebook.'"[39] If Malamud often asked a great deal from his characters, he always asked a great deal from himself.

In 1950 he published "The Cost of Living" in *Harper's Bazaar,* "The Prison" in *Commentary,* and "The First Seven Years" in *Partisan Review.* The quality of both the periodicals and of the stories themselves ended the ten-year apprenticeship: a powerful and original presence was emerging on the American literary scene. Two of the products of the apprenticeship, "Benefit Performance" and "The Place Is Different Now," were published seven years earlier in obscure periodicals. While both stories have their strengths, what most distinguishes them are the ways in which they anticipate the far superior fiction of the 1950s. In response to a query about the apprentice fiction, Ann Malamud wrote

> His first novel was written in the mid-1940's; he called it *The Light Sleeper.* I regret I cannot recall much about it except that the protagonist was a young struggling man probably Jewish. Bern destroyed the *ms.* in a trash can that was in the backyard of a house we were renting in Corvallis, around 1952. During the 1940's about 2 dozen stories were never printed. There are 3 or so early stories, vignettes mostly, that went to the *Washington Post.* Fourteen of these very early *mss.* are in the "I" person, perhaps 6 others have Jewish protagonists (from the names he gave them, not necessarily from their speech patterns). Who knows how he developed his own "style" except that we know he was very persistent, very determined, and was willing to work hard and do a lot of rewriting always. I always considered "The Place Is Different Now" his best early story. However it would seem that he found an intensity and richness of "voice" and depth of characterization when he began to cull from his early life among his Jewish relatives and some of his storekeeper neighbors.[40]

In "The Place Is Different Now" Malamud tried to mine some of the non-Jewish possibilities of his Gravesend neighborhood. In fact, of the thirty-three published stories that are set in America, this one, far more than any other, tries to gain verisimilitude through the use of street names and references to local landmarks, like the cut made by the Long Island Railroad. Moreover, one of the story's two primary characters is a familiar figure in the later fiction (and I would wager in Malamud's own past): the ethical, soft-hearted, immigrant shopkeeper who offers advice to a troubled young man. The locale of *The Assistant* (where the interactions of Frank Alpine with Morris Bober help to transform the young drifter's life) is a spectral version of "Place's" setting. But what can the kindly barber, Mr. Davido, do for someone as far gone as Wally Mullane, the protagonist?

Wally is the ancestor of Ward Minogue, Frank Alpine's evil double in the novel. Besides the same initials, Wally and Ward are bloated, unemployed alcoholics who have been driven from the neighborhood by the clubs of policeman relatives: Johnny, Wally's brother; Ward's father. Both suffer from an illness—unnamed in Ward's case, diabetes in Wally's. He learned of the diabetes in the welfare hospital where he recovered from Johnny's blows to his legs, and where he was told that he was fortunate the beating did not give him gangrene.

The action of the story occurs a week after Wally has been released from the hospital and encompasses about twelve hours of a hot July night and the following morning. The vagrant caps years of self-destructive behavior—stealing money at his job to play the horses, buying whiskey with the money Johnny gave him to find a job—by ignoring his brother's threats and returning to his old neighborhood, in search of place to sleep. Mr. Davido would have offered Wally a barber chair for the night, but his windows are dark and his door is locked, as are the ones to the stores, cellars and garages in which he would otherwise sleep. Consequently, Wally walks the streets all night and finally rests by the El station, intending to panhandle money for beer and breakfast from the early morning commuters. But he falls asleep just before daybreak and the workers who recognize him are disgusted by the sight of the filthy and unshaven neighborhood bum, sitting "heavy-bellied on the milk box, with his head leaning back against the elevator pillar and his mouth open."[41]

Three conversations occur between the time that Wally wakes up after eight, with the commuters long gone, and the moment the story moves toward and away from: the confrontation with Johnny. The first exchange is with Mr. Davido, who kindly urges the derelict to keep off the liquor, to get out of the neighborhood before Johnny finds him, and to find a job and a furnished room. The barber even tells Wally what employment agency would be best. Wally responds by exhibiting the only gleam of self-respect that surfaces in the story: he does not try to beg money. Davido seems to try to reward this flickering of restraint by offering to shave Wally after he opens his shop.

Then comes a brief, skillfully rendered squabble with the Jewish owner of the candystore by the El. Wally is literally pulled out of the quarrel (and into terror) by a strong hand that grasps his shoulder and swings him around. However, the hand belongs not to Johnny but to Agnes, his powerfully built sister, who is taking their half-blind mother to the eye hospital. Agnes can only berate her brother but Mrs. Mullane succumbs to her son's sly wheedling and, with her daughter's grudging help, gives Wally twelve cents to get a clean shirt out of the laundry. Her hopes that appearances can to some extent be kept up are unfounded: there is no clean shirt, only Wally's intention to use the twelve cents for beer and pretzels.

But Johnny, drinking in uniform at nine in the morning, is at the bar. In one long, cascading paragraph he runs down his fleeing, terrified brother and again clubs his legs and buttocks. The policeman finally yields to Wally's moans and pleas that the beating will give him gangrene but, before leaving, Johnny swears to murder his brother if he ever returns to the neighborhood.

Early in the story, before he sits down by the El station, Wally sadly thinks of how "the neighborhood looked the same, but it wasn't. He thought of the fellows who were gone now, and he thought of his friend Vincent Davido, the barber's son, who had been gone since 1937. He thought of himself, not having set foot in his own house for the past six years, and it made him feel sorry for himself, almost like crying" (231). Wally's associations of Vincent as a part of a better past, one in which he, Wally, found some acceptance in the neighborhood, reoccur as he lies bloodied and in great pain in the backyard in which his brother left him. His first memories seem to be of a lost innocence, though both are tinged by the grimness of the neighborhood: playing with Johnny in the very coalyard they had just raced through, sledding with unnamed neighborhood boys down the sides of the railroad cut. Then come two scenes of idleness, both associated with Vincent. The first contains the only pleasant imagery in this grim story: "Then he thought of standing in front of the candy store on quiet summer evenings, with his shirt sleeves rolled up, smoking and fooling around with

The Short Fiction: An Essay

Vincent and the guys, talking about women, good times, and ball players. . . ." Like the teenaged Malamud, "they all waited for the late papers to come in with the complete box scores."

The final memory is of Vincent's last day on the block. Time has passed, more innocence has been lost. The sidewalk sages are now designated as "the unemployed fellows" and "like Wally, Vincent had quit going to the agencies, and he stayed on the corner with the rest of them, smoking and spitting on the sidewalk." When Mr. Davido looked up from the haircut he was giving to see the other loiterers laughing at a presumably offensive comment his son has made to a passing girl, the barber, red-faced, charged out of the the store, "grabbed Vincent by the arm and struck him hard across the face, shouting 'You bum, why don't you go look for a job?' Vincent's face turned very white. He didn't say anything, but he walked away, and they never saw him again" (240).

Pulling himself from his memories, Wally then manages to stumble to the barbershop, where the pitying barber shaves him. The sight of how much the outcast has changed over the years causes Mr. Davido to recall, as he often does, "how things used to be," when Vincent lived at home. Then he thinks "how wonderful it would be if Vincent came home someday—maybe after the war. He would put his arms around his boy and kiss him on the cheek." Meanwhile, the futureless Wally—hated by his family, his health ruined—can only long for the time when he owned expensive suits and smoked good cigars, when he was able to admire himself in the mirror before he went out on a Saturday night.

We then move into the story's coda. So many later Malamud stories culminate with hard-won, wonderfully convincing pathos. This early attempt fails:

Wally opened his eyes.
"You know," he whispered, "Everything's kinda changed. The place is different now."
    "Yes," said the barber, looking out of the window.
    Wally closed his eyes.
    Mr. Davido looked down at him. Wally was breathing quietly. His lips were pulled together tightly, and the tears were rolling down his cheeks. The barber slowly raised the lather on Wally's face until it mixed with the tears. (241–42)

14

The final paragraph is perhaps saved from sentimentality by the closing image of the wet blend of tears and shaving cream—we're brought back to Wally's repellent messiness—but this is not enough to redeem the sentimental obviousness of the preceding three paragraphs, in which we're supposed to sympathize with Wally. On the one hand the closing captures Malamud's ambiguous attitude toward his protagonist. It's as if he tried hard throughout the story to harness his considerable capacity for sympathy and, as did so many others of his generation, write a tolerant study of a true down-and-outer. But here was this boozing, filthy goy, with no capacity for self-respect or self-discipline. Malamud must have experienced a certain relief when, years later, he added the desires to rape Jewish girls and to beat and rob from Jewish storekeepers to Wally's flaws, and sent him forth as Ward Minogue.

This is not to say that Malamud's characters should not reflect his ambivalence toward them. His ability to dramatize convincingly their contradictions, their strengths and weaknesses, will become a crucial component to his success. But in this early story, Malamud tried to plaster over with sentimentality his confused sense of Wally's claim to our sympathy. We're to feel that, although what Wally misses is clearly inferior to what Mr. Davido misses, he's doing the best he can. But it's also suggested that Wally does have some finer stuff in him, that he also profoundly misses Vincent. The story works best if we respond to Wally's life-threatening return to his neighborhood not as the simple search for a place to sleep but, in this time of desperate extremity, as the pathetic attempt of a damaged animal to return to a place where he had once been contented, accepted. Vincent would seem to have been the most admirable peer who ever accepted him—though this does not come through as clearly as it might.

Beneath the facade of social realism that covers "The Place Is Different Now," we can detect the penchant for doubling characters and dramatic situations, and for blurring family lines that help bring to *The Assistant* a sense of uncanny interrelatedness. Neither Wally nor Vincent has been in his family home for six years, since 1937, and the families strangely complement one another: Wally's father is never mentioned; Vincent and his father are the only Davidos we hear of. Malamud will play fascinating variations on the massive theme of a father's search for a son or a son's for a father. In "The Place Is Different Now," the quest is handled ironically. Vincent's idleness might at one time have matched Wally's, but the Davidos are much finer stuff than the brutish Mullanes. The barber gets not his son (who after his humiliation behaved with a style Wally never matched) but the unregenerate, even loathsome, Wally.

Unfortunately, Malamud's uncertain handling of Wally weakens the irony just as the tangled relations between the Mullanes and Davidos weaken, rather than strengthen, the whole of the story. It's almost as if the character Malamud really wanted to have at the center of the story was Vincent, the young Italian-American with the capacities for extreme gestures and, perhaps, for overcoming his flaws. Is the absent Vincent the germ of Frank Alpine?

Malamud used his Jewish contacts much more fully in "Benefit Performance," the other story published in 1943. The protagonist is Maurice Rosenfeld, a first-generation actor in the Yiddish theater. Before we finish the first paragraph we realize that he makes no attempt to separate the histrionics of his profession from the rest of his life:

> Maurice Rosenfeld was conscious of himself as he took the key from his pocket and inserted it into the door of his small apartment. The Jewish actor saw his graying hair, the thick black eyebrows, the hunch of disappointment in his shoulders and the sardonic grimness of his face, accentuated by the twisted line of the lips. Rosenfeld turned the key in the lock, aware that he was playing his role well. Tragedy in the twisting of a key, he thought.
> "Who's there?" said a voice from inside the apartment.

The interrogator is Sophie, his twenty-eight-year-old daughter, apparently home early from work. (We soon learn that she's discomfited by the onset of her period.) Her question cuts into the little melodrama that her father is playing for himself, but the aging egotist soon begins to perform for her. The announcement of a lull in production becomes "The Jewish theayter is deep in hell. . . . Second Avenue is like a tomb." When Sophie, who has been assimilated into less extreme ways of thinking and talking, tries to reassure him with "Don't worry . . . you had a good season last year," Rosenfeld haughtily replies, "I'm too young to live on memories." Malamud nicely counters what Rosenfeld thinks of as his resounding rhetoric with the meager reality of the dinner of carrots and lumpy potatoes waiting for him on the stove. Of the hamburger waiting for him in the broiler he says, "No, it burns me my stomach when I eat chopmeat."[42]

With the arrival of Sophie's suitor, Ephraim, a well-built, decent enough man, we have the basic conflict of one of the Yiddish plays that Rosenfeld might have acted in, or that Malamud might have seen as a boy. For the unimaginative Ephraim is a plumber, or "plum-ber" in the actor's sarcastic pronunciation, and Rosenfeld claims to want for his daughter someone who can give to his wife the kind of cultured contacts he feels he gave to his wife and daughter. (The characterization is too thin for us to know whether or not Rosenfeld actually gave these cultural advantages to his family or, indeed, whether or not his possessiveness of his daughter is so great that no son-in-law would be acceptable to him.)

Rosenfeld relentlessly goads the normally good-natured plumber until the latter is driven to defend himself with "At least a plumber can support a wife and doesn't have to send her out to work for him." Rosenfeld is so shaken by this act of lèse–majesté that he is first silent, then stutters "You nothing, you. You nothing." Then, as he gathers his forces, this slice of the Yiddish theater in prose moves into its climax:

> He rose slowly. Rosenfeld crossed his arms over his breast, then raised them ceilingward and began to speak deliberately in fluent Yiddish.
>
> "Hear me earnestly, great and good God. Hear the story of the afflictions of a Second Job. Hear how the years have poured misery upon me, so that in my age, when most men are gathering their harvest of sweet flowers, I cull nothing but weeds."

On rants this Lear of the Yiddish stage (with no more knowledge of possible oedipal desires than the king) to commend his own attempt to give to his daughter "every opportunity for growth and education," and to claim ludicrously that his reasonable, almost stolid daughter— who tries to appear more attractive to her suitor by adding a hair ribbon to match the blue of her housecoat—"has become so mad in her desire for carnal satisfaction that she is ready to bestow herself upon a man unworthy to touch the hem of her garment, to a common, ordinary wordless plum-ber who has neither ideals nor—." Here, Sophie's plea for him to stop succeeds, Ephraim curses Rosenfeld and leaves, Sophie withdraws, and the actor, "his shoulders hunched in disappointment[,] . . . sees himself with his graying hair, a tragic figure."

How can his carrots and potatoes be worthy fare for such a grand figure? Still on stage but forced to constitute the whole of his audience, Rosenfeld ends the story with the sotto voce utterance "Tonight I will eat chopmeat" (22). Since the reader already knows that hamburger "burns me my stomach," the silly melodrama of the line is clear enough. Contemptuous of contributing to a benefit performance for one Isaac Levin, Rosenfeld performs for the benefit of himself in more ways than one.

Malamud's control of the characters and of their interactions is much more sure than in "The Place is Different Now," but then "Benefit Performance" is a much less ambitious story. In fact, it is much more a local color sketch than a short story that tries to chart a crisis in its protagonist's life. As was the case in the sketches of most local colorists, or the Mark Twain who wrote "The Notorious Jumping Frog of Calaveras County," a grammatically correct narrator scrupulously reports to the reader the patois of his quaint protagonist. Mark Twain's great fictional breakthrough came when he made Huck Finn the narrator of his adventures, allowing Huck's wonderful voice and sensibility to pervade the whole of the novel that Hemingway claimed to be the ancestor of all modern American literature. This was not the vernacular solution Malamud would take. According to Ann Malamud, all of the early first person stories are narrated in standard American English,[43] and the mature Malamud did not find the first person particularly congenial: none of the eight novels, and only four of forty-five stories—one of the first thirty-one—use this point of view.

However he managed it, by 1950 Malamud had learned to blend the Yiddish residue of his early years with English and thus consolidate the most crucial component of the style that made *The Assistant* and the majority of the stories of *The Magic Barrel* distinctively, arrestingly, his own. He created an extremely diverse narrative voice, one that could range in the same paragraph from formal American English, to colloquial American English, to the syntax and diction of Yinglish. We would do well to consider at some length the first paragraph of the most linguistically idiosyncratic of the 1950 stories—and one of the best Malamud ever wrote—"The First Seven Years":

> Feld, the shoemaker, was annoyed that his helper, Sobel, was so insensitive to his reverie that he wouldn't for a minute cease his fanatic pounding at the other bench. He gave him a look, but Sobel's bald head was bent over the last as he worked and he didn't notice. The shoemaker shrugged and continued to peer through the partly frosted window at the near-sighted haze of falling February snow. Neither the shifting white blur outside, nor the sudden deep remembrance of the snowy Polish village where he had wasted his youth could turn his thoughts from Max the college boy (a constant

visitor in the mind since early that morning when Feld saw him trudging through the snowdrifts on his way to school) whom he so much respected because of the sacrifices he had made throughout the years—in winter or direst heat—to further his education. An old wish returned to haunt the shoemaker: that he had had a son instead of a daughter, but this blew away in the snow for Feld, if anything, was a practical man. Yet he could not help but contrast the diligence of the boy, who was a peddler's son, with Miriam's unconcern for an education. True, she was always with a book in her hand, yet when the opportunity arose for a college education, she had said no she would rather find a job. He had begged her to go, pointing out how many fathers could not afford to send their children to college, but she said she wanted to be independent. As for education, what was it, she asked, but books, which Sobel, who diligently read the classics, would as usual advise her on. Her answer greatly grieved her father.[44]

Phrases like "He gave him a look" or "she was always with a book in her hand" could have been uttered by Feld, the Polish immigrant. But Malamud does not consistently gather Yinglish into the narrative voice any more than he has two immigrants converse in Yiddish, as they naturally would in "real life," or as Rosenfeld does when his limited control of English denies him the eloquence to which he aspires. Some of the language of the paragraph is Yinglish, which helps to bridge the gap between the sensibilities of the narrator and of Feld— a closing of narrative distance that also makes it easier for the reader to identify with the shoemaker. But the majority of the phrases in this paragraph, as in almost all of Malamud's narrative ones, are not exclusively Yinglish but one of the following: standard American English; some idiosyncratic or colloquial form that might to varying degrees be touched by some aspect of Yinglish—the clumsiness or the terseness, for example—but could still not be called Yinglish; and an idiosyncratic form that has nothing to do with Yinglish.

"Would as usual" in the next-to-last sentence strikes me as an example of the second group; "near-sighted haze" in the third sentence is an example of the third group. The preceding examples are from separate sentences, but the pleasing quarrel between the different narrative voices can occur within a single sentence. In the opening lines the idiomatic "wouldn't for a minute" yokes word choices—"insensitive to his reverie" and "cease"—which would never be Feld's. The most charged word in the sentence is "fanatic." Were a "real" Feld to have articulated the thought, he would probably have substituted some Yiddish word—*meshugganah,* for example.

Some contemporary Jews who have mastered American English, as Feld has not, seek to bring color or humor or intimacy to their conversation by sprinkling in Yiddish phrases or words. In fact, the popularity of Jewish culture in recent decades has been substantial enough for some gentiles to adopt the same conversational strategy. When Malamud writes in his immigrant mode, he sprinkles his paragraphs not with Yiddish words proper—there are surprisingly few in the whole of his writing—but with the occasional Yinglish of the narrator and the much more consistent Yinglish provided by the statements of the immigrant characters. For using Yiddish words or sentences to spice one's prose is finally a losing battle: unless one is writing for an extremely limited audience the insertions are usually clichés; the strategy has been worn to weariness by comedians and inferior Jewish writers in the last few decades. As Daniel Stern has observed, "Malamud is to be read as being first and foremost a 'modern' writer. Modern in the sense that he comes after Pound's dictum 'Make it strange, make it new.' Brooklyn, Oregon and Vermont may give rise to the strange and new as well as Montparnasse. But instead of the poetic imagination in the service of the pure universe of art, it is newness and strangeness in the service of how men should live so as not to cause pain, so as to be the best they can be."[45]

The author of "Benefit Performance" was a competent but unexceptional local colorist. The author of "The First Seven Years" was an impressive modernist who related his art to the world through what the Russian formalists call "defamiliarization." By undermining and estranging a conventional sign system—in this case American English—Malamud forces us to attend closely to the workings of the language he puts before our eyes and, if the reader is fully attentive, of language itself. Thus our perceptions of the possibilities of language and of the world the language tries to represent are renewed, made much more immediate.

We can speak of Malamud's stylistic modernism more specifically. One of the dominant influences upon Malamud during this stage of his career was that massive pioneer of modernism, Dostoyevski. Though both authors' use of doubling, their sympathy for outcasts, and their fondness for grinding studies of sin and salvation quickly come to mind, we might also consider a formal similarity. Perhaps more than any other novelist, Dostoyevski was able to get stunningly different characters and plots to cohere somehow in the same work. Moreover, as Mikhail Bakhtin has brilliantly demonstrated, "contradictory accents intertwine in every word of his works."[46] The more a work keeps tensions in controlled counterpoise, the more power it will have. If Malamud's fiction cannot compare in dramatic and thematic polyphony with Dostoyevski's, his technique of blending markedly diverse accents in his narrative helps to bring nervous tension and movement even to the scenes of apathy and enervation he often dramatized. Put differently, the often centripetal plots are charged by language so subtly varied that they strain toward the centrifugal. And the "narrative music" is usually augmented and complicated by the varying accents of the characters' speeches, just as their more positive strivings are heightened by the straining language. Malamud had to have an uncannily accurate ear for the sonic force field of a story or novel to keep it from veering in more narrative directions than the reader could absorb. As we shall see, sometimes he was unable to harness the divergences of tone, but usually his strategies were most successful.

For example, Malamud often uses Yinglish to drive us deep within a character, and the final sentence of the paragraph closes with the reader pushed close to Feld's grief at his daughter's attachment to Sobel. Yet the sentence is the most austerely "correct" one in the paragraph: "Her answer greatly grieved her father." On the one hand, it is as if Malamud perceived that the reader might be tiring of all the assimilation he was asked to do and wrote a sentence as brutally direct as the pain Feld experiences. On the other, the reader is asked to assimilate in a new way. Feld's sorrow is amplified by the r's in every word and by the double alliteration of "greatly grieved": the "most simple" sentence is also the most consciously poetic one. As an orchestrator of what we might call the music of pathos, Malamud—of all American writers of his generation—most reminds us of another Russian modernist master: Chekhov.

Malamud's stylistic blendings and evolutions are subtle and various in many more ways than I have suggested; we shall be unpacking a fair number of them subsequently. Here we might consider two more aspects of the 1950 stylistic breakthrough before we turn to the thematic content of "The First Seven Years." First, Yinglish shapes the syntax as much as it does the diction. The fourth sentence of the first paragraph is long—seventy-eight words—and extremely clumsy: on and on it goes as the narrator inserts distracting modifying clauses and pastes on new clauses with the apparent artlessness of an inept sausagemaker adding to his string of knockwurst.

If we consider the sentence in isolation, its ungainliness is not exclusively characteristic of a native speaker of Yiddish who is attempting to communicate in English, or of a narrator who is trying to push us into the crowded inner life of a Jewish immigrant. But the tortured syntax does become Yinglish or something very close to it when we consider the linguistic context: the Yinglish diction of the first paragraph, and Feld's characteristic syntax when he finally does speak: "Ever since you went to high school . . . I watched you in the morning go to the subway to school, and I said always to myself, this is a fine boy that he wants so much an education" (*TMB*, 5). The primary use of the Yinglish is not to heighten local color verisimilitude as it was in "Benefit Performance."

All of the speakers of Yinglish who find their way into print after Rosenfeld suffer from one or more of the following afflictions: sorrow, depression, baffled longings for a better life, poverty, ill health, guilt, or hunger. With the exception of "The Last Mohican," all of the stories in which speakers of Yinglish appear are set in America, and the failure of the speakers to gain a native's control of American English works to emphasize their inability to gain a comfortable foothold in the New World: we are reminded of Malamud's parents in particular, and, more generally, of the hard realities of immigrant life. Significantly, the least vulnerable of the speakers of Yinglish in the stories and in *The Assistant* is Shimon Susskind, the refugee from Israel who surfaces in the Rome of "The Last Mohican." His dialect mostly works in the story to emphasize his manipulative cunning. Elsewhere Yinglish usually works to heighten the pathos of largely ineffectual characters. In "The First Seven Years" the clumsy syntax in which Feld's judgment of Max is cast anticipates his inability to understand or effectively control Max, his daughter, or Sobel.

Our second consideration follows from the way the variousness of the narrator's tones and distances of identification from the character being described often creates an ironic commentary. This ironic distance modifies the pathos even as it is being developed, and keeps it from becoming cloying. Though the third sentence of the first paragraph—"The shoemaker shrugged and continued to peer through the partly frosted window at the near-sighted haze of falling February snow"—is an arresting, "defamiliarizing" one, and though it connects the Yinglish diction of the preceding two sentences and the Yinglish syntax of the succeeding one, it owes none of its sense of newness to Yinglish. Most obviously, the way in which Feld looks through the distorting lens of the window doubles the sense of the visual strangeness of the snowy haze.

So far we have an example of Malamud's penchant for describing transformed ways of viewing. (Someone who knows his work is perhaps reminded of a dream Frank Alpine has in which he's in the street, viewing through a window the glowing flesh of a woman he loves but who now hates him, while the window is gradually covered with ice.) The estrangement of the sentence in "The First Seven Years" is heightened when we consider the curious personification of "nearsighted haze": people, not hazes, are nearsighted. We can easily recast the phrase so that it makes sense—the world looks as it might to a nearsighted person. But as we read on, the irony of calling not Feld but the snowy haze nearsighted is brought home to us. However the shoemaker might fare on a vision test, he is experientially nearsighted: he will not let himself perceive the love of Sobel and Miriam for one another, the hopeless inadequacy of Max as a mate for Miriam, or what that word which is so crucial to Malamud—education—might entail. With his bad heart, wasted youth, scant future and desire that his daughter have a better life than he has had, Feld engages our sympathy. But this compassion is compromised by his experiential myopia. In this case the complication follows from an estranging strategy in which the narrator has moved further from Feld's sensibility than he did in the preceding sentences, shaped as they are by Yinglish.

Malamud's characteristic ironic treatment can also occur during narrative closeness. For example, in the preceding sentences, Feld is annoyed at Sobel's insensitivity to his, Feld's, own inner life, but it is Feld who is imperceptive of his tangled motives. Because it's not in his economic interest to let his recognition of Sobel's attachment to Miriam reach his consciousness, Feld instead explains in the following way why Sobel works so hard for the small salary Feld pays him: "the man, no doubt because of his terrible experiences as a refugee, was afraid of the world" (*TMB*, 8). Thus Feld disingenuously fails to realize that it is precisely Sobel's fanatic pounding that gives him the emotional ease to daydream of his past or plan for Miriam's future. Correspondingly, after he furtively encourages Max to call Miriam, Feld cannot understand why the jealous and furious Sobel so increases the force of his pounding that he smashes his last and runs from the store.

Toward the end of the story, when Feld next sees Sobel, he tells the refugee that he had treated him like a son. The ironic truth is rather that Sobel had behaved more like the son (or son-in-law) of an improvident father, carrying the sickly shoemaker, his wife, and his daughter on his broad back for most of the five years he had worked in the shop. Sobel shatters his employer's delusion by telling him that he toiled for Miriam and adds that he didn't have to tell Miriam that he loved her because "She knows who I am and what is in my heart." Feld finally comes to perception: the way to that heart was through

> his books and commentary [with which] Sobel had given Miriam to understand that he loved her. The shoemaker felt a terrible anger at him for his deceit.
>
> "Sobel, you are crazy," he said bitterly. "She will never marry a man so old and ugly like you." (*TMB*, 14)

While Sobel had silently made clear what was in his heart, Feld hid from himself the truth that was in his.

In *Billy Budd* Melville argues that "Passion and passion in its profoundest, is not a thing demanding a palatial stage whereon to play its part. Down among the groundlings, among the beggars and rakers of the garbage, profound passion is enacted. And the circumstances that provoke it, however trivial and mean, are no measure of its power."[47] Perceived from one perspective, the circumstances are not at all mean: a father frantic for his daughter to have a better life than he did; an improbable but passionate and narrowly profound suitor, who had his youth torn from him by a monstrous regime. From another perspective they are: these are economically and socially marginal people cursing each other in a shabby store in the grim, placeless locale Malamud hit upon for the majority of the stories he would collect in *The Magic Barrel*. But the passion is as powerful and as believable as it is subject to subtle modulations (all of which the preceding shifts and combinations of the narrative voice helped prepare the reader to accept). Sobel moves in a few moments from a rage that turns him black, to sobbing, to reading peacefully. Feld bounces from a vindictive fury to a grinding pity in which he finally permits himself to recognize the emotional intensities Sobel had been carrying within him: "How strange and sad that a refugee, a grown man, bald and old with his miseries, who had by the skin of his teeth escaped Hitler's incinerators, should fall in love, when he had got to America, with a girl less than half his age. Day after day, for five years he had sat at his bench, cutting and hammering away, waiting for the girl to become a woman, unable to ease his heart with speech, knowing no protest but desperation" (*TMB*, 15).

Having confronted some of the truth in his heart, Feld is now free to confront as well the compassion and moral intelligence that also lie there. But lyrical realist that Malamud so often is, the shoemaker's sudden moral surge is no unmixed blessing. To recognize the validity of Sobel's claim for his daughter is also to experience "a strange and gripping sorrow, as if she were already Sobel's bride, the wife, after all of a shoemaker, and had in her life no more than her mother had had. And all his dreams for her . . . all these dreams of a better life were dead" (*TMB*, 15). Feld might be mistaken about the life that awaits Miriam. Then again he might not be and, as Malamud well knew and as a hardheaded candystore owner tells Frank Alpine, poverty "ain't beautiful, kiddo. To be poor is dirty work" (*TA*, 31). Still, there is a certain rightness to Sobel's claim to Miriam (which I'll consider more closely in the next chapter), and Feld can only ask that Sobel wait two years to ask for Miriam's hand, until she is twenty-one. Having behaved like the essentially moral man that he is, Feld, who was recently driven to a heart attack by Sobel's thieving replacement, is able to walk home "with a stronger stride" (*TMB*, 15). For once, Malamud quickly rewards ethical behavior in material terms. When the "heavy-hearted" Feld arrives to open the store the next morning, "he saw he needn't have come, for his assistant [Sobel] was already seated at the last." But Malamud characteristically takes away some of the relief he provides. The image captured by the final words of the story, of Sobel "pounding leather for his love" (*TMB*, 16), captures an energy that is more sexual than vocational. Feld has reason to be discomfited by his helper's triumphant assertion.

The Magic Barrel

In 1944, two years after he published *On Native Grounds*, his precociously learned overview of twentieth-century American prose, Alfred Kazin expanded the grounds of his cultural formation to include the Jews of East Europe and their orthodox, Zionist, and socialist traditions: "I admire these. I have been influenced as a writer and as a person by the idea of them—I only wish I knew how much." But "I have never seen much of what I admire in American Jewish culture, or among Jewish writers in America generally. . . . Who is he [the American Jew]? What is Jewish in him? What does he believe, especially in these terrible years that separates him at all from our national habits of acquisitiveness, showiness and ignorant brag?"[48] Fifteen years later Kazin concluded an attack on the majority of contemporary novelists for their inability to create morally informed, socially meaningful actions by offering as a contrast "the tangibility, the felt reverberations of life that one finds in a writer like Bernard Malamud." Kazin went on to argue that such fiction "can elicit and prove the world we share[;] . . . it can display the unforeseen possibilities of the human—even when everything seems dead set against it."[49]

There was no need for a significant enlargement of Kazin's sympathies by 1959 for him to offer as testimony of the continuing power and value of fiction the work of a Jew—one who was just one year older than the critic and also raised in Brooklyn by immigrant parents. For Malamud's emergence was just one manifestation of a massive enlargement of the presence of Jews in the contemporary literary scene during the preceding fifteen years. (Given Kazin's tastes he could have substituted Saul Bellow's or Grace Paley's or Philip Roth's name for Malamud's.) By 1959 a disproportionate percentage of our most respected fiction writers were either Jews who often wrote of their ethnic experience (like Malamud, Bellow, Roth, Edward Wallant, Wallace Markfield, Herbert Gold, and Paley) or who did not (like Norman Mailer and J. D. Salinger). There have been many explanations for this stunning emergence, ranging from the mention of the traditional respect for the written word in Jewish culture to the claims that Jewish were unfairly favored by the relatively high percentage of Jewish critics and Jews with power in the publishing business. Here I would like only to consider some aspects of the unique combination of assimilation and alienation in mid-century American culture.

First, the emerging writers combined a number of the following characteristics: as the children of struggling (often immigrant) parents they were extremely eager to rise in the world; the fervor that might have gone into religion (particularly Zionism) and social reform went into a love affair with literature; in spite of their respect for modernist masters, they felt their experience was worth writing about; the vigorous immigrant speech they had absorbed was an important part of that experience.

Second, we should consider a highly predictive paradox that the critic and fiction writer Isaac Rosenfeld offered at the same 1944 symposium that elicited Kazin's dismissal of contemporary Jewish culture: "Since modern life is so complex that no man can possess it in its entirety, the outsider often finds himself the perfect insider."[50] Of course, cultural distance from things American has heightened the powers of observation and conjecture of such distinguished foreign-born observers as de Toqueville, Frances Trollope, and Gunnar Myrdahl. But Rosenfeld was referring to American-born outsiders—to Jews. In the forty-odd years since Rosenfeld hinted at the possibilities of apartness, a good many commentators have observed in different ways that the vein of cultural alienation that the Jews had experienced in this culture has widened to become a fissure in which a majority—if not all—Americans foundered. As the tensions of the cold war and the homogenization of 1950s America deepened, and a substantial number of thoughtful Americans found themselves increasingly distanced from what was nourishing in our culture, such Jews as David Riesman, Norman Mailer, Paul Goodman, Daniel Bell, and Irving Howe found appreciative audiences for their analyses of our culture.

But I am not so much concerned with large-scale cultural description and prescription as with the sense that the Jew—both victim of the Holocaust and expert in improbable survival—seemed to many for several decades to be the most appropriate instructor of the possibilities of connection within contactlessness. If, as Malamud said in 1959, "each of us in his secret heart knows . . . his image as a human being,"[51] it seemed that the Jewish writer who happened to be connected to a longstanding spiritual tradition had a headstart in finding his or her way to that image. In the fifties and sixties Bellow, Malamud, and Roth—writers so often lumped together that Bellow and Malamud have described the trio as the Hart, Schaffner, and Marx of American literature—created characters who seemed to find their way to a moral identity that existed independent of the assaults of contemporary American culture. We might call this ultimate center the nourishing heart. Tommy Wilhelm, in Bellow's *Seize the Day,* thinks of it as the realm of the "real soul," from which we can say "plain and understandable things to everyone," where "truth for everybody may be found and confusion is only—only temporary."[52]

The news that we are all powerfully, meaningfully connected through our common and innate moral centers can be a heartening antidote to the way we sometimes, or usually, or almost always feel about ourselves and our fellow humans, and a good many authors and readers have explored the possibilities of "Jewishness." The moral assertions in the most important fiction were more often than not associated with a character's acceptance of his "Jewishness" or of his communion with his "Jewish heart." As Joseph Landis has written, "the efforts to describe the nature of the Jewish writer's Jewishness, the distinctively Jewish qualities of his writing, have covered a range from the very general qualities of moral sensitivity and intellectuality which Maxwell Geismar sees as the distinguishing characteristics to the very specific responses to 'a series of moments in the search for God,' which Irving Malin uses as his touchstones."[53]

This celebration of the spiritual uses of "Jewishness" met varied resistance. First there were the critics who deplored what they felt was the arrogance of suggesting, for example, that Jews had a particular gift for putting suffering to spiritual use, or the ones who attacked what they felt was the vagueness and illogic of suggesting that "an ethic of hard work, integrity, acceptance of responsibility, forebearance in distress and so forth" had "a necessary connection with being a flesh and blood Jew."[54] At times Malamud has seemed to argue for the singular moral endowment of Jews in a way that supports Philip Roth's claim "for the characteristic connection . . . in Bernard Malamud's work . . . between the Jew and conscience, and the Gentile and appetite."[55] For example, in 1974 Curt Leviant asked him "What besides their names and milieu makes your characters Jewish?," to which Malamud responded, "Their Jewish qualities, the breadth of their vision, their kind of fate, their morality, their life; their awareness, responsibility, intellectuality, and ethicality. Their love of people and God."[56] How are we to reconcile this with the fact that a good many of Malamud's

Jewish characters are in no way admirable, and that words like *fate* and *life* often mask qualities like masochism, ineptness, self-pity, and timidity in the more admirable ones?

An art dealer who bought a reputed Picasso was later told by the painter that the work was not a true Picasso. "But I saw you painting it!" exclaimed the dealer. "I often fail to paint true Picassos," replied the painter. In somewhat the same way, some of Malamud's Jews lack *Jewishness*—his term both for the attempt to understand those negative forces within and without that would drive a man to a degraded conception of himself, and for the need to behave in a moral fashion in spite of those forces. To put Malamud's metaphorical use of Jewishness in a recognizable historical context, during a 1968 lecture tour in Israel, less than a year after Israel was threatened with extinction in the Six Day War, he said "I try to see the Jew as universal man. Every man is a Jew though he may not know it. The Jewish drama is a . . . symbol of the fight for existence in the highest possible human terms. Jewish history is God's gift of drama."[57] For Malamud it is not common genes that bond humanity but common experience. Unified as we are by the agonies and defeats of the past, the limitations of the present, and the threats of the future, we must still struggle to keep in our minds and instill in our acts "what it means human"[58]—to quote one of Malamud's most noble strugglers for a humane scale in a universe that is essentially inhumane.

Not all of Malamud's moral strugglers are Jews, but the majority are. His most probing studies of the workings of moral transformation understandably occur in his novels—for by its very length a novel can trace pervasive moral shifts in ways a story cannot—and it is significant that though the first four of his seven novels are to varying degrees structured around the need for the protagonist to grow morally, the only sensibility that fails to develop is that of the gentile (Roy Hobbs in *The Natural*).

It is no coincidence that Malamud came fairly late both to the study of Judaism and to writing successful fiction: the former contributed substantially to the latter. His father's leanings were more socialistic than Talmudic, and Bernard was never bar mitzvahed. Then again, certain aspects of Judaism can be better learned through experience than through books. Several critics have written about the similarities between Malamud's work and the ideals of Hasidism, the eighteenth-century movement that transfigured the ghettos, and particularly the shtetls, of Eastern Europe in the eighteenth century, and that emphasized inner salvation, the finding and heeding of the truths of the heart. One of these critics, Marcia Gealy, interestingly speculates that the young Bernard learned the ideals of Hasidism from his parents.[59]

The early years of his apprenticeship coincided with the increasing horror of what was happening to Jews in Europe, and Malamud began to read books by and about them. In October 1943, for example, he wrote to the woman he was to marry two years later, "I've also been reading a book on 'what a Jew believes' about which I know very little."[60] Paradoxically, marrying a gentile intensified his brooding over the nature of his Judaism, for it made Malamud "ask myself what it is I'm entitled to in Jewish experience."[61] The most productive entitlement was the repeated and powerful kindling of his imaginative powers by his identification with the often terribly oppressed Jews of the Pale—"in particular the . . . immigrants of my father's and mother's generation." Malamud has also said that he was "deeply moved by the Jews of the concentration camps, and the refugees moving from nowhere to nowhere,"[62] though he never took on camp life in his fiction and only one character in the stories is explicitly identified as a survivor of the camps: Isabella della Seta in "The Lady of the Lake."

In six of the stories in *The Magic Barrel* ("The First Seven Years," "The Mourners," "Angel Levine," "Take Pity," "The Loan," and "The Magic Barrel"), two in *Idiots First* (the title story and "The Cost of Living"), and in *The Assistant*, Malamud combined his capacities for fantasy, his modernist, experimental urge, and his profound respect for the continuities of Jewish experience by creating a folk terrain, one in which, as Philip Roth put it, his characters "live in a timeless Depression and a placeless lower East Side."[63] In varying degrees, these abstractions of time and place combine with the Jewish characters' situations and sensibilities to superimpose their twentieth-century American experience upon that of the inhabitants of the ghettos and the more intensely religious shtetls within the Pale, over the past two or three centuries.

Malamud was particularly taken with the ability of the Old World Jews to exercise their moral freedom within confinement, to realize a heightened inner life in spite of severe material privations. Sometimes one of his characters' heightened inwardness follows from his or her proximity to the Old World culture. For example, there are a number of reasons why Sobel enters "The First Seven Years" with a moral depth, a strong sense of "who I am and what is in my heart" (*TMB*, 14) that Feld lacks. His reading and voluminous commentary are of course quite traditional, and, as a recent refugee, he embodies more of the experience of the Diaspora than Feld. The Eastern European culture he recently left was one that still felt the effects of Hasidism and, to some degree, brought its emphasis on the truths of the heart all the way to the gas chambers that destroyed it. When Malamud touches upon the theme of the assimilation of Jews into American culture, it is often to deplore the process. Feld lacks Sobel's moral intensity and the American-born Max is so thoroughly assimilated into materialism that he's more moved by the bang-up job Feld does on his shoes than he is by Miriam's good looks and depths of feeling.

Many of Malamud's stories are, as Earl Rovit has written, "within the tradition of the Yiddish teller of tales—tales narrated with a discernible echo of the eternal chant, tales of misery . . . [of] man's inhumanity to man."[64] But there are often positive strains to the "Thus was it always" echo. The title "The First Seven Years" ironically contrasts Jacob, the father of the twelve tribes of Israel, toiling under Laban, with poor Sobel, toiling under Feld. But it also asserts that paupers as well as patriarchs can combine passion with self-discipline and loyalty, now or 3,500 years ago.

The ability of so many Jews of the Pale to cultivate their inner lives while their outer ones were so relatively impoverished exercised understandable appeal to a Jew who has described himself as "a real child of the Depression."[65] Recalling this time of few jobs and little money, Malamud said in 1980, "The good thing about the Depression was everything went down to bedrock[;] . . . Experience that deprives you of something can make you realize what it is that you need most, and it sends you inward."[66]

Paradoxically, the emergence of this poet of material scarcity came in the latter part of a decade—the fifties—when our gross national product doubled, and when the consequent complaints that our spiritual lives were being vitiated by our attachment to material goods and physical comforts more than doubled. To the expected attacks upon the shifts in values, a number of social critics added a line of reasoning that helped to explain some fiction writers' complaints about the difficulty of getting a hold on post–World War II America. Since one of the primary human realities, if not the dominant one, has been material want, our sense of reality is being diminished to the degree that the new prosperity seems to be lessening our sharp responses to want. As a way of describing the situation in America in 1959, Irving Howe referred to this hyperbolic but still relevant comment by an unnamed

German novelist: "There's no longer a society to write about. In for-mer years you knew where you stood: the peasants read the Bible; the maniacs read *Mein Kampf.* Now people no longer have any opinions; they have refrigerators. Instead of illusions, we have television, instead of tradition, the Volkswagen. The only way to catch the spirit of the times is to write a handbook on home appliances."[67]

Few of the characters in what I might call the stories of the folk ghetto are distracted from the workings of their "inner bedrock" by distracting commodities, for Malamud usually created privations that keep them in dramatically painful contact with their desires and frus-trations. Often material want largely shapes their distressing world. But if the little businesses in the stories are finally going fairly well, Mala-mud finds other ways to keep the proprietors from straying very far beyond their painful limits. Because of Sobel, Feld can afford to send his daughter to college, but he's frustrated by her refusal to go, and then there's his heart condition. In "The Loan" "the sweet, the heady smell of Lieb's white bread drew customers in droves" (*TMB*, 183). But as the baker—his eyes clouded with cataracts, the button of his truss pressing into his stomach—explains, "For thirty years . . . he was never with a penny to his name. One day, out of misery, he had wept into the dough. Thereafter his bread was such it brought customers in from everywhere" (*TMB*, 185).

Roth's reference to the timeless depression and the placeless Lower East Side came in his 1961 essay "Writing American Fiction," in a context that enclosed his convincing assertion that "the American writer in the middle of the twentieth century has his hands full in trying to understand, describe, and then make *credible* much of the American reality."[68] Often Malamud's fictive solution was to disregard such aspects of this reality as the effects of affluence, the cold war, the struggle for integration, and Jewish assimilation. If Malamud found Jews the very stuff of drama, no headlines, news reports, or radio or television programs intrude to distract the characters of the stories of the folk ghetto or the reader from the theater of the self that they fill with their vivid emotions. So rigorous is Malamud's selection in these eight stories that twentieth-century history is a silence broken only by mention of a few eruptions that kill Jews: "the war" (*TMB*, 43) in "Angel Levine;" Bolsheviks and typhus in "The Loan"; Hitler or his incinerators in "The First Seven Years," "The Mourners," "Take Pity," and "The Bill."

In their splendid introduction to *A Treasury of Yiddish Fiction*, Irving

Howe and Eliezer Greenberg wrote, "*The virtue of powerlessness, the power of helplessness, the company of the dispossessed, the sanctity of the insulted and the injured,* these finally are the great themes of Yiddish literature."[69] These are are also themes that lie at the center of much of Malamud's best work—as we would expect of an author who argues through the title and epigraph of his second collection, that idiots, not women and children, should get preferential treatment. And there's a good deal of bitter humor, irony, and fantasy in both Malamud's fiction and Yiddish literature. But Malamud's claims that his short fiction has been far more influenced by Joyce, Hemingway, and Anderson than by Peretz or Scholem Aleichem are surely justified by his experiments with point of view, by his terse economy, and by the way in which he created webs of symbolic interrelationships among thoughts, acts, and objects both in fiction that dealt with Jews and fiction that did not.

And there are profound differences between Malamud's New York Jews and the inhabitants of Yiddish fiction or the actual ghettos and shtetls. Though the Jews of the Pale were isolated from gentiles, their communal bonds were very strong. In contrast, Malamud's Jews tend to be, as Joseph Featherstone has put it, "on the edge of urban disintegration."[70] Moreover, as Howe and Greenburg have argued, their political powerlessness and their precariousness—for a conclusive pogrom might wipe them out at any time—encouraged a good many of the inhabitants of the Pale to live in "an almost timeless proximity with the mythical past and the redeeming future, with Abraham's sacrifice of his beloved son to a still more beloved God and the certain appearance of a cleansing Messiah—for heaven was *real,* not a useful myth, and each day that passed brought one nearer to redemption."[71] The pasts that the denizens of Malamud's folk ghetto look back to are usually so far from being mythically satisfying that they tend to add to the pathos of the present. Feld thinks of his youth in a Polish shtetl as wasted. All that seems to redeem the youth of Lieb and Kobotsky in "The Loan" is that they still had hope and, in night school, memorized a poem about nature at play even as the prisons of their lives closed around them. There is no Messiah in the folk ghetto, and Malamud's heaven is emphatically unreal, peopled as it might be in "Angel Levine," by Jewish Negroes who, once back on earth, can give way to boozing, wenching, and anti-Semitism.

But if Malamud brought to his quasi-timeless, quasi-placeless, quasi-legendary New York the shtetl's sense of enclosure and limited worldly possibility, its expert knowledge of hunger and suffering, he also sometimes brought the possibilities of inner transcendence, whether with sudden moral fervor or with prolonged discipline. And the shtetl affinity to the miraculous asserts itself in what Marcus Klein has called Malamud's "special note . . . a mysticism which compels all the discrete actualities of his knowledge to extremes. The fiction hurries reality into myth, or into parable or exemplum or allegory, and its typical process has been a sudden transition of particularities."[72] More often than not in the stories of *The Magic Barrel* the hurrying, generalizing movement suddenly concludes with a frozen, epiphanic image.

For example, toward the end of "The Mourners" Kessler, a mean-spirited, retired egg candler confronts for perhaps the first time in his life the wrong he has done. Smitten "to the heart," his self-hatred is so great that he rocks back and forth, moaning and tearing at himself with his nails. Gruber, the landlord who has driven Kessler to this state through his repeated attempts to evict the old man, mistakenly interprets Kessler's behavior as a mourning for the death of Gruber himself. After "an enormous constricted weight" rises from chest to head, so that Gruber awaits a stroke for a full minute, the feeling passes and the still miserable landlord looks around the room to find that its unpleasant particularities—its filth and stench—are miraculously transformed: the room is "clean, drenched in daylight and fragrance." Then, suffering "unbearable remorse for the way he had treated the old man," Gruber tears the sheet off Kessler's bed, wraps it around himself and, "sinking heavily to the floor . . . [also becomes] a mourner" (*TMB*, 25–26).

The story several times refers to Gruber's bulk, and his name (which in Yiddish would signify "the gross one") emphasizes both his physical and moral grossness. Though not needy, he has let himself become imprisoned by the pressures, some of them financial, that he feels bearing down on him. The penetrating of the fat around his moral center had begun the preceding day when the landlord was temporarily shaken by Kessler's asking him if he was "a Hitler or a Jew." On the final day Gruber takes the first halting step toward his metaphorical Jewishness when he decides "to get the old man into a public home" (*TMB*, 23–24). He is driven much closer with the piercing fear that he experiences when the janitor tells him that spying through the keyhole of Kessler's door has failed to reveal any movements. The fear crescendos in the uncanny experiencing of his own death, but then the terror modulates into his radiant transforming of the room. A benign reading would have it that this signals at the least Gruber's belated spiritual transformation. The final frozen image—Gruber's mourning for what he has become—is one of the authorial sleights of hand that close a good many of Malamud's stories. By the very nature of his act, Gruber is transformed into a mourner for the dead or dying insensitive bully that he was just a short time before.

"The Mourners" is about spiritual transformation, but it is also about how a fat businessman's error drives him to wrap a sheet about himself and sink in ritual posture in a stinking tenement room. Gruber is that stock figure in Yiddish and Malamudian fiction, a schlemiel—a bungler who could fall on his back and break his nose. But the schlemiel is often a sort of holy fool, whose inappropriate acts and statements have an experiential wisdom about them that the "rational" world lacks. Malamud sometimes extends to his schlemiels "rewards" that, like so much Yiddish humor, mock and celebrate simultaneously. Ruth Wisse has observed that "the classic expression of Yiddish irony is the saying . . . 'Thou hast chosen us from among the nations—why did you have to pick on the Jews?'"[73]

Consider, for example, the closing of the title story of *The Magic Barrel*. With imagery that Malamud has said was inspired by that transcriber of shtetl miracles, Marc Chagall, violins and lit candles revolve in the sky as Leo Finkle, with flowers outthrust, rushes forward to meet the prostitute he intends to save with his love. He is simultaneously inspiring and a sort of silly stagedoor Johnny, rushing with roses to the stripper's door.

The rabbinical student was even more of an ʼinnocent at the beginning of the story—the only main character of the ten *Magic Barrel* stories set in the United States who enters the story with no particular history of suffering behind him. In "The Magic Barrel," as in "The Last Mohican," Malamud drops the guarded protagonist into the educating crucible of pain by bringing him into contact with an uncanny older man who is a recurrent figure of Yiddish folklore. Less than a week after he consults the *schadchan* (marriage broker), Pinye Salzman, Leo Finkle learns that

> he did not love God so well as he might, because he had not loved man. . . . He saw himself for the first time as he truly was—unloved and loveless.
>
> The week that followed was the worst of his life . . . however he drew consolation that he was Jew and that a Jew suffered. (*TMB*, 204–5)

In 1973 Malamud said, "I don't believe in the supernatural except as I can invent it. . . . I write fantasy because when I do I am imaginative and funny and having a good time."[74] Often much of the imaginative pleasure that comes from Malamud's sudden or prolonged surges into the uncanny would seem to follow from his sense that he is capturing with arresting metaphors both the ultimate unknowability of things and the possibilities for moral assertion within that unknowability. For example, Klein offers Salzman's improbable appearances in "The Magic Barrel" as instances of the sudden transition of particularities. Much more contributes to the marriage broker's ultimate mutability than his explaining an impossibly prompt appearance in Leo Finkle's room with "I rushed" (*TMB*, 211).

At first reading Salzman has his complexities but is still the "commercial cupid" (*TMB*, 199) who, with the enthusiasm of a used-car salesman, overpraises his male clients to his female ones and vice versa. If his eyes are mournful, it may be because, for all his enthusiasm, he does not do well, or because his profession is no longer honored, or because his daughter Stella reminds him that he is merely a peddler of flesh when she begins peddling her own. Perhaps he intentionally leaves his daughter's picture with Finkle because the approval he feels for the rabbinical student's face, both ascetically innocent and latently sensual, is his approval of a manageable victim. Whether or not he intentionally leaves the picture, he is in the placement business, and he finally places his daughter. Are the prayers for the dead that he chants in the last line of the story (as Leo rushes forward to meet Stella) for his own moral self? For Leo's future? Other readings offer themselves but, within this line of reasoning, all lead to King Frederick William of Prussia's comment about the sympathy that Catherine II showed for Poland when the third partition erased that country from the map of Europe: "She wept but took."

But there is a second way to read the story. As Yakov Bok, the protagonist of *The Fixer*, sighs when he learns how he is being framed, "So that's how it is. . . . Behind the world lies another world."[75] Behind the world of Salzman, the endearing but scheming pimp, lies the world of Salzman the holy spirit, placed on earth to bring Leo Finkle from an arid knowledge of the law to the perception that he can fulfill the spirit of the law only by loving in this world. Thus Salzman arranges the meeting between Leo and Lily Hirschorn because he knows it will drive the rabbinical student to the shattering admission that "I came to God not because I loved Him but because I did not" (*TMB*, 204). As Leo becomes stronger in his resolution to save himself by saving

Stella, his need for Salzman grows less. By the time the latter agrees to arrange the meeting he is "transparent to the point of vanishing" (*TMB*, 213), for his work in this world is almost finished. Leo has learned of the universality of suffering, manifested by the terrible pain in the eyes of Salzman and his daughter, and he is determined to do what he can about it. And so, for the first time in the story, Salzman stops eating his fish before he has finished it—one must eat to survive—and it remains only for him to chant the death of the old man and the birth of the new.

With Salzman as spirit, his improbable manifestations become a matter of course. His wife's accusation of her *luftmensch* husband with his office "in the air . . . in his socks" (*TMB*, 210–11) becomes a happy metaphor for the way the spiritual must be grounded in the physical. Correspondingly, the fish that Salzman devours could, as the early Christians believed, symbolize immortality of the spirit. Yet the fishy odors that cling to him and to his pictures of unfulfilled women could, and certainly seem to, come from the magic barrel of life itself, with all its sad experience, desperate innocence, improbable hopes, and teeming sexual odors.

But in a way that reminds us of Malamud's frequent mirror images, or optical confusions, or characters whose separate eyes do separate things, each reading keeps swimming back into the other. For example, the story is crowded with biblical allusions or unintentional recastings (for Malamud's imagination was strongly folkloristic),[76] but do these reinforce or ironically undercut Salzman as an improbable but intentionally redeeming angel? In the face of irresolvable ambiguity, Leo makes his decision and so too can the reader choose a "majority reading." As we regard the story, its "reality," like life itself, is likely to shift in a way that inspires both delight and frustration.

Because the terms of "Angel Levine" are more consistently those of fantasy—which is to say they partake somewhat less dizzily of the world's ambiguity—the terms of the choice that the afflicted tailor Manischevitz must make are, though complex, much more clean-cut:

> Tears blinded the tailor's eyes. Was ever a man so tried? Should he say he believed a half-drunken Negro to be an angel? . . . a wheel in his mind whirred: believe, do not, yes, no, yes, no. The pointer pointed to yes, to between yes and no, to no, no it was yes. He sighed. It moved but one had still to make a choice.

> "I think you are an angel from God." He said it in a broken voice
> thinking, If you said it it was said. If you believed it you must say
> it. If you believed, you believed. . . .
>   Levine burst into tears. "How you have humiliated me." (*TMB*,
> 55)

Twice before this climatic scene, Manishevitz has been unable to
believe that the Negro is an assisting angel. Consequently, several
nodes of meaning cluster here. In terms of interdependency, the tailor's inability to be fully human and give credit (to recast a statement
from "The Bill") drives Levine into the stereotypes of a *shvartzah* (Negro) joke: from a worried if somewhat sententious correctness to a
heavy Negro dialect, from shabbily dressed dignity to lust and drunk-
enness in a sort of Sporting Life costume. In terms of the workings of
faith, the inability to make a difficult assertion only renders it yet more
difficult: since Manishevitz cannot accept a sober Levine in his apartment, he has to accept the stage Negro while they are surrounded by
anti-Semites in a Harlem dive. But as with the Jews of the shtetl or
ghetto, catastrophe may make the impossible possible, the irrational
reasonable. With his wife "at death's door" (*TMB*, 51), the irrational
speaks: the tailor dreams of Levine preening his wings. From this follows the final trip to Harlem, the leap of faith, and Levine's winged
ascension.

The shtetl dynamics that inform some of Malamud's fiction can in
good part be described as a simultaneous holding on and letting go.
One clings to the possibility of the miraculous, to the value of the
morally developed self, to the value of the other. But to make any one
of these assertions one might have to disregard what the order of things
before our eyes obdurately proclaims to be "reality." This is why the
suggestion that Manischevitz is less than human is by almost any other
standard unfair. With his addressing God as "sweetheart" (*TMB*, 44),
his fearful bewilderment as he pushes himself through a Harlem of
trousers with a razor slit in the seat, or a group of blacks, comically,
uncannily, engaged in Talmudic exegesis, the tailor is most humanly
endearing. But the pressure of his need, which in this case derives from
his love for his dying wife, drives him to be still more human and give
still more credit.

Malamud also used fantasy to excavate less benign human strata.
"Take Pity" is set in a sparsely furnished institutional room in a gray,
embittered afterworld. The grimness of the locale and of the emotions

that surface there work within the fantasy to freeze for eternity the comparable earthly grimness of act, place, and emotion. The terrestrial story emerges as "Rosen, the ex-coffee salesman, wasted, eyes despairing" recounts to Davidov, "the census-taker" (*TMB*, 87) the process that finally drove him to take his life.

Rosen's narrative centers on his attempts to help Eva Kalish and her two slowly starving young daughters. But Eva will not accept help, out of what combination of twisted pride, self-hatred, death wish, and sense of fatality we can never know. The ambivalent possibilities of the title, with the assertion of "Take" and the sympathetic merging of "Pity," seem to have exhausted themselves by the time Rosen recounts how he said to himself, "Here . . . is a very strange thing—a person that you can never give her anything.—*But I will give.*" He gives up his possessions by willing them to the widow and to her two girls when she dies; he gives up his life by putting his head in the oven. But Rosen only drives Eva deeper into her compulsion: she kills herself, probably kills her children, and the story ends as they continue their struggle in the afterworld—but with the new twist that she now seeks him out with raised arms and "haunted, beseeching eyes" (*TMB*, 94).

The final description of her eyes reminds us of Rosen's "despairing ones" and deepens our sense of the perverse collaboration between the salesman and Eva, a more grimly comic version of what seems like the perfect marriage between the sadist and the masochist. "Beat me!" the masochist luxuriantly pleads on their wedding night. "No!" the sadist triumphantly replies, as their folie à deux, like Rosen and Eva's, continues. Some critics feel that Rosen's sense of charity is at fault, that he offers Eva only money—which could demean any reasonably proud person.

But their colliding motivations shape a more complicated interaction. After Axel Kalish's death, Rosen first offers Eva advice as he tells the widow to take the $1,000 insurance money and her children, run from her "graveyard" (*TMB*, 89) grocery, find a job and, eventually, someone to marry. Malamud has said that he's obsessed with the drama of character fulfilling itself and he has been praised for bringing to much of his fiction a sense of the transforming force of character more present in nineteenth-century fiction than twentieth. Eva's character has this relative autonomy, but her wilfullness is finally perverse: "With marriage I am finished. Nobody wants a poor widow with two children. . . . In my whole life I never had anything. In my whole life I always suffered. I don't expect better. This is my life" (*TMB*, 89).

Rosen attempts to distance his generous impulses from the cash nexus with his subsequent gifts of food and his offering living space and childcare payment so that she might get a job and pay from her earnings for their own food and clothing—and save some money that would bring her some independence in a subsequent marriage. But her resistance drives him to steadily greater insensitivity. The offers of marriage—"What did she have to lose?" (*TMB*, 91)—and to pay for her dowry so she could marry a "strong, healthy husband that he will support you and your girls" (*TMB*, 92) could offend someone whose independence has taken a less maddened form than Eva Kalish's. It is after her refusal of the dowry money and her demand that he leave her store and never return to it that anger begins to replace his compassion—"I felt like to pick up a chair and break her head" (*TMB*, 93)—and it is increasingly from this anger that Rosen tries to give with money—first through impersonating a nonexistent friend paying back a debt to her dead husband and then through his suicide.

Rosen's original compassion for the slowly starving girls is genuine, and he justifies bringing them "a nice piece sirloin" in words that powerfully resonate in a work by Bernard Malamud: "So what else could I do? I have a heart and I am human" (*TMB*, 90). That the ex-salesman then interrupts his narrative to weep supports his claim that he is "human." But then we would have to say that being "inhuman" is just a way of being "human, all too human"—to use Nietzsche's appraisal of human frailty. Dahfu, the brilliant, eccentric African king in Bellow's *Henderson the Rain King*, feels that all humans receive blows, but "A brave man will try to make the evil stop with him. He shall keep the blow. No man shall get it from him, and that is a sublime ambition."[77] Eva is all too willing to pass on the misery of her life to her children, and Rosen gradually becomes willing to pass back to Eva, in the form of despotic generosity, the blows he has received from her—blows that have affected his ability to eat and sleep, hurt his back "where was missing one kidney" (*TMB*, 92), hurt his sense of himself as a kind, effectual person.

Davidov also passes on the blows he receives; in fact, much of the power of the story follows from the ways the incidents that emerge from the narrative frame collide with and comment upon the details of the story that Rosen tells. Consider the first sentence of the story: "Davidov, the census-taker, opened the door without knocking, limped into the room and sat wearily down. Out came his notebook and he was on the job." His Yinglish and eccentric ways—like writing in an archaic language—tend to obscure how sharply Malamud has caught with his characterization the mean-spirited *fonctionnaire,* whose inability to extend sympathy interestingly counterpoints Eva's and Rosen's. Davidov doesn't knock because he's overworked—limping and weary—and he's just passing on the little blows he feels. He's on the job immediately because even someone exuding as much painful eloquence as Rosen has to him very little, if any, worth or interest as a person or former person. Davidov's heart has run as dry as his pen. Like the protagonist of Tolstoy's overwhelming indictment of bureaucratic banality (and so much more), "The Death of Ivan Ilych," Davidov tries to strip all professional inquiries of any existential content. Like the terrain surrounding the room, his mission is a bit vague, but one can piece it together. He knows just how Rosen and Eva killed themselves; his task seems to be to discern just how Rosen's and Eva's interaction caused their suicides. But he is granted no knowledge of deaths apart from suicides. Thus, his attempts to discern how Axel Kalish died are unusually persistent:

> "How did he die?" Davidov spoke impatiently. "Say in one word."
> "From what he died?—he died, that's all."
> "Answer, please, this question."
> "Broke in him something. That's how."
> "Broke what?"
> "Broke what breaks. He was talking to me how bitter was his life, and he touched me on my sleeve to say something else, but the next minute his face got small and he fell down dead, the wife screaming, the little girls crying that it made in my heart pain." (*TMB*, 87–88)

The pain of Kalish's life, annihilating death, and then the anguish of the survivors: all of this indicts the inhumanity of the order in which we live. Ginzburg, the exterminating angel in "Idiots First," defends it as "the cosmic universal law, goddamit, the one I got to follow myself" (*IF*, 13). Such concerns are lost on the surly bureaucrat, unaffected by anything but Rosen's failure to give him the desired one-word reduction of the cause of Kalish's death. (Davidov's other evident response to Rosen is a negative one: perceiving that Rosen covets the chair he's sitting on—the only one in the room—he pettily refuses to give it up.) Far from being moved by the powerful conclusion of the ex-salesman's narrative, Davidov is bored: the information he needed for his spectral "census" has been gathered.

Davidov writes "in an old fashioned language that they don't use it nowadays" (*TMB*, 94), which is to say that tales of bureaucratic inhumanity, the inhuman order of things, and the amount of damage that two people of strong, conflicting wills can inflict on each other are very old tales indeed. That one can leave "Take Pity," surely one of Malamud's best stories, thinking of Ugolino and Ruggiero, near the bottom of Dante's Inferno, gnawing each other's heads until Judgment Day, suggests its force.

Davidov's inability to give Rosen any of the pity he seeks is in keeping with the implicit critique of institutionalized assistance in *The Magic Barrel*. Either Malamud denies to his desperate Jews any of the support structures depression America offered or he suggests that they're worthless. The doctor in "Angel Levine" can do nothing to ease Manishevitz's physical and emotional pain save to think that "he would someday get him into a public home" (*TMB*, 51). More tellingly, before his conversion Gruber decides to offer to get Kessler out of his apartment by offering to get him into a public home. Whether spiritually or economically, a character's situation can be bettered only by treating someone else as an end and not a means—by disregarding what the other might do for oneself—or by finding someone who will treat him or her in the same way.

Thus Kobotsky, the arthritic ex-furrier whose "face [glitters] with misery," goes to Lieb for the $200 for the tombstone he has, for the past five years, been unable to provide for his dead wife's grave. In Charles May's words, "Lieb's crying into his bread to make it sell reflects the broader irony of the traditional Jewish experience of misery—an historical misery that instead of defeating one makes one strong."[78] Kobotsky would seem to have gone to the right man, since what has become strong about Lieb is not his body—weakened as it is by a hernia and cataracts—but his desire to act in accordance with the meaning of his name—with love. Since May's fine discussion of the workings of the "The Loan"—in terms of the colliding strengths and needs of Kobotsky, Lieb, and Bessie (Lieb's ferociously self-protective wife)—is included in part 3, I turn now to the three stories in *The Magic Barrel* that deal with New York gentiles: "A Summer's Reading," "The Bill," and "The Prison."

In 1950, the year of Malamud's emergence from his apprenticehood, he published three stories: "The First Seven Years" and "The Cost of Living" are stories of the folk ghetto; the protagonist of "The Prison" is Italian, and the treatments of setting and diction consequently vary.

Between 1950 and 1956 Malamud published roughly one story that did not deal with a New York Jew for every two that did. Between 1956, which saw the publication of "A Summer's Reading," and 1958, when *The Magic Barrel* was released, Malamud published only two stories in periodicals: "The Last Mohican" and "Behold the Key." Both came out in spring 1958, shortly before the collection was released, and both were set in Rome, as Malamud began to mine the experience gained during 1956–57 when he lived in the Eternal City and traveled throughout Europe.

I mention all this because, as the fifties unfolded, the great success of the experiments with Yinglish, and with temporal and spatial abstraction in the tales of the folk ghetto and in *The Assistant*, must have posed a genuine problem to Malamud. So technically innovative and ambitious an author, one so concerned with the need to grow, was not about to let these strategies harden into a formula as he attempted to replicate his greatest successes in the short story or novel form. (Each of Malamud's novels is technically different from the others to a degree that is not the case with the novels of such leading contemporaries as Bellow, Roth, Updike, Cheever, Tyler, Percy, and Vonnegut.) One solution was to move from the calculatedly impoverished New York setting to ones of headswimming plenitude by having the protagonists collide with the cultural complexity and diversity of Italy, as Malamud himself did. Or there were the impressions of his months in Washington with the census bureau, which inspired "The Girl of My Dreams." But if he was to continue to set stories in such a comfortable fictional terrain as New York, save that the stories revolved around gentile sensibilities, what strategies from the tales of the folk ghetto would be appropriate? What other strategies might he come up with to bring to these stories the immediacy and power of works like "The First Seven Years," "Take Pity," or "The Loan"?

The abstractions of time and place in the tales of the folk ghetto bring to them some of the emotional residue of centuries of Jewish experience. But some of the strategies of the realistic tradition—in particular, the precise but evocative notation of surrounding objects, manners, and actions—can bring the reader to at least as full a sense of shared experience. This Malamud achieved in "A Summer's Reading" by returning to his geographical instead of his ethnic origins. Since no street names are offered we cannot place the locale as precisely as we could that of "The Place Is Different Now." In fact, from the internal evidence we know only that the story is set in Queens or in Brooklyn.

The way in which Malamud gains verisimilitude by combining dramatized and remembered acts with scenic detail (instead of dropping place names) is one of the story's primary strengths. "A Summer's Reading" is set in a working-class neighborhood in which the nineteen-year-old protagonist, George Stoyonovich, had as a boy played punchball and been given nickels for lemon ices, in which "during the sultry days some of the storekeepers and their wives sat on chairs on thick, broken sidewalks in front of their shops, fanning themselves," and where, in a lovely urban portrait that Ben Shahn or Reginald Marsh might have painted, "Nights, during the hot weather, he [Mr. Cattanzara] sat on his stoop in an undershirt, reading the *New York Times* in the light of the shoemaker's window. . . . And all the time he was reading the paper, his wife, a fat woman with a white face, leaned out of the window, gazing into the street, her thick white arms folded under her loose breast, on the window ledge."

The reader, Mr. Cattanzara, is "a stocky, baldheaded man who worked in a change booth in an IRT station"; his cultural yearnings are suggested by the fact that he reads the *Times* "from the first page to the last" (*TMB,* 136–37) instead of tabloids like the *News* or the *Mirror* as typical neighbors like the Stoyonovichs do. We might see the wife as either the attending muse of her husband's aspirations or a seeker gazing out into the street with her own undisclosed yearnings. Since Cattanzara functions as the muse of George's emotional growth, the first reading is particularly apt.

The opening words of the story obliquely describe George's predicament: "George Stoyonovich was a neighborhood boy who had quit high school on an impulse when he was sixteen." Three years later, the consequences of this action—shame at having to tell possible employers and neighbors that he had not finished school—have created so low a sense of self-worth that George stays "off the streets and in his room most of the day" (*TMB,* 135). When he does go out in the relative cool of the evening, he doesn't join the "guys hanging out on the candy store corner. A couple of them he had known his whole life, but nobody recognized each other" (*TMB,* 136). We cannot tell if these peers share George's low opinion of himself or if they pick up from his body language his desire to remain apart from them.

Unemployed, George could fill his yawning days, enrich his future, and rejoin the community by attending school. But he is filled with rationalizations. In summer school "the kids in his classes would be too young. He also considered registering in a night high school, only he didn't like the idea of the teachers always telling him what to do. He felt they had not respected him."

The narrative voices of the gentile stories lack the tonal variety of those of the folk ghetto, but they have their own quieter, usually functional, disjunctions. To continue with the story's opening paragraph, the next sentence is "The result was that he stayed off the streets and in his room most of the day." Though the matter-of-fact voice is the narrator's, the irrational causality—immure yourself because teachers of years past might not have respected you?—pulls us into the irrational, confused workings of George's mind. The operative word is in the earlier sentence: respect. George, who fears both the negative evaluations he might receive in school and the new demands to which completing his education might subject him, does not respect himself. Consider the rest of the paragraph: "He was close to twenty and had needs with the neighborhood girls, but no money to spend, and he couldn't get more than an occasional few cents because his father was poor, and his sister Sophie, who resembled George, a tall bony girl of twenty-three, earned very little and what she had she kept for herself. Their mother was dead, and Sophie had to take care of the house" (*TMB*, 135).

This is actually the language of self-derogation. We learn in the next paragraph that George does indeed clean their five room flat, though probably so sporadically that his sister often has to add housework to her already long working day. George's guilt for this surfaces with his refusal to take any credit for helping. The description of Sophie tells us that George feels *he* is unattractive. In fact the first two paragraphs of the story subtly suggest that George feels that he is the most inferior member of an inferior family: he does not work and they have to rise early or travel far for what little they make. The lack of money is an excuse for not having to meet the rejection that George expects from girls.

On his nightly walks, he leaves the neighborhood that he feels defines him as a loser, and, "in a darkly lit little park with benches and trees and an iron railing, giving it a feeling of privacy," the yearnings that exist beneath the self-derogation emerge. Encouraged by this touch of the urban pastoral, George likes himself enough to air desires for "a good job . . . a private house with a porch, on a street with trees. . . . some money in his pocket to buy things . . . a girl to go with, so as not to be so lonely, especially on Saturday nights. He wanted people to like and respect him. . . . Around midnight he got

up and drifted back to his hot and stony neighborhood" (*TMB*, 137)—
or back to his stifling sense of being imprisoned in failure and the consequent way he runs his life. The way that the quoted cadences capture George's heavy sense of his own failure typifies Malamud's
splendid control of tone throughout the whole of "A Summer's
Reading."

But by meeting Mr. Cattanzara during one of his nightly walks,
George interacts with the neighborhood that lies between his flat and
the park. Ashamed to tell the changemaker that he is out of work,
George instead announces that he is reading "a lot to pick up my education. . . . Maybe about a hundred [books]" (*TMB*, 138). Cattanzara
spreads the lie around the neighborhood, and George enjoys unearned
respect from both neighbors and family, who generously see in his supposed project a disciplined realization of their own desires for a better
life.

As the summer wears on George feels good enough about himself to
clean the house every day. Earlier he had cleaned only "when it got
on his nerves" (*TMB*, 136), or when his guilt had grown too strong even
for him. Sophie now gives him a dollar a week allowance, which
George feels he manages shrewdly (though he is not about to try to
take a girl out). Best of all being "regarded . . . highly . . . in the
neighborhood, where people had known him from the time he was a
kid playing punchball," he sometimes feels "so good that he [skips]
the park at the end of the evening" (*TMB*, 140). But George's self-
regard stops short of permitting him to read books that might justify
the neighbor's regard by, in one way or another, bettering himself. At
one point, Malamud tells us that "lately he couldn't stand made-up
stories, they got on his nerves" (*TMB*, 136). It is the "made up" in
fiction that, as Malamud said in 1959, "must remind man that he has,
in his human striving, invented nothing less than his freedom."[79] Fearful of the possibilities of his freedom, George reads no books, story
books or otherwise.

The bill comes due one night when a tipsy Mr. Cattanzara chal-
lenges George to name one book he has read. The superbly rendered
scene closes when George, who can only close his eyes, opens them to
find the older man gone, but his closing words still in his ears:
"George, don't do what I did" (*TMB*, 143). For Cattanzara, who seems
to drink as a way of dealing with his vocational imprisonment in the
change booth, the mistake would seem to have been accepting too low
an evaluation of his abilities, too enclosed a vision of the future.

With his fear that all will know he took credit where none was due, George's proper, Malamudian education begins—not in school or even in books, but in suffering. Feeling that he has lost the right to appear before neighbors or family, "He stayed in his room for almost a week . . . though the weather was terrible and his small room stifling. He found it very hard to breathe, each breath was like drawing a flame into his lungs" (*TMB*, 143).

We remember that Malamud listed Sherwood Anderson as one of the short story writers who influenced him. This story, centering on a lie told by a nineteen-year-old who tends to rationalize and has a low opinion of himself, is reminiscent of Anderson's "I'm a Fool." But unlike Anderson, Malamud ends his story happily, by bringing a development to his protagonist that is both emotional and moral. Cattanzara extends yet more credit to George, spreading the rumor that he has completed his book list. The narrative then jumps a month or two. The pressure to start paying off his bill to the neighborhood presumably built within him during the time because, "one evening in the fall" George runs out of the flat, not to the park to spin fantasies about a better life but to the library, where he begins to work toward it. There, George finally overcomes his fears of a more elevated conception of himself as, "struggling to control an inward trembling he easily [counts] off a hundred [books], then [sits] down at a table to read" (*TMB*, 144).

The title is ironic, for the only books that George read that summer were the metaphoric ones of psyches—his own, and those of the people with whom he came in contact. From this "reading" he was finally able to perceive some of what he owed to himself and to others. The metaphorical reading, which made possible the encounter with literal books, was ballasted by the weight of the neighborhood's moral support—unmatched by any of the locales in all of the Malamud fictions set in the United States—and as palpable, as convincing, as the weight of Mrs. Cattanzara's loose breast upon her thick white arms. Although not as idiosyncratically startling as "The First Seven Years," "The Magic Barrel," or "The Last Mohican," "A Summer's Reading" is an evocative, profound, and beautifully made story.

As a writer with a strong naturalist bent—it is no accident that he wrote his M.A. thesis on the novels of Thomas Hardy—Malamud often explored the possibilities of freedom within powerful, shaping forces. In the stories of the folk ghetto the spectral neighborhoods seem more to confirm or deepen the inner lives of the characters: truly twisted psyches like Eva Kalish's or Bessie Lieb's were bent before they arrived in America. For all of the suffering that George has gone through, he is young and malleable; his emotions are often painful, but like the neighborhood, they are a part of a mid-range of experience. The neighborhood has a shaping force that the folk ghetto lacks; in this case the force is benign. The locale of "The Bill," first published three years earlier, in 1953, is also a determiner, but one that is far from benign.

The block on which the story is set is not so much a place as a metaphor of baffled existence. The use of locale and the language in which the locale is rendered are two of the reasons that "The Bill" has much more of the "bittersweet" quality so many critics associated with Malamud's best fiction of the fifties and early sixties, and why this story is so much closer in feeling and theme to the stories of the folk ghetto than "A Summer's Reading." The urban poetry of "A Summer's Reading" is lovely, but one could imagine Updike or a slightly updated Howells writing it. Only Malamud could have begun a story in this way: "Though the street was somewhere near a river, it was landlocked and narrow, a crooked row of aged brick tenement buildings. A child throwing a ball straight up saw a bit of pale sky" (*TMB*, 145). Philip Roth's search for a sentence that perfectly expressed his sense of Malamud as a "sorrowing chronicler of human need . . . of blockaded lives racked with need for the light, the lift, of a little hope"[80] led him to quote the preceding one.

But the quest for light is baffled on the landlocked street of the story—as blasted a terrain in its way as Melville's Encantadas is in its. The spirit of the place is a deforming, darkening malignity, whose force has bent the row of houses crooked. It has blackened the building in which the story's central intelligence, Willy Schlegel, works as a janitor, as it has the building across the street. In the basement of the second building is a "small dark delicatessen owned by Mr. and Mrs. F. Panessa, really a hole in the [blackened] wall." Though Willy is "tall and broadbacked," the building in which he lives and toils has imposed its own dark image upon him. His "heavy face" has been "seamed dark from the coal and ashes he shoved around all winter, and his hair often looked gray from the dust the wind whirled up at him out of the ash cans." The contagion of the place has made the eyes of his wife, Etta, "gaunt"—a surrealistically apt adjective—and it seems to have killed their four-year-old child of diphtheria, a contagious disease.

Theodore Solotaroff has observed that "the resonance of such brief tales as 'The Loan,' 'The Bill' and 'Take Pity' results mainly from Malamud's uncanny sense of what types of people belong in the same story, of the subtle and unexpected ways in which relations bind and influence.[81] Willy's dramatic complements are the Panessas, a beautifully mannered, elderly couple whose innocence and independence brought them into this block of corrosive experience. Because they did not want to depend upon their daughters—whose characters they feel have been damaged by their marriages to selfish men—they talked over the purchase of the basement store "for many nights and days" before concluding that it "would at least give them a living." Therefore, in a few phrases whose clumsy earnestness anticipates the couple's pathos, "Panessa, a retired factory worker, withdrew his three thousands of savings and bought this little delicatessen store" (*TMB*, 145–46).

The Panessas' vulnerability and Willy's deformity fatefully mesh one day while the janitor is so absorbed in airing his complaints about "how the tenants goaded him all the time and what the cruel and stingy landlord could think up for him to do in that smelly five-floor dungeon" that he runs up a bill for three dollars—six times the amount of money he has on him. Unwilling to have Willy continue looking "like a dog that had just had a licking" Mr. Panessa responds with the hopefulness of the child seeking the bit of pale sky between the darkened walls. "Willy could pay the rest whenever he wanted . . . Mr. Panessa [chirps][;] . . . everything was run on credit, business and everything else, because after all what was credit but the fact that people were human beings, and if you were really a human being you could give credit to somebody else and he gave credit to you" (*TMB*, 146–47).

As much as Morris Bober's frequently quoted credo, which is at the center of *The Assistant*,[82] Panessa's words express what is for Malamud ideal human relationship. One of the more telling images in American literature of the way in which the ideal can deteriorate in the crucible of experience is the valley of ashes in *The Great Gatsby*: "a fantastic farm where ashes . . . take the forms of houses and chimneys and rising smoke, and, finally, with a transcendent effort, of men who move dimly and already crumbling through the powdery air."[83] The image of the human within Willy, the man of the ash cans, has survived enough for him to be moved by Panessa's recognition and for him to trade on it by demanding more and more credit. But it has deteriorated too much for him to behave responsibly. The Willy who crosses the street to the Panessas, "who were always waiting for him to come in" (*TMB*, 147), is an addict pulled toward his fix.

Malamud interestingly complicates our response to Willy's obsession. In their innocence, kindness, and eagerness to please, the Panessas feed Willy's addiction. And money that might have gone to the Panessas is consumed by Willy's desire to buy something for Etta that he thinks is beautiful. The package he takes from the furnace room and gives her contains a black, beaded dress, which captures both his deformed or blackened condition and his touching aspirations for elegance. Malamud pushes the reader deeper into the tangle of human motivation by having Etta say she would not wear the dress "because the only time he ever brought her anything was when he had done something wrong" (*TMB*, 147). But she now begins to collaborate with her husband's obsession: she lets Willy do all the shopping and no longer nags when he does buy "on trust" at the Panessas. One day, when the bill had risen to over eighty-three dollars—a formidable sum in the world of this story—Mr. Panessa, smiling, asks Willy for some payment, and this is the last day that either Schlegel shops in the basement grocery.

Willy's response to the bill moves through two phases: resistance to paying and hopeless attempts to pay. The first phase both peaks and ends when, after a month, his wife reminds him of the bill. Like Eva Kalish and Bessie Lieb, Willy parades his disfigurement instead of his humanity:

> "What have I got that I can pay? Ain't I been a poor man every day of my life?"
>
> She was sitting at the table and lowered her arms and put her head down on them and wept.
>
> "With what?" he shouted, his face lit up dark and webbed. "With the meat off my bones?"
>
> "With the ashes in my eyes. With the piss I mop up on the floors. With the cold in my lungs when I sleep." (*TMB*, 149)

From hatred of the Panessas to a night drunk in the gutter and sobbing repentance to his wife, he moves to the second phase. But financial pressures drive the landlord to cut Willy's already slender salary and expense money. And so he and Etta extend the credit of their intensified labors to the tenants, but are no more paid for it than the Panessas were by Willy. Finally, the janitor responds to Mrs. Panessa's poignant request for ten dollars by pawning his overcoat for just that amount. He gleefully runs back to the grocery—perhaps the world is a place in which he can meet his debts—but meets two men in black carrying to a hearse the "small and narrow pine box" that holds Mr. Panessa. We learn at the end of the story that "Mrs. Panessa moved away to live first with one stonefaced daughter, then with the other. And the bill was never paid."

Like "Take Pity" and "The Loan," "The Bill" is simultaneously a perfectly integrated, modern short story and a grim parable. The ways in which essentially decent people can damage each other, and in which some lapses can be irreparable are but two of the parable's many readings. Malamud's control of his language was never more sure than in this echoing of the eternal chant over the interactions of four gentiles. In his tribute to Malamud's life and career, Philip Roth observed that in Malamud's "most consciously original moments, when he sensed in his grimly-told impassioned tales the need to sound his deepest note, he remained true to what seemed old and homely, matter-of-factly emitting the most touchingly unadorned poetry to make things even sadder then they already were."[84] Though there are no Jews in "The Bill," the story is so quintessentially Malamudian that Roth chose as an example of this deepest note Willy's response to Mrs. Panessa's telling him her husband had died of old age: "He tried to say some sweet thing but his tongue hung in his mouth like dead fruit on a tree, and his heart was a black-painted window" (*TMB*, 153).

The story is crowded with such bittersweet poetry, much of which emphasizes the way in which the burly Willy brutalizes the fragile, diminutive Panessas. The janitor comes to see the Panessas as "two scrawny, loose-feathered birds"—so much for their earlier chirping hopefulness—and then as "two skinny leafless bushes sprouting up through the wooden floor. He could see through the bushes to the empty shelves." The imagery of vegetation is continued in the next paragraph when Willy's commitment to pay the Panessas rises along with the "grass shoots . . . sticking up from the cracks in the sidewalk" (*TMB*, 150). His moral future *is* bound to their survival. Not having the built-in resonance of centuries that his Yinglish provides, Malamud accentuates the story's lean toward timelessness, toward the emblematic, by occasionally using the language of the Old Testament, of the fable. For example, he explains the landlord's cutbacks with the short statement "Hard times set in" (*TMB*, 150). The felt life of the story is so close to that of the tales of the folk ghetto that, in his chapter on

Malamud's stories, Sidney Richman assumes that the Panessas are Jewish.[85]

Published as it was in 1950, "The Prison" is such a relatively early story that the issue is not so much Malamud's consciously rejecting or employing a strategy that experience had proved successful as his trying, for the first time in a published work, to place a vivid image from his Jewish past in the altered circumstances in which he found himself. That is, Malamud attempted in "The Prison" to place the image of the store as a prison in which moral behavior might flourish within the Italian-American culture, which he has said his marriage opened to him. For author and character alike, this is a neighborhood story. The protagonist's store is on largely Italian Prince Street, hard by largely Italian King Street, where Malamud lived during or shortly before the composition of the story.

Like "The Bill," "The Prison" emphasizes the deforming power of the locale more than the ghetto stories do. But instead of the aching poetry of the later story, flattened general statements—"this tenement crowded, kid-squawking neighborhood, with its lousy poverty"—and careful notation of manners render the neighborhood of "The Prison." Like George Stoyonovich, Tommy quit school when he was sixteen, but this only served to absorb him more fully into the company of the neighborhood bravos. He "began to hang out with the gray-hatted, thick-soled-shoe boys, who had the spare time and the mazuma and showed it in fat wonderful rolls down in the cellar clubs to all who would look . . . who had bought the silver caffe espresso urn . . . and had the girls down" (*TMB*, 97). The critique of working class morality is far less favorable than the one in "A Summer's Reading." Tommy's neighborhood involvements led him to a participation in a holdup, to an arranged marriage to an unlovable woman, and to working seventeen hours a day in a candy store where "usually the whole day stank and he along with it. Time rotted in him." In this story there is neither the urban poetry of "A Summer's Reading"—in the course of the story Tommy leaves the store only through recollection—nor Cattanzara's paternal success with George: Tommy fails in his attempt to keep a neighborhood girl from making his own mistake of stealing.

Malamud's 1950 attempt to fuse the Jewish and Italian aspects of his experience was much less successful than it would be in *The Assistant*, published seven years later. The story's language of baffled ambitions for a better life and the rotting time of one's present could be taken from the novel, but Tommy does not seem sufficiently driven by the combination of weaknesses or commitments or compulsions that implacably turn a Morris Bober or a Frank Alpine or an Eva Kalish into a prisoner. Only twenty-nine, relatively intelligent, filled with street smarts, Tommy often thinks of taking off. Why doesn't he? We can come up with an explanation, beginning with Tommy's sadness over the bitter old age of his Uncle Dom, his role model, and add to it his lack of a profession, and his timidity before the disapproval of others. And surely in the "real world" are people as relatively undamaged as Tommy who accept as bad a life situation from depression or guilt or whatever. But tortuous explanation is an inadequate substitute for the reader's sense of the driven personality fulfilling itself.

It has been said that the principle of a successful short story is that of an explosion: the most force is concentrated in the least space. Much of the success of stories like "The Magic Barrel," "Take Pity," or "The Loan" follows from Malamud's ability to fill the stories with the force—sometimes mysterious like Salzman's, sometimes twisted like Eva Kalish's, sometimes radiant like Lieb's—of the inhabitants of their small spaces. Perhaps Edward O'Brien, who included "The Prison" among the best short stories of 1950, felt that Tommy's interaction with the thief liberated within him the obsessive energy that grows out of the characters' collisions in Malamud's best stories. But just as I feel the closing, ephiphanic image of the girl to be forced, consciously "artistic" ("The girl, like a grotesque dancer, half ran, half fell forward, but at the door she managed to turn her white face and thrust out at him her red tongue" [*TMB*, 104]), so do I feel that Malamud tells us that this obsessive tangle exists, but he does not realize its compulsive force on the page.

Apart from the deepening of the shaping force and concrete reality of the environment, the language of these two gentile stories—"The Prison" and "A Summer's Reading"—most distinguishes them from the six in the collection that deal with New York Jews. (Such common themes as the imprisoning force of one's past and the possibilities of interdependence and suffering are also those of the stories of New York Jews.) In these stories, Malamud still wrote colloquial prose, but he had to forgo in the different narrative and dialogic colloquies the particularly terse, strident tonalities of Yinglish that he rendered so well. Both protagonists are neighborhood losers, but since Tommy is more streetwise, more aggressive than George, the narrative colloquialisms have much more edge to them. Compare, for example, "He [Tommy] wouldn't spit on a candy store, and Rosa was too plain and lank a chick for his personal taste, so he beat it off to Texas and bummed around in too much space" (*TMB*, 98) to the tone that captures George's greater helplessness: "He wished he had some hobby to work at—as a kid he was good in carpentry, but where could he work at it?" (*TMB*, 136). As I suggest above, the more heightened verbal effects of "A Summer's Reading" rise from the descriptions of communal life above the heavy, broken sidewalks. Since Tommy is precisely imprisoned in the store, the poetic effects of "The Prison"—save for the closing image—are the ones that capture not a potentially nourishing neighborhood but Tommy's unhappiness: "his mind was like a dark, empty room" (*TMB*, 102); "he would wake with the sour remembrance of the long night in the store ahead of him" (*TMB*, 99).

Arthur Fidelman, Carl Schneider, and Henry Levin, the protagonists of "The Last Mohican," "Behold the Key," and "The Lady of the Lake," respectively, are relatively young men (in their twenties or thirties) whose varying kinds of innocence are tested against some extremities of the European experience. Since experience is for Malamud in good part the experience of suffering, it is no coincidence that the characters' pasts seem to have been far less damaging than those of the collection's other protagonists, with the exception of Leo Finkle. Moreover, all three live in worlds of secular possibilities at a considerable remove from those of all the collection's overburdened New Yorkers save for Finkle.

But we should not confuse their wealth and ease with that of Jamesian sojourners like Christopher Newman or the postinheritance Isabel Archer. Since Malamud tended much more than James to test the possibilities of moral assertion in the face of material encumbrances, Fidelman and Carl, the flawed but more admirable protagonists, bring limited funds, deadlines, and family obligations to Italy. Carl has two small children he must house with himself and his wife; Fidelman had to borrow part of the money for his trip from a harassed sister with five children. The most callow is the freest: "Having recently come into a small inheritance," Levin quit his job and "went abroad seeking romance" (*TMB*, 105). The secular wealth of the other two follows more from their formal educations and abilities, which they hope will produce extended scholarly studies (of Giotto in Fidelman's case, of the Risorgimento in Carl's).

Though not as battered as a Feld or a Rosen, Fidelman bears his bruises. We learn in the first sentence of "The Last Mohican" that, like the protagonists of Malamud's first four novels, he has gone on a journey in search of a second chance in life after earlier inadequacy: "Fidelman, a self-confessed failure as a painter, came to Italy to prepare a critical study of Giotto." When we first see him as he stands in front of the Rome train station he is clutching a briefcase in one hand. It contains what is, as far as we know, the only testimony he has of his new competency as an art historian: the opening chapter of his study. This "he had carried across the ocean" (*TMB*, 155) like the treasure he thinks it is: "how painstakingly he had built each idea, how cleverly mastered problems of order, form, how impressive the finished product. Giotto reborn!" (*TMB*, 177).

Proud of his ability to get "himself quickly and tightly organized" (*TMB*, 161), Fidelman bustles about Rome during his first eight or nine days there, devoting his mornings to searching catalogs and archives, his afternoons and early evenings to looking at paintings in museums and churches. Sometimes he works on his notes through the night until morning. Though inspired by the wealth of culture, the depth of history around him, Fidelman is also oppressed by it:

> History was mysterious, the remembrance of things unknown, in a way burdensome, in a way a sensuous experience. It uplifted and depressed, why he did not know, except that it excited his thoughts more than he thought good for him. This kind of excitement was all right up to a point, perfect maybe for a creative artist, but less so for a critic. A critic he thought, should live on beans. . . . Once, after a couple of days in the Vatican Museum, he saw flights of angels—gold, blue, white—intermingled in the sky. "My God, I got to stop using my eyes so much," Fidelman said to himself. (*TMB*, 162)

Malamud needed his considerable self-discipline, for he was powerfully aware of the conflict between the demands of artistic creation and those of immediate experience. In the later Fidelman stories and the novels *The Tenants* and, particularly, *Dubin's Lives*, he made it one of his master themes. But here we are concerned with a man who mistakenly, fearfully, tries to wall up the inspired responses to the past and the present that make heightened life, heightened art, and heightened criticism possible. This man, who thinks critics should live on beans, who has such fussy pride in what he thinks is his distinguished appearance, in his organizational ability, even in his "cotton-dacron underwear, good for quick and easy washing for the traveler" (*TMB*, 155), is never going to write a book that does justice to one of the great artists of Western culture. First Fidelman will have to confront aspects of himself he will never find in library catalogs and archives: his ability to sink into the common life around him; the tragic and comic aspects of the Jewish past that have gone into him; the paradoxical nature of reality, including his own reality. For this he needs the intercession of Shimon Susskind, an even more improbable ministering angel than Pinye Salzman.

Susskind enters the story early, while Fidelman, still in front of the train station, is moved by the sight of the remains of the Baths of Diocletian and by the knowledge of Michelangelo's role in its conversion into a church and convent: "Imagine," he mutters, "Imagine all that history." The moment has the optical confusion Malamud often employs to signal mysterious eruptions. Already undergoing a sort of double vision (he admiringly sees himself seeing the baths), the unusual moment becomes truly uncanny when Fidelman becomes "aware that there was an exterior source to the strange, almost tri-dimensional source of himself he had felt as well as seen." The third dimension is provided by Susskind, seeing Fidelman while the latter is admiring himself and his surroundings.

That the two are the same size and that the refugee sees Fidelman at the same instant the latter sees himself suggests that he is, among other things, a double for the American, an aspect of his psyche with which Fidelman will have to come to terms. As Freud observed, the perception of doubling is a primary source of the uncanny, and Malamud heightens our initial sense of the refugee's essential weirdness by giving him an appearance not quite of this world. He wears "brown knickers and black, knee-length woolen socks drawn up over slightly bowed, broomstick legs, these grounded in small, porous, pointed shoes" (*TMB*, 155–56). Our sense of his uncanny nature is heightened when we realize that with the description of this mysterious traveler, whose shirt is open over his corded neck, Malamud is tipping his hat to the death-double figure in "Death in Venice," Thomas Mann's modernist classic that also contains a protagonist who confronts his double and goes on to relinquish his tight control over instinctual demands while in an Italian city.

But Susskind's origins are not in Mann or in Dante (he will later be referred to as Virgilio Susskind) as he leads Fidelman through the nether regions of Rome, but in the culture and literature of the ghetto and the shtetl. It is a part of his strange particularity that he is a Jewish refugee from Israel; his claims to have fled "Germany, Hungary, Poland. . . . Where not?" (*TMB*, 158) recapitulate much of the experience of the Diaspora. He is the *luftmensch* who claims he lives literally on air. Most of all he is, as Fidelman immediately realizes, a *schnorrer* (beggar, freeloader)—one with "all the bravado, all the *huzpah* (arrogance), associated with the common beggar or *schnorrer* of East European *shtetl* society."[86]

During their first meeting he pockets the fifty cents Fidelman gives him and then asks the American for a suit. Between the time Fidelman refuses and flees to his hotel, the refugee uses his knowledge of the Italian currency exchange to effect his own version of the exchange system: he relinquishes the half dollar for a dollar. Doubles have a way of demonically invading one's space, one's life. A week later Fidelman looks up from his reading to find the refugee in his room, where he again asks for a suit. Four dollars for a warm sweater only brings a request for another dollar, then for the suit again, then for a twenty thousand lire loan (about thirty-one dollars) capped by the apparently shameless claim that Fidelman is responsible for him "because you are a man. Because you are a Jew, aren't you?" (*TMB*, 165). The next day at lunch Fidelman looks up to find not the waiter, but Susskind, who again asks Fidelman to stake his business ventures. That night Susskind enters Fidelman's room and, unable to invade the locked armadio that holds the American's clothing, steals the briefcase and the chapter within it. After a night of tortured dreams in which he pursues an unfairly knowledgeable and evasive Susskind, "the student arose in the morning" (*TMB*, 171). This is the first time Fidelman is described in this way: the most crucial phase of his education has begun.

Having wedged himself so tellingly into Fidelman's life, the schnorrer now retreats, pulling after him the student desperate for the return of his chapter. His search, which lasts from late September into December, teaches him "the face of Rome" as he wanders through second hand fairs and vegetable markets and dawdles "on busy street corners after dark, among beggars and fly-by-night peddlers." In an image characteristic of Malamud's splendid evocation of the locale, he seeks Susskind in the faces of the chestnut sellers, "huddled over pails of glowing coals" (*TMB*, 173). His search takes him to local reminders of the fateful intertwinings of Jews with Italians and their Nazi allies: to a synagogue where a beadle laments the Nazi's murder of his son; to the Jewish cemetery where one gravestone commemorates "My beloved father / Betrayed by the damned Fascists / Murdered at Auschwitz by the barbarous Nazis / *O Crime Orribile*"; to the ghetto where, in an image that picks up both the spiritual possibilities of suffering and the image of the faces huddled over the glowing coals, he sees "impoverished houses . . . dark holes ending in jeweled interiors, silks and silver of all colors" (*TMB*, 175–76).

The double pulls Fidelman's appearance closer to his own. The searcher takes to wearing a beret (as does Susskind) and pointed shoes, for now he hates "his burly oxbloods which overheated his feet and whose color he detested" (*TMB*, 173). Mentioned in the second sentence of the story's opening paragraph, the recently purchased shoes combine with the new pigskin briefcase (mentioned in the opening sentence) to suggest a crucial immaturity. To do justice to Giotto, Fidelman must sink more into the experience of a people who shunned the pig from which the briefcase is made. A more profound Fidelman stays on in Rome "to know man" (*TMB*, 177), to know why Susskind stole the chapter. By the time he meets the refugee in mid-December, he has developed a street cunning that enables him to mask his consuming hatred of the thief. He is more comic manipulator than the butt of the author's derision as he dissembles "the Unified Man," uttering "cagily whispered" (*TMB*, 178–79) bribes in his attempt to get the chapter back.

It is his new cunning that leads him to track Susskind to the icy hovel in which he lives and later to search it for the briefcase and chapter. But it's the awakening Jew in him that is so moved by the hard realities of Susskind's life. From this continued deepening comes his dream: first of Virgilio Susskind hinting (by way of Tolstoy) at the communal and moral basis of all true art, then of the Giotto ceiling fresco of St. Francis giving his cloak to the poor horseman. The Fidelman of September resisted angelic promptings (which are really metaphors for the promptings of the heart within); the Fidelman of December does not. The wonderful story quickly moves to its close as the student gives a suit to Susskind and even forgives the refugee for burning his chapter. For Fidelman has acquired enough depth to appreciate the truth of the fleeing refugee's last words: "The words were there but the spirit was missing" (*TMB*, 182).

But are these words uttered out of the corrosive cynicism that one could argue was the constant beneath all of Susskind's gestures to Fidelman before the chapter was stolen, or out of the generosity of the guide, the ministering angel, who intentionally brings Fidelman to a much deeper appreciation of the demands, paradoxes, and possibilities of existence? In her helpful discussion of the Hasidic element in Malamud's short stories, Marcia Gealy admits that, like "the wandering beggars and fools of Hasidic folklore [Susskind] is demonic as well as saintly." But Gealy's reading emphasizes his latter aspect: "Because he is a product of [East European shtetl] society, Susskind knows that as a beggar he is an occasion for *mizvos* (good deeds) and thus, an instrument of grace. If he feels himself at an advantage, if he does not hesitate to demand his due, it is because he realizes that the more fortunate need him as an object of charity. In the culture of the *shtetl* it is the *schnorrer* who opens 'the portals of heaven' for the more fortunate man. . . . Susskind . . . with all his grotesque humor, can be identified with the wandering beggars and fools of Hasidic folklore. Like them, he is an enigmatic mixture of the commonplace and mysterious . . . like them, he makes people dream and leads them to themselves."[87]

To quote the last line in another fine work about Americans abroad, "Isn't it pretty to think so?"[88] One could as easily attribute the stealing of the manuscript to Susskind's demonism, which is quite possibly behind the manipulativeness and aggression that bubble out of the man. On his way to being Malamud's quintessential schlemiel, Fidelman made his choice. We must make ours, as we did with the much gentler Salzman. I find the schnorrer even harder to read than the *shadchan*: though we were able to enter Salzman's mind for part of "The Magic Barrel," the psyche of the more relentless "other" is, for the whole of "The Last Mohican," appropriately closed.

Like Fidelman, Carl Schneider, the protagonist of "Behold the Key," is excited by the sensuous flow of history pouring out from "the variety of Roman architecture from ancient to modern times" (*TMB*, 67). Unlike Fidelman, he arrives in Rome eager to sink himself into the paradoxes and intrigues of the past, as must any responsible researcher of the Risorgimento, the movement to liberate Italy from foreign domination and to unify the country, lasting from about 1796 to 1870. What he wants no part of are the intrigues of the present, represented by the lies of the agents and caretakers he has met during this month-long search for an apartment for himself and his family, and then by a demand for a bribe. After the search has cost him almost a month of his precious time for research he has a chance to rent the perfect apartment if he will pay 15,000 lire (reduced from 85,000) to Del Vecchis, the apartment's former tenant. Though the final offer is only about twenty-three dollars, Carl refuses "to be a party to a bribe"

(*TMB*, 78) as he primly put it. In revenge, Del Vecchis destroys the apartment's furnishings, defaces its walls, and hurls the key, which hits "Carl on the forehead, leaving a mark he could not rub out" (*TMB*, 83).

"Behold the Key" is the only story in the collection Malamud loaded with more symbolic freight than it could bear. The central meaning seems clear enough: the love Carl claims he bears for all things Italian is abstracted from the realities of Italian life. Del Vecchis puts his finger on Carl's unreasonable fastidiousness: "It is people like you who drive us to the hands of the Communists. You try to buy us—our votes, our culture, and then you dare speak of bribes" (*TMB*, 78–79). So far the story works well: Del Vecchis and his attitude toward Americans balances that of Bevilacqua, Carl's endearing Italian agent who bears affection for the country that makes Marilyn Monroe movies. Each sings his brief aria in the trio that occurs just before Del Vecchis hurls the key

> "Assassin!" shouted Bevilacqua. "Turd!" May your bones grow hair and rot."
>
> "He lives for my death," he [Del Vecchis] cried to Carl, "I for his. This is our condition."
>
> "You lie, said Carl. "I love this country." (*TMB*, 82–83)

Does Del Vecchis's "he" refer to Carl or Bevilacqua? If Carl, as is probably the case, is Del Vecchis merely engaging in characteristically Italian emotional inflation (which Carl should have anticipated); or, if Bevilacqua, is Malamud belatedly insisting upon the kind of negative symbiosis between two characters that propels so many of his stories? If so, what are its cultural reverberations? Is the mark of Cain that the key leaves on Carl's forehead supposed to symbolize his failure of humanity or the way in which he is implicated in Italian life whether he likes it or not? The interpretive problems increase exponentially when we realize that the aria might be a duet and not a trio, that the second speaker might be Bevilacqua and not De Vecchis. As Huck Finn would say, "It's too many for me."

For the final Italian story of *The Magic Barrel* Malamud again employed the motif of the protagonist seeking a second life but this time encased the quest with some of the Jungian symbolism present in a fair amount of his work, particularly *The Natural*. Unlike Fidelman,

Henry Levin of "The Lady of the Lake" does not come to Italy bearing the scars of vocational failure. Instead, his vocational past suggests the way he has floated through life, ethically and vocationally unmoored. Books seemed to hold no more value to Levin than as the locus in which he moved: he "walked the floors in Macy's book department, wearing a white carnation." If we hear in the course of the story that he had often been in love, we are never told that Levin suspects that he might have shared in the failure of all the relationships. Instead the women of the past "had come to less than he expected" (*TMB*, 105).

Kierkegaard might have said that Levin had lived his life on the aesthetic level: he seems only to have sought sensuous satisfaction, which the Danish philosopher observed is an inevitably frustrating approach to existence. Since he has not made his way into the next Kierkegaardian level, the ethical, he happily accepts the financial inheritance—surely from a Jewish relative—but wants no part of the ethical imperatives or the suffering Malamud implicitly argues are also a Jew's inheritance. He feels that his being Jewish has brought him only "headaches, inferiorities, unhappy memories" (*TMB*, 126), and while in Paris, that secular city, he embarks on a second identity, signing the hotel register as Henry Levin but calling himself Henry R. Freeman. The narrator seems to acquiesce in his character's wish, for he's known to us as Freeman from the third sentence of the story on, but he arranges encounters for Freeman that make the punning hopefulness of the name increasingly ironic.

Having made his way to Stresa, he introduces himself as Freeman to Isabella del Dongo, the beautiful resident of the mansion on Isola del Dongo, in Lake Maggiore. Her social rank and beauty, the beauty of the lake, the history of the family, and the magnificence of their mansion, particularly of its gardens, all combine with her immediate interest in Freeman to present romantic possibilities beyond even his unrealistic hopes. During their first conversation her first three sentences are questions: "Si è perduto?" (Are you lost?), "Are you an American?," "Are you, perhaps, Jewish?" (*TMB*, 113). Freeman denies both that he is lost and that he is Jewish—the irony need not be explained—and his broodings over whether he should risk rejection by admitting his origins provide much of the story's conflict. Even after Isabella tells Freeman that her last name is della Seta not del Dongo and that her father is no nobleman but a poor caretaker and guide, Freeman cannot match her partial shedding of false identity. During their final meeting, when he hopes she will agree to marry him, he again denies that he is Jewish. Then she both literally and figuratively bares her breast, displaying "a bluish line of distorted numbers"—her legacy as a Jew who survived Buchenwald. Malamud's desire to give the pretender his comeuppance propels Isabella into an annoying explicitness as she explains that she can't marry Freeman because "We are Jews. My past is meaningful to me. I treasure what I suffered for" (*TMB*, 132). Then she disappears into the mist before Freeman can reveal that he too is Jewish.

Isabella, then, is the moral presence who could bring Freeman to claim his place as a man in the world, were he as worthy of her as Arthur was of receiving Excalibur from his lady of the lake. From a Jungian viewpoint, she is *magna mater*, the positive maternal archetype, whose acceptance permits our vital energies to flow unimpeded into the world. She is water or the mother as the source of life, as opposed to *mater saeva* (the terrible mother), who will dam up our energies and engulf us (death by drowning that symbolizes the consequence of capitulation to the negative maternal archetype). In *The Natural* the *magna mater* figure is Iris Lemon, who speaks so knowingly about the possibilities of suffering, and who is consequently associated with life-giving fluids and physical, as well as ethical, life. The negative archetype is Memo Paris, associated with stagnant waters, with sick breasts. There is no *mater saeva* in "The Lady of the Lake," only the dual aspect of Isabella's breasts—disfigured yet beautiful. Edwin Eigner has interestingly argued that in her guise as the loathely lady (whose apparent ugliness the hero must love before she reveals her actual beauty to him), Isabella "tests shallow Levin-Freeman with the sight of her desecrated breasts, and, stuttering, he fails."[89] I would argue that Levin has conclusively failed his tests before he even sees Isabella's disfigurement and that—like the bread in "The Loan" that nourishes because it is salted with human tears—Isabella's breasts are lifegiving precisely because they show the signs of suffering. If the Jungian mother has two aspects, so does suffering for Malamud: the ennobling and the crippling. Freeman is too immature, too ethically undeveloped, to perceive any of this.

Malamud told one of his bibliographers that "The Girl of My Dreams," the only story in *The Magic Barrel* not set in New York City or Italy, was "suggested by an experience he had as an aspiring and lonely young writer in a strange city."[90] Whatever the inciting experience, the story's locale is not so much Washington, D.C. (though it could be), as a place where the protagonist does not confront the cultural collisions of the three Italian stories, and where the protagonist can escape the oppressions of his needs far more easily than the New Yorkers of *The Magic Barrel*. These thematic axes are replaced by a different one: "Girl" is Malamud's first published work to turn upon that conflict present in so much of his later fiction—the colliding demands of art and life. Having had his novel rejected by "more than twenty publishers over an eighteen month period"—a rate that makes it seem the manuscript's failings emanated through its wrappings—Mitka burned it in a trash barrel one autumn day. With the sparks went "all his hopes, and the proud ideas he had given his book," and "with a twist of the key [Mitka] locked himself a prisoner in his room, only venturing out after midnight for crackers and tea and an occasional can of fruit" (*TMB*, 27).

Not too long before he wrote the story Malamud also burnt the bulky manuscript of a novel in a trash barrel, but any pain he might have experienced is, like Mitka's suffering, diffused by the narrator's stance toward the protagonist. Of all the interments in Malamud's fiction, Mitka's is the most unnecessary. Upon beholding "his meager thighs as he dressed, if he were a weeper he would have wept." No need for the silly schlemiel to grow lank. Mrs. Lutz, his adoring landlady, daily "tried tempting him down to her kitchen with spry descriptions of lunch: steaming soup, Mitka, with soft white rolls, calf's foot jelly, rice with tomato sauce, celery hearts, delicious breasts of chicken—beef if he preferred—and his choice of satisfying sweets." She even tries to woo him back to the dance of life with news of "a new guest on your floor, girl by the name of Beatrice—a real beauty . . . a tender twenty-one or -two, pinched waist, firm breasts, pretty face, and you should see her little panties hanging on the line—like flowers all" (*TMB*, 29–30).

Reading a paper one day Mitka mistakes for the real thing a fiction about the accidental destruction of a nearly completed novel—just as he has mistaken the life of art for the whole of life. Still, his pity for the author, one Madeleine Thorne, is rending, and this first step out of his solipsism stumblingly leads to the second one of arranging a meeting with her. He finds no Madeleine but an Olga, a woman who is "marvelously plain" (*TMB*, 36) and decades older than he instead of the attractive girl in her early twenties he has expected. The inspirational nourishment she offers—her frequent pleas for him to persist with his writing—do little for apparently untalented Mitka. Her true wisdom consists of a Brechtian "First one must eat" approach to existence. She brings to the library where they meet and to the bar where they go her own magic barrel: an almost bottomless shopping bag full of tasty food, which Mitka largely devours. Not hungry for the first time in months, "gripped and held by the spring night," by the re-awakened possibilities of what the present might hold for him, we leave Mitka as he heads home intending to drape "Mrs. Lutz from head to foot in flowing white . . . then swing her across the threshold, holding her where the fat overflowed her corset as they waltzed around her writing chamber" (*TMB*, 41). If Mitka cannot write good fiction he can still enjoy food and sex, and the girls of his dreams turn out to be the ones who lead him back to quotidian existence. There's much to be said for Mark Shechner's claims for Malamud's distrust of instinctual desires (see his essay in part 3), but in this story they certainly win out over the self-skewerings of the failed artist.

The nature of the story's persistent irony renders impossible any identification with Mitka's suffering, which is also to say that since the author was not following his homing signals of strongly realized sorrow or frustration or longing, the pages of the story lack the inevitability of almost all the others in the collection. For a Malamud story, the whole of "The Girl of My Dreams" has an improvisational feel to it.

Published in November 1951, fourteen months before "The Girl of My Dreams" first saw print, "An Apology" is a more characteristic *Magic Barrel* story than the later one, save that Malamud did not include it in the collection. "Early one morning, during a wearying hot spell in the city," a zealous young policeman named Lou arrests a shabbily dressed old lightbulb peddler for peddling without a licence and then for refusing to give his address. On the way to the station they detour across the Brooklyn Bridge so that Walter, Lou's older partner, can wash and change his shirt at home. But on the return trip the peddler takes advantage of the slowly moving traffic on the bridge to bolt from the police car and to try to leap to his death from the railing. Lou is able to pull him to the sidewalk where he lies "moaning and tearing with his fingers at his chest and arms."

Both policemen are baffled until a passing pretzel peddler identifies the old man as Bloostein and tells the two policemen that after he lost his store, his wife died and his daughter was killed in a fire. "Now he's got the seven years' itch and they can't cure it in the clinic." Walter, who had disagreed with the arrest from the start, convinces his partner to release the peddler. When the older policeman returns home that night Bloostein is waiting in front of his house, demanding the return of "my little box lights,"[91] a carton of bulbs left behind during his arrest. Since Walter's first attempts to find the bulbs yield nothing, he offers to pay for them but Bloostein refuses the proffered five dollars: he unreasonably wants "my little box lights" (462). The two continue to drive about lower Manhattan as Walter makes further inquiries but—like Bloostein's store, wife, daughter, and good health—the bulbs have disappeared.

Walter would seem to have freed himself when he buys and gives to the old man the same number and kind of bulbs that were lost, drives home, and finally goes to bed. He is unable to fall asleep, however, and he gets up and goes to the window: "the quiet street was drenched in moonlight, and warm dark shadows fell from tender trees. But in the tree shadow in front of the house were two strange oblongs and a gnarled, grotesque-hatted silhouette that stretched a tormented distance down the block. Walter's heart pounded heavily for he knew it was Bloostein"—who continues, for perhaps five more hours, to invade the summer night normality outside the house and the steadying continuities inside it: the wife sleeping beside Walter, the son sleeping down the hall. The afflicted old man disregards Walter's threat to call the police as well as the summer blanket the policeman throws down when it rains during the night; only when Walter apologizes, "from my heart" (463–64), will the bitter old man leave, taking the blanket with him as additional payment.

It was probably Bloostein's resemblance to Breitbart, the uncanny lightbulb peddler in *The Assistant,* that kept Malamud from ever collecting so good a story. Vulnerable to the heat in a way his partner Lou is not, Walter is also vulnerable to the terrible power the injured and the insulted can exercise over a humane person. (Walter has six or seven beers at two different bars and buys and opens a bottle of whiskey during his peregrinations with Bloostein.) But the peddler has come to the sidewalk before Walter's window as much from a ghetto or shtetl as from the pages of a Dostoyevski novel. The little Yinglish he speaks and Walter's attempt to justify himself during the arrest—"If you were in Germany they would have killed you" (461)—add to

Malamud's successful thrusting of some of the extremities of the Jewish experience upon the policeman reflector, one who occupies a more central place in American society than any other protagonist in *The Magic Barrel*. The Malamud of the fifties was a very talented writer indeed if "An Apology" was one of his lesser efforts.

Idiots First

By the late 1950s Malamud likely felt that the characteristic strategies of the fiction of the folk ghetto would serve more to imprison his imagination than release it, and it was time to move on. On the whole he moved into more realistic modes. Unlike his first two novels, *A New Life,* which he wrote between 1958 and late 1960 or early 1961, is set in a particular time, and in a particular political climate. When the novel's protagonist, S. Levin, steps off a train on the last Sunday in August 1950, he has to add to his own "backlog of personal insecurity his portion of the fear that presently overwhelmed America. The country was frightened silly of Alger Hiss and Whittaker Chambers, Communist spies and Congressional committees, flying saucers and fellow travelers, their friends and associates, and those who asked them for a match or the time of day."[92] The setting is neither the surreal product of the collision between the contemporary mythology of baseball and past mythologies (as in *The Natural*) or the folk ghetto of *The Assistant.* Even if we did not know from Malamud's life or the geographic and academic details that Eastchester, Cascadia, *is* Corvallis, Oregon, we can recognize the setting easily enough: a mediocre English department of the state agricultural college, in an attractive small town, in beautiful natural surroundings. In short, Malamud tried for the first time to dramatize his abiding moral concerns against the manners and relative affluence of a representative slice of post–World War II America.

The novel completed, Malamud turned again to writing stories. In the first of these, "Idiots First," which was published in *Commentary* in December 1961, he temporarily retreated from realism and set the tale in a New York that is even more expressionistically abstracted than the stylized New Yorks of the earlier stories of the folk ghetto or of *The Assistant.* But "Idiots First" proved to be the last fictional work set in a folk New York. Later stories, like "The Jewbird" (1963) and "The Silver Crown" (1972), contain Jews (one of them a talking bird) who do—or seem to do—amazing things in New York, but the setting is very much a recognizable, contemporary New York, with Jewish leading characters who have assimilated into vocations like teaching high school or selling frozen foods.

When Malamud's second collection of stories, *Idiots First*, came out in 1963, the degree to which he was setting his moral fables in the here and now was somewhat obscured by the fact that he included two stories of suffering Jewish shopkeepers—"The Cost of Living" and "The Death of Me"—that he had published in the early 1950s. But Malamud's tendency to write in a more realistic mode than he employed in the fifties makes itself felt in all of the other stories save "Idiots First." "Black Is My Favorite Color" deals with interactions between New York Jews and blacks, as does "Angel Levine," but no softening gauzes of fantasy and dialect humor are laid over the hard realities of their interactions. "The German Refugee" once again recounts the grim consequences of not extending enough credit, but in a context of precisely noted historical and cultural dislocation. In "A Choice of Profession" the protagonist seeks a new life in the same profession and in the same general locale as the protagonist of Malamud's most recent novel.

As for the four stories in the collection that are set in Italy, Malamud used Italian life somewhat differently than he did in the Italian stories of *The Magic Barrel*. In each of the three earlier stories a relatively young American male must confront the moral consequences of his Jewish or American identity. "Still Life" and "Naked Nude," which I discuss in the next chapter, do not particularly deal with moral concerns. In "The Maid's Shoes" an American law professor is, like Carl Schneider of "Behold the Key," unwillingly pulled into the complexities of Italian life, but no moral revelations surface for him. He is sixty and seems to have had a good sense of the limitations of his sympathies before he arrived in Rome. No American appears in the fourth story, "Life Is Better Than Death."

Though the characters of "Idiots First" uncharacteristically roam through the city, the story culminates some of the earlier strategies of the fiction of the folk ghetto. More than all of the earlier protagonists save Manischevitz of "Angel Levine," Mendel is driven by an immediate need for an ironically qualified end, and it is this need that propels the story's feverish physical movement. The old, wasted man must on the last night of his life raise the thirty-five dollars he still needs to send Isaac, his thirty-nine-year-old idiot son, to the improbable care of an eighty-one-year-old uncle in California. But the minute that he needs to put his son on the train is denied him in the name of "the cosmic universal law, goddamit, the one I got to follow myself" (*IF*, 13). The speaker is Ginzburg, the angel of death, at that moment in the uniform of a ticket collector in Pennsylvania Station. Unmoved by Mendel's pleas that his lifetime of suffering has earned him the minute's respite, Ginzburg refuses to open the iron gate. "You bastard, don't you understand what it means human?" Mendel incongruously cries as he tries to choke the angel of death.

Like Hawthorne, Malamud often uses visual or reflecting images to signal that a particular degree of realism is swerving further into fantasy or allegory. At this point, as Ginzburg is blasting the old man with his icy, killing gaze, Malamud pushes a story that is already fantastic into one of his most extended reaches:

> Clinging to Ginzburg in his last agony, Mendel saw . . . that Ginzburg, staring at himself in Mendel's eyes, saw mirrored in them the extent of his own awful wrath. He beheld a shimmering, starry, blinding light that produced darkness. . . .
>
> His grip on the squirming old man slowly loosened, and Mendel, his heart barely beating, slumped to the ground.
>
> "Go." Ginzburg muttered, "take him to the train." (*IF*, 14–15)

Who is the "he" who beholds the starry blinding light? The story works best if it is Ginzburg, particularly since Malamud brilliantly relates the many light-dark images in the story to the angel of death. But have we for the only time in the story moved into someone else's mind besides Mendel's? Or are we to believe that the old man has seen what Ginzburg is seeing (as well as his own reflected image in the angel of death's eyes)? The *reality* of the moment becomes as evasive as the color we see when we close our eyes. It is during this breakdown of our resolutely binary, either-or mode of thinking that Malamud, like the nineteenth-century Russian and Yiddish writers he loved, seems to be asking us to believe, for an instant, that even a human, inhuman universal law must for an instant bend and recognize "what it means human" if the petitioner has suffered enough and is desperately enough committed to his just cause. Manishevitz lunges into irrationality, Mendel into violence; but each release is actually a clinging, a heightened commitment to otherness—for Malamud the glue that holds together the moral world.

The spiritual quests of some of his characters have caused some critics to place Malamud in the Kafka tradition.[93] For me Malamud is most Kafkaesque when, as in "Idiots first," he transforms the external world so that it mirrors his characters' troubled inner lives and, above all, when he creates a fictional world that emphasizes the human animal's radical homelessness in the world. Two of the authors' aphorisms—Kafka's "In the fight between you and the world bet on the world"[94] and Malamud's "Der oilem iz a goilem (The world is a monster)" (*TA*, 17)—have a good deal in common. But we must be aware of a crucial difference. For all of his pessimism, Malamud possessed a humanist streak that the Czech genius lacked. Either Malamud's spiritual strugglers never seek supernatural comfort and validation or they eventually realize that the ethical and spiritual exist only through human efforts.

"Idiots First" strikes me as Malamud's most heightened plea for human possibility. Mendel is pitted against natural law, the physical world, and contemporary manners. Even the idiot son he is trying to help symbolically opposes his father, yet Mendel "wins." The primary adversary is, of course, Ginzburg, but Malamud also bestows various attributes of the angel of death to all but one of the other humans Mendel meets during the three main encounters that precede the climactic one with Ginzburg: with a pawnbroker, with the philanthropist Fishbein and his servant, and with an aged rabbi, his sexton, and his wife. The exception is the rabbi, who donates the coat that Mendel pawns for the rest of the money he needs for Isaac's ticket. The rabbi shares what we know of Mendel's appearance: Mendel has wasted arms, the rabbi is skinny; both are old and have weak hearts. Apart from his arms, we only know that Mendel's lips are cracked. Since the story is so clearly an allegory, with the party of humane concern (Mendel and the rabbi) pitted against the party of indifference (Ginzburg and all other characters in the story), the stripping from Mendel of physical attributes—save a few details that emphasize his vulnerability—achieves several purposes. First, the strategy asserts the force of his inner life, best expressed by his commitment to place his son before he dies. Second, it allies all others, with their more detailed physical attributes, with Ginzburg and places them in the party of death, of annihilation of the moral urge.

In his guise as a ticket collector, Ginzburg is "a bulky, bearded man with hairy nostrils and a fishy smell" (*IF*, 13). His beard is black, his eyes glitter, and he cynically disclaims responsibility, usually by uttering clichés: "The law is the law. . . . You ain't the only one[;] . . . some got it worse than you. That's how it goes in this country" (*IF*,

14–15). He is associated with food, both by the fish smell and by the fact that Mendel and Isaac are driven from a cafeteria by the sight of him eating as he sits.

His black beard is echoed by the red one of the pawnbroker, who will give Mendel only eight dollars for his gold watch, his hairy nostrils by Fishbein's. In fact, enough is made of the black hair of Ginzburg's beard and nostrils to associate with him all possessors of hair: Fishbein's servant with his long sideburns; the rabbi's gray-haired wife who fights with Mendel for the coat. She also shares Ginzburg's bulkiness and glittering eyes. The pawnbroker also eats fish. Apart from Fishbein's name, his concern with his dinner, his "fixed policy" (*IF,* 8) of denying individual requests for charity, and his paunch also ally him with Ginzburg.

Even Isaac is of the party of resistance. His concern about eating, the references to his eyes and thick hair, his idiot's ignorance of what his father has done for him ally him more with Ginzburg than with his father. Much of the moral grandeur of Mendel's commitment follows from the absurdity of expecting any gratitude from his son. The dying man's last two statements in the story are to tell Isaac to remember his mother and father, and to tell the conductor "Be nice to him, . . . Show him where everything is." But as the train leaves, Isaac does not even turn to say good-bye to his father; his face is "strained in the direction of his journey" (*IF,* 15). All Mendel has left is Ginzburg, whom he seeks in the last sentence of the story.

What is nonhuman in the story seems icily or malevolently resistant to Mendel's attempt to assert the humane in the inhuman world we inhabit. The clock that stops in the first sentence of the story, the "cold embittered clothing" (*IF,* 3) the old man puts on, the remote stars and moon, the uncanny tree whose surrealistically altered branches serve to shorten the amount of time Mendel has left,[95] the gates over the pawnbroker's windows—all these point toward the iron gates of Pennsylvania Station that block Isaac's way to the train. My discussion of this great story gives little sense of its visionary intensity, and the wonderfully apt gradations of tone and image within its rush toward the moment of Mendel and Ginzburg locked in each others' arms before the closed gates.

Just as the last of the tales of the folk ghetto pits two frail people against the full weight of the external, so did the first that saw print: "The Cost of Living," first published in June 1950 and collected thirteen years later in *Idiots First*. Here the monstrousness of the world, its ultimate indifference to Sam and Sura Tomashevsky's needs and claims for justice, follows from the other characters' adherence to the profit motive. On the whole, though, "characters" overstates. With the exception of I. Kaufman, the crude but well-to-do acquaintance who refuses to keep a competing grocery out by putting in a shoe store, Sam's adversaries are nameless. We no more know the names of the longtime customers who have no loyalty to Sam than we do those of the carpenters, painters, electricians and fixtures men who transform the dark space next door into a brightly colored, up-to-date food market, or the manager and two clerks who busily wait on customers all day while the Tomashevskys despair in their empty store. We're never told the landlord's name, though we learn that he's a barber of Italian descent, that he's been deeply saddened by losing his son in the war, that he would rather not lease to a competitor who will put Sam out of business but eventually succumbs to the business-is-business ethos that serves as the Prime Mover in the world of this story. We also know that he feels enough guilt and sorrow about what he has done to close his eyes while he cuts Sam's hair on the December day the grocer's store goes at auction.

I devote this much space to the barber because he is the most likely candidate for an embodied antagonist with whom Sam might develop the kind of obsessive relationship that, to varying degrees, propels all of the other stories of the folk ghetto. But the barber is a sympathetic figure, a fellow sufferer, and Sam seems to be angry at him for only a few moments during the seven months of his hopeless struggle to survive the new store's competition. His namelessness helps him to swerve toward the generic. Like Sam and Mr. Pellegrino, the ex-shoemaker who was the previous inhabitant of the adjoining store, the barber is one of the decent little people who is damaged by the cash nexus. The impersonality and pervasiveness of Sam's adversary, our sense of the grocer's blamelessness, and the hopeless pathos of his attempts to woo back customers, economize, and so keep his sorry niche in the world, place "The Cost of Living," more than any other Malamud story, in the tradition of literary naturalism.

If the stories of the folk ghetto brilliantly bridged Malamud's immigrant origins and literary modernism, both are present to an unusual degree in "The Cost of Living." As did Malamud's grocer-father, Sam Tomashevsky grew up in or around the city of Kamenets-Podolsky in the western Ukraine. The way in which Malamud renders Sam's recollection of his childhood and the thematic uses to which he puts it help to place "The Cost of Living" in one of the modernist mainstreams: the victorious artwork transcends the destruction of its characters by the modern world.

The symbolic center of the story is the store that adjoins Sam's poor grocery and that had become a magically charged place for Sam the previous summer when Mr. Pellegrino stopped trying to compete with the "streamlined shoe-repair shop [which had] opened up next block where they had three men in red smocks hammering away in the window and everyone stopped to look. Pellegrino's business slackened off as if someone were shutting a faucet." After reading this, for the only time in the story we move into another sensibility besides Sam's. Having fallen into a terrifying economic reality, the phenomenal world in which the shoemaker worked was altered: "one day he had looked at his workbench and when everything stopped jumping it loomed up ugly and empty." His place in the world dissolving around him, Pellegrino tried to regain it by seeking work with his former customers. We learn, in the most disjunctive sentences in the story, ones that capture Pellegrino's new instability, that he collected only three pairs. The following month he "sold everything to a junkman and bought candy to peddle with in the streets; but after a while no one saw the shoemaker any more, a stocky man with round eyeglasses and a bristling mustache" (*IF,* 142–43). The vigor of his mustache, the solidity of his body are illusory; Pellegrino has been emptied out along with his store.

During the seven months between the time the shoemaker left and the sign for the new grocery appeared, Sam often stares at night into the store's dark emptiness and broods over the radical transience it bespeaks. For the grocer the store is paradoxically inhabited by absences: the memories of all the shoes hammered upon, the customers "who had left something of themselves in the coming and going" but who will never come again. For Sam the disappearance of what was good is as frightening and evil as the residue of what was bad, in this case the way the silence of the "haunted house" back in Kamenets-Podolsky—where "there had once been a ghastly murder"—becomes "a pit of churning quiet from which . . . all evil erupted" (*IF,* 143). As he stands on the dismal New York street, fearing his own displacement—the resident evil in a "free," capitalist society—Sam feels as he did when he stood before the haunted house in the Ukraine.

The color symbolism in the story is consciously and consistently used: the redness of capitalist success creates the blackness of individual transience. The red aprons that heralded Pellegrini's departure begin the process that culminates in Sam's slow descent into blackness. With Pellegrino driven out and his store blackened, the jolly red plague spreads there, with the sign and the streamers that announce the coming of the market that causes Sam, as one of his desperate economies, to turn off half his lights. I. Kaufman's wart glows red as he refuses to save Sam by putting in a shoe store; the other man who refuses to consider putting a store next door has red hair. "A red auction flag [flaps and furls] in the icy breeze as though it were a holiday" (*IF*, 152) as Sam's store goes at auction. Our sense that the Tomashevskys will be victimized by the happy red glow—which, after all, encourages customers to share the sense of success while they purchase—is established in the story's opening sentences. Sam has just seen the sign, a promiser of heightened buying experiences for others, a vocational death sentence for him: "Winter had fled the city streets but Sam Tomashevsky's face, when he stumbled into the back room of his grocery store, was a blizzard. Sura, who was sitting at the round table eating bread and salted tomato, looked up in fright and the tomato turned a deeper red" (*IF*, 141). It is characteristic of Malamud's attempt to "make it new," to practice verbal estrangement, that he renders the Tomashevsky's white faces indirectly, without using the adjective.

Of all Malamud's stories "The Cost of Living" most vividly dramatizes what is perhaps Kafka's master theme: a character's psychic disintegration as he is pushed into increasing isolation. As Sam lies awake nights he sees what the workmen who are readying the fancy grocery have achieved though he has never looked through the window. Sam's participation in the slow process that will destroy him is reminiscent of Kafka's "The Burrow," in which the molelike narrator devotes his life to creating an invulnerable underground fortress for himself, but hears, as he tells us of his efforts, the digging of the larger creature coming to devour him. The grocer tries to "bet on the world": "He whispered to himself this [the competing store] would be good if it was for me, but then the alarm banged in his ear and he had to get up and drag in the milk cases" (*IF*, 150). Malamud spares Sam the most extreme agonies of a Joseph K or a Gregor Samsa but not the terror of losing one's center. Sam had looked into the evil of the deserted store through the image of its inhabitant: the "image of the grocer gazing out" (*IF*, 143). The story's closing sentence is "So long as he lived he would not return to the old neighborhood, afraid his store was standing empty, and he dreaded to look through the window" (*IF*, 152). The cost of Sam's remaining life is the terror that his deepest reality is to be what no longer is. At hasty perusal a thirties-type tearjerker about capitalism's destruction of the little people, close reading reveals "The Cost of Living" to be a brilliantly crafted and profound study of psychic and physical dislocation.[96]

The symbolism and subtlety of "The Cost of Living" make its attack upon capitalism peripheral. "The Death of Me" is a frontal assault on the aggressive impulse. For more than a year, Josip Bruza and Emilio Vivo, presser and tailor for the clothier Marcus, worked side by side without incident. "Then one day, as though an invisible wall between them had fallen, they were at each other's throats" (*IF*, 61). For all of the attempts of the kindly and eloquent Marcus to make peace, there the Pole and the Italian remain until Marcus has a carpenter build a thick partition to separate their working spaces. This gains a week of silence. But in a perverse version of the way the work of a genius like Mozart grew independent of his life, their genius for hating grows independent of their separation. Their truce ends in hideous escalation, with Josip driving a knife into Emilio's groin as Emilio opens "a smelly purple wound" (*IF*, 66) on Josip's arm with his burning iron. After Marcus fires them and withdraws they choke each other. This time Marcus's attempt to part them causes a heart attack and his death; "You'll be the death of me"—the bromide that gives the story its title—becomes a wrenching reality.

The story's unusual power follows in large part from the superb characterizations of the adversaries, particularly from the imagery with which they're rendered. So much about the "heavy, beery, perspiring Pole, who worked in undershirt and felt slippers, his pants loose on his beefy hips" (*IF*, 57) adds to the sense of his wet grossness: the dozen bottles of beer he keeps with ice in a rusty pan and guzzles while he works; the cabbage he sometimes cooks in the back of the store; the way "oily tears [smear] his cheeks and chin so that it looks as though he had been sprayed with something to kill flies" (*IF*, 59) when he reads letters from his wife, back in Poland with their tubercular son. In combat with Emilio he might breathe "like a dog in heat" (*IF*, 61), or he might shout in Polish that "he would tear off someone's genitals and rub the bloody mess in salt" (*IF*, 63). The violence of this imagery sometimes modulates into blendings both Dantesque and surreal, like the depiction of Marcus's vision of the adversaries' world as one "of gray grass and green sunlight, of moaning and blood-smell. . . . Skirting the lit and smoking sands, they scrambled high up on a craggy cliff, locked in many-handed struggle, teetering on the ledge, till one slipped in slime and pulled the other with him" (*IF*, 62).

Everything is compressed, centripetal in Josip's adversary, "a thin, dry, pigeon-chested Sicilian, who bore or returned the Pole a steely malice" (*IF*, 58). The Pole, on the other hand, is centrifugal. He responds to Marcus's questioning him about why he fights by hugging "the old Jew into a ponderous polka, then with a cackle, [pushing] him aside and, in his beer jag, [dancing] away" (*IF*, 64). True to the reputation for brooding and plotting of his people, the Sicilian constantly whispers to himself. The whispering is as much an unexplainable given as the hatred the two have for each other. At one point Marcus thinks that the whispering is about Emilio's wife, who has left him five times, but on the same page he conjectures that the wife leaves him because she cannot stand the whispering.

Marcus believes that the combatants could be united by their common suffering, and he holds before them the imagery of his own family's suffering, just as Etta Shlegel held before her husband the picture of their dead son in "The Bill." Malamud believed that suffering cripples at least as much as it ennobles but what makes this story so upsetting is the sense that the characters' capacity for hatred is innate, at least as much a part of "what it means human" as nobility. During the week of silence, the adversaries' most consistent habits are suspended. Emilio no longer whispers; Josip touches no beer and brings the letters from Poland home to read. Their bloodlust is precisely what is natural; the two are suffering the dislocation of being temporarily deflected from what is at their core. As Freud argued in perhaps his grimmest book, *Civilization and Its Discontents*, "It is clearly not easy for men to give up the satisfaction of this inclination to aggression. They do not feel comfortable without it."[97] "The Death of Me" is thematically a trial run for *God's Grace* (1982), as implacable in its way as late Freud. In this allegory, a chimpanzee argues that slaughtering a baby female baboon and eating its delectable brains is a "perfectly natural, naturally selective thing to do. The hunt was stimulating and the flesh delicious."[98] The other chimpanzees side with the orator and eventually sacrifice Calvin Cohn, last living human and, in spite of a few slips, a good man. Their aggression is *natural;* his attempts to control it are secondary, not primal. Had he known the theories of anthropologists like Konrad Lorenz, who argued that aggression is acquired and not innate, Malamud—at least the Malamud that wrote this story—would likely have rejected them. "The Death of Me" supports Mark Shechner's claim that Malamud distrusted the instinctual and Philip Roth's point that Malamud habitually posited Jews as creatures of restraint, sublimation, and moral aspiration, and gentiles as often dangerous creatures of instinctual release. For all of the power of the characterizations, they are schematic enough for the grossness of one, the hissing malice of another, and the lyrical humaneness of the third to seem representative of what it is for many to be a Pole, a Sicilian, a Jew.

It is tempting to compare this story—of one employee who is fleshy and drinks and another who is thin and talks to himself—with Melville's masterpiece "Bartleby the Scrivener." The comparisons and contrasts are many and fascinating, but I will only suggest that Turkey's and Nipper's unhappiness is easily explainable and, until Bartleby appears in the office, the lawyer-narrator is just able to harness their eccentric ways so that he runs a smooth if somewhat zany operation. Real strife only comes to the office with the arrival of Bartleby, that "bit of wreck in the mid Atlantic,"[99] and the apparently perverse uses to which he puts his free will. The closing line of the story—"Ah, Bartleby! Ah, humanity!"[100]—is first of all an evocation of the forlornness, the essential contactlessness of the human condition. "Monstrous employees! Monstrous humanity!" is the implicit closing line of "The Death of Me."

Although hesitant to discuss the sources of his stories, Malamud did offer some background for "The Jewbird." Upon reading Howard Nemerov's "Digressions Upon a Crow," a sketch the poet published in the spring 1962 *Carleton Miscellany*, Malamud "said to myself, thinking of a jewfish, suppose the bird had been Jewish. At that point the story came to life."[101] Schwartz, the Jewbird of Malamud's story, would have fared well had he flown into the home of the narrator of Nemerov's sketch. But instead of finding a haven in the suburban or rural house of Nemerov's bookish, witty man—so kindly that he has fed the area's grosbeak population for years and is horrified by a gamekeeper's suggestion that he wring the neck or run his car over a sick gull that he has been nursing—Schwartz flies into Harry Cohen's apartment, on the east side of Manhattan. There he lands "if not smack on Cohen's thick lamb chop, at least on the table, close by" (*IF*, 101). The thickness of his chop, like the thickness of his hairy-chested body and his up-to-date job selling food frozen in hardened masses, complement Cohen's gross, obdurate sensibility; "Grubber yung [slob, lout]" (*IF*, 108), Schwartz later caws at the frozen food salesman. When Schwartz responds to Cohen's first gestures—a curse and a missed blow—with "Gevalt [heaven], a pogrom!," Cohen's wife, Edie, and Maurie, his ten-year-old son, are appropriately astonished. But Cohen has little time for the improbabilities of either the physical or moral world and can only demand to know what the bird wants. Correspondingly, when Schwartz proves he's a Jew by fervently dovening (or praying in Hebrew), Cohn wants to know why the bird wears no hat and no phylacteries, as the ritual requires, and if he's not "some kind of ghost or dybbuk" (*IF*, 102–3).

Schwartz is neither, just somebody's cranky, sly, Old World Jewish uncle who moves into crowded quarters for a while and who, at his advanced age, likes "the warm, the windows, the smell of cooking . . . to see once in while the *Jewish Morning Journal* and have now and then a schnapps because it helps my breathing, thanks God." He is also a bird with dusky, bedraggled feathers and, like Susskind, that other skinny-legged fugitive from anti-Semitism, an opportunist, though he uses wheedling instead of Susskind's arrogant onslaughts. On the surface Schwartz is one of those "just boil me a potato" visitors: "whatever you give me, you won't hear complaints." But when Cohen brings home a bird feeder full of dried corn, Schwartz rejects the food with a haughty "Impossible" (*IF*, 105). Still, the old bird is physically and emotionally vulnerable in many ways that Susskind is not, and it is the combination of the bird's fragility, decency, and opportunism that tests the humanness of each member of the Cohen family.

If the story mixes modes in a new way, with the Jewish uncle/talking bird dropped into a realistic setting, the ethical framework is familiar: each character is defined in terms of his or her Jewishness. For once, Malamud associates morality with response to ritual: Cohen is unmoved by the bird's praying, but Edie bows her head and Maurie rocks back and forth; mother and son want to offer the weary traveler the traditional sanctuary the father would deny. Edie and Maurie are able to house Schwartz for four months for two reasons. First, Cohen's relationship to his mother preserves a vestigial tie to his Jewish past. On the August night that Schwartz first flies through their open window, the Cohens have returned early from vacation only because Harry's mother is ill. Second, "though nobody had asked him, Schwartz took on full responsibility for Maurie's performance in school," and the good-hearted but unintelligent boy's grades improve enough for Cohen to boast "If he keeps up like this. . . . I'll get him into an Ivy League college for sure" (*IF,* 106–7).

To an unusual degree for a Malamud story, "The Jewbird" deals with that great theme of twentieth-century Jewish-American fiction, assimilation. Malamud's usual position is that the degree to which a Jew is assimilated corresponds to the degree that he has been corrupted by contemporary American society, and he does not deviate from this stance in the story. Racism in large part follows from the projection onto others of qualities that secretly frighten or shame the racist, and Schwartz does embody to Cohen the Jewish origins that he would like to expunge. The bird also represents difference—in the workings of the story a comically uncanny sort—that excites the racist's characteristic xenophobia: "whoever heard of a Jewbird?" (*IF,* 110) is one of Cohen's many objections to the bird's presence. Malamud interestingly complicates things by making the Jewbird seem to Cohen able to help complete his flight from his Jewishness. To have a son in an Ivy league school would extend his, Harry Cohen's, rise in WASP society and for this he needs the more patient, erudite Schwartz—though the bird tries to puncture his grand design for Maurie's academic future.

Of course the qualities that make Schwartz a fine companion for Maurie and Edie also threaten Cohen's sense of himself as the dominant male in the house. In a characteristically comic but telling moment, he accuses Schwartz of wanting to sleep next to his wife. The bird's reply typifies the way in which the comic possibilities of his characterization usually work to lessen the seriousness with which we respond to the conflict between him and the frozen food salesman: "Mr. Cohen, . . . on this rest assured. A bird is a bird" (*IF,* 108).

Though Cohen's solution is similar to that of a good many anti-Semitic countries, who permitted the Jews to stay but subjected them to increasing torments, the comic slipperiness generated by Schwartz's dual identity as bird and Jewish uncle lessens the pain of the parable. Malamud finally explodes the strange blend of the antic and the upsetting by having Cohen's mother die on the same day Maurie receives a zero on an arithmetic test. Cohen's restraints are loosed as surely as were those of the Cossacks or a gentile mob before they descended upon a shtetl; he either kills "the broken hearted bird" or badly damages Schwartz and leaves him for the other predators of the world to finish off. When Maurie finds, with the melting of the snow in the spring, "a dead black bird in a small lot near the river, his two wings broken, neck twisted, and both bird-eyes plucked clean," the reader suddenly falls through the comic afterglow to the painful remembrance of what many humans have done and what many humans (and perhaps animals) have suffered. Edie tells her son that Schwartz was killed by "Anti-Semeets" (*IF*, 112–13), but the implicit accusation of her husband does not at all suggest that "Edie, in skinny yellow shorts" will now be able to stand up to her husband "with . . . beefy shorts" (*IF*, 102). Beneath all of the story's wonderful comedy is the sense that the brutes still run things.

Another way that some of Malamud's short stories of the early sixties differ from those of the late forties and the fifties is in their use of point of view. When "Black Is My Favorite Color" appeared in the *Reporter* of 18 July 1963, it marked the first time that Malamud published a story told in the first person. The monologue of Nat Lime, a forty-four-year-old bachelor who owns a liquor store in Harlem, is a prolonged lament over the different ways in which blacks have rejected his offers of assistance, friendship, and love. Although Nat volubly asserts moral truths (like the importance of brotherhood and the need to communicate the truths of one's heart) that the author holds, his insight into himself and others is not high. The distance between what Nat is aware of and what the careful reader perceives brings added tension and hopelessness to a narrative already crackling with the racial tensions of the early 1960s.

In the first of his recollections, Nat relates how "once in the jungle in New Guinea in the Second War, I got the idea when I shot at a running Jap and missed him, that I had some kind of a talent" (*IF*, 19). The talent for valuing all kinds of humans, whether their skins are yellow, black, or white, is a worthy one, but some of the causes of the valuation are not as admirable as the sentiment Nat expresses.

The son of an arthritic, unemployed cutter and a mother who supported the family by selling paper bags from a pushcart, the young Nat moved with his parents from Manhattan to a "not-so-hot" section of Brooklyn. He perceived that the block inhabited by blacks was much grimmer than the others: "In those days though I had little myself I was old enough to know who was better off, and the whole block of colored houses made me feel bad in the daylight. But I went there as much as I could because the street was full of life." This sort of ambivalence toward black behavior and appearance is repeated so many times in the story that it is indicative of Nat's confusion and lack of insight. For example, he never perceives that his feeling bad about the life situation of blacks was really a way of feeling good about himself: as little as Nat's family had, it was more than blacks did. He picked out Buster, a lonely black boy who was two years older, "because I had no . . . [friends] then, we were new in the neighborhood (*IF*, 19–20). Having so little, the son of an alcoholic, usually unemployed barber who cut another black with a half-inch chisel one weekend, Buster could not very well refuse Nat's treating him to movies, candy bars, his best comics.

Nat comes closest to understanding the source of his affection for blacks when he muses that perhaps he and Buster never got to be friends "because it was a one-way proposition from me to him" (*IF*, 22). In his perceptive reading of the story, Merrill Skaggs writes, "the point is not that Nat deceives himself about the intensity of his feeling for Negroes—there is no reason to doubt his love—but that he never searches beyond the emotion to understand that it originates in a need to be charitable, and therefore to be morally, socially, or economically superior.[102] Although I feel that Skaggs sometimes pushes too far, suggesting for example that Nat should address his black employees as Mister (when a black employer surely would not), his premise that blacks "eventually reject Nat because they perceive his offer of friendship is based on their racial rather than individual identities"[103] is borne out by the story.

But "Black Is My Favorite Color" also captures Malamud's sense that the racial situation is so volatile, so incendiary, that more tactfully tendered, generously based gestures of friendship than Nat's might also be refused. Toward the end of the story Nat tells us that he recently tried to help a blind man—not a black blind man—on the sidewalk. But that the blind man was black has become an inescapable social fact; consequently a heavy black woman pushed Nat away so hard that he hurt his leg on a fire hydrant. There's some justification for his self-pitying next statement: "That's how it is. I give my heart and they kick me in my teeth" (*IF*, 30). But in a closing gesture reminiscent of Rosen's *"But I will give"* in "Take Pity," Nat demands that he be joined in the kitchen by the black maid, Charity Sweetness, who would rather eat her lunch in the bathroom than at the same table with him.

Nat's ambivalence extends to his feelings about black violence—which he seeks out though it horrifies him—and his relationship with Ornita Harris, a black widow about fifteen years younger than he is.

The Short Fiction: An Essay

Nat, who several times mentions his bald spot and extra pounds, thinks on his first date with her how strangers looking at them might notice "how pretty she was for a man of my type" (*IF*, 24). The covert suggestion that he would not have a chance with a comparably attractive white woman compromises the worth of both of them. But since the racial situation is the social fate bearing down on the mixed couple, she does reject Nat after they're attacked by three black youths one cold February night.

Malamud also experimented with tense in the early 1960s. Nat's attempt to get Charity Sweetness out of the bathroom, which frames "Black," is narrated in the present tense. The frustration of this situation presumably triggers Nat's recital, in the past tense, of all the rejections he's met from blacks. This told, he returns to the frustration of the present and we leave him suspended there. "Naked Nude," published in August 1963, a month after "Black," is wholly in the present tense, as if to emphasize the uncertain future of Fidelman, a captive in a brothel. The present tense is used in the first paragraph of "The German Refugee," as it was in the narrative frame of "Black," to register a pervasive lack of connection. Each of the paragraph's three sentences carves an image at a temporal distance from the others as the narrator vividly "sees" his first meeting with Oskar Gassner in a way that registers part of the disconnections of the time:

> Oskar Gassner sits in his cotton-mesh undershirt and summer bathrobe at the window of his stuffy, hot, dark hotel room on West Tenth Street while I cautiously knock. Outside, across the sky, a late-June green twilight fades in darkness. The refugee fumbles for the light and stares at me, hiding despair but not pain. (*IF*, 195)

Save for one phrase, when the present tense is used to register the apparent endlessness of Oskar's functional paralysis, the rest of the story is in the past tense.

The time of this first meeting is late June 1939. Hitler is demanding the return of Danzig to Germany and the right to build a road and railway across Poland to connect East Prussia with the rest of the country. England guarantees support for Poland's rejection of the demands, and when the German army crosses the border into Poland, on 1 September, World War II is under way. No other Malamud story is as firmly welded to precise historical events as "The German Refugee," and though there are many refugees in Malamud's stories, this one is unmatched as a study of culture shock. Just as Hitler seems to hold history in his demonic grip, Oskar and the narrator, the only two characters who appear for more than a paragraph in the story, are held throughout the summer by a heat wave that objectifies the refugee's stifling inner life. The pressures of the immediate history of Germany have driven the Jewish Oskar, a prominent critic and journalist on a Berlin paper, to a disordered, stifling hotel room in New York. In the more expensive rooms he had before and in the apartment he soon moves to, he experiences the "refugee's displacement, alienation, financial insecurity, being in a strange land without friends or a speakable tongue" (*IF*, 205).

Having gained a job lecturing throughout the coming academic year on the literature of the Weimar Republic, Oskar can write his lectures in German but he must deliver them in English. Unable to master English pronunciation or to write more than a page of his first lecture, he exudes despair and melancholy through most of the story. But Oskar seems to be on his way to acculturation when, largely through the efforts of the narrator, he sufficiently overcomes his loss of self-esteem and hatred of the language of the Nazis to write a lecture in German, and when he ostensibly demonstrates his acceptance of his new state by so improving his pronunciation that he delivers the lecture successfully in English.

But Oskar has not lived, only written and spoken about his topic—the effect of Whitman's *Brudermensch* (brotherhood) upon the Weimar writers. Having threatened to commit suicide if he does not write the lecture, he instead takes gas when he learns what has happened to his gentile wife, to whom had had been married for twenty-seven years but abandoned in Germany as a part of the hated country. Having failed in her letters to convince Oskar of her loyalty, she coverted to Judaism, was arrested, and underwent the hideous brotherhood of victimization that characterizes so much of twentieth-century life when she toppled (in the last sentence of this splendid collection) "into an open tank ditch, with the naked Jewish men, their wives and children, some Polish soldiers, and a handful of gypsies" (*IF*, 212).

Since Oskar is the main character of the story, and one whose situation carries considerable dramatic and thematic charge, Malamud made the narrator, Martin Greenberg, much more reliable, a far more transparent lens, than Nat Lime. Moreover, Martin might have changed a good deal from the brash, skinny, twenty-year-old who tutored Oskar in English, but to have considered his evolving story would have been to diminish Oskar's. The only Martin that we see is one whose characterization interestingly counterpoints Oskar's. "A skinny life hungry kid . . . palpitating to get going," Martin regards the imminent war as "a goddamn cheat" (*IF*, 195), which blocks his happy movement out into the wide world. A part of the world Martin has not experienced has left Oskar consumed with hatred for the Nazis "for destroying his career, uprooting his life after half a century, and flinging him like a piece of bleeding meat to the hawks." Malamud gets a good deal of leverage from the contrast between the energetic and optimistic American—as at home in New York as a fish in the sea—and the defeated, sodden German. Oskar moves down the stairs so slowly in his inappropriately heavy, formal dress that he seems to Martin "always suspended between two floors" (*IF*, 203). The more meaningful suspension is between two cultures. The contrast between Martin's extraordinary kindness toward Oskar and the older man's failure of generosity toward his wife is to some degree also the contrast between the possibilities of innocence and the potentially crippling effects of the experience of suffering.

Though sharply written, "A Choice of Profession' blends so many of Malamud's characteristic motifs that it has a programmatic quality to a reader familiar with his work. Like the protagonists of "The German Refugee," *The Fixer*, and "Life Is Better Than Death," Cronin feels he has been betrayed by his spouse, whom he discovers has been having an affair with a friend. After living through a good many degrading emotions, particularly jealousy, Cronin, like S. Levin, heads into the mythic and pastoral west from a huge city—Chicago instead of Levin's New York. What both are searching for serves as the title of Levin's quest: a new life. Like Levin, Cronin is striking out in the newly adopted profession of teaching, and at a college in beautiful natural surroundings—Northern California to Levin's Cascadia (or Oregon). Like the protagonists of *The Natural* and "The Lady of the Lake," he is powerfully attracted by a woman who has come to terms with a damaging past and who is associated with the spiritually rejuvenating possibilities of water. During an outing on a particularly lovely spring day, Cronin and Mary Lou Miller, his twenty-four-year-old student, pause "by a long blue lake shaped like a bird in flight." There Cronin, who had about six weeks earlier been sickened by Mary Lou's confessing that her manipulative ex-husband had set her up as a prostitute, reflects, "in the present a person is what she is becoming and not what she was" (*IF*, 80). The description of the lake reminds one of the redemptive woman of *The Assistant,* who has "breasts like small birds in flight" (*TA*, 75) and who realizes that another sexual transgressor (former rapist and thief Frank Alpine) "had changed into somebody else, no longer what he had been. . . . What he did to me he did wrong, she thought, but since he has changed in his heart he owes me nothing" (*TA*, 243). Mary Lou then becomes Cronin's nature goddess (in her avatar as the lady of the lake) by stripping and going swimming. The comedy Malamud brings to the story is only a little less grotesque than in *The Natural,* in which the water goddess tells the protagonist— after a nude swim together and during intercourse—that she's a grandmother. While driving to Mary Lou's apartment to make love, she offhandedly tells the groaning Cronin that she had been raped by her brother when she was thirteen.

Although Mary Lou can formulaically announce that her past no longer bothers her, Cronin is not so fortunate. Consumed by jealousy when he later mistakenly thinks a friend is having an affair with Mary Lou, he tells the friend of her career as a prostitute. Malamud then plays a variation on his familiar theme of practical, as opposed to formal, education. Unlike Mary Lou, Cronin has not learned from his past suffering. Insufficiently giving and excessively jealous in past and present, he perceives he is not morally qualified to teach literature, while in the last line of the story we learn that Mary Lou "hoped some day to teach" (*IF*, 87).

Its mainstream realism is what makes the story an experimental one for Malamud. That is, he tried to give familiar motifs a new spin by having them dramatized by WASPs whose expressive ranges are relatively limited compared to many of the vivid Jews, Italians, Poles, and Russians of his other fiction. Admittedly, the control of settings, of the shifts in Cronin's inner life and, in particular, of the interactions between the hulking but extremely vulnerable Cronin and Mary Lou— by turns blunt, resolute, tentative, vulnerable—are well done. But the story lacks the incandescence, vivid or muted, that he brought to the Jewish and Italian stories in the collection.

Malamud said that because of his Italo-American wife he was able to sink into Italian family life during his stay in Rome.[104] Both "The Maid's Shoes" and "Life Is Better Than Death" register Malamud's imaginary immersion into the lives of typical Italians with a low-keyed realism that differs from the tones of the other eight stories that are set in Italy. Since Malamud found Italians at least as histrionic, as demonstrative as the Jews, his Italian connection was a particularly fortunate one for him.

Though the first name of Orlando Krantz, the legal scholar of "The Maid's Shoes," is Italian, the varying degrees of repugnance with which he confronts what he feels is the messiness, the chaos of Italian life is no more Italian than his last name. Interviewing for a maid to clean his rented apartment, he rejects the first, sixteen-year-old candidate because he's put off by the way the aunt who accompanies her "[plays] up certain qualities of the girl" (*IF*, 154). Are some of these qualities her sexual desirability or accessibility? The fine story would work even better if they were. When Krantz tells the portinaia that he wants an older woman, she remembers the forty-five-year-old Rosa. It is she the professor hires and it is she who, after drawing the guarded professor much further into her unhappy life than he ever wanted to go, reveals to him that she is pregnant. She also tells Krantz that when her son finds "out his mother's a whore . . . he'll break my bones, if not with his hands, then with his teeth" (*IF*, 167).

When we first see Rosa in the story's opening paragraph, we learn that though her bad teeth and long, bitter widowhood have made her look older than her years, "her hair [is] black, and her eyes and lips . . . pretty," her legs "heavy but well-formed" (*IF*, 153–54). With the detail of the way the seam in her worn black dress has split open on the hip, exposing about two inches of her white underwear, Malamud fuses her "messiness" and—as with the description of Ornita Harris's layerings in "Black Is My Favorite Color" (*IF*, 25)—her sexuality. The two-inch opening symbolizes her still-yearning vagina. For a while Rosa brings Krantz dirty eggs laid by her daughter-in-law's hen, but he finally tells her that the yolks are too strong for him, just as the persistence of sexuality in the Italian peasantry is too strong for his highly sublimated nature. To his "It hardly seems likely that you can conceive, considering your age" Rosa responds, "My mother gave birth at fifty" (*IF*, 167). It turns out that Rosa is not pregnant, but the professor, who likes to deal with human entanglements at the abstracted distance his legal research provides, cannot stand the agitation caused by the consequences of the persistence of Rosa's sexuality. When Rosa departs she takes with her all her possessions save the pair of sensible shoes Krantz had given her a few weeks earlier to replace the battered torn pair she had worn for the past six years. For Rosa, to accept the shoes would be to accept the fact that she is no longer a sexual being who can attract men, only a toiler, a drudge. And neither will the portinaia accept this definition of herself, for after Krantz gives her the shoes she passes them on to her daughter after wearing them for only a week.

Earlier, Krantz had felt that his giving her the shoes was "a psychologically proper move in more ways than one." Rosa had come to him one morning and told him that her married friend Armando wanted to give her a pair of shoes to replace the ones that looked "as though they've been chewed by goats" (*IF*, 162–63), but that she feared the shoes would then lead her to Armando's bed. Should she accept the shoes from Armando? With flushed face and head, Krantz tries to avoid responding, finally urges her not to accept them, then tries to solve the situation equitably by purchasing the sensible shoes for Rosa. That he enables Rosa to keep free from sexual entanglement, provides her with good shoes, and acts with intelligently informed generosity seems to constitute the psychological rightness of his behavior. But Italian life is not so easily managed by rational behavior. Rosa had already accepted "a pair of dressy black needlepoint pumps" (*IF*, 164). Had she accepted them before the preceding day and been trying to squeeze money for shoes from Krantz? Had she been sleeping with Armando before she spoke to the professsor? The reader is no more able to penetrate the intrigues of Italian life than is Krantz, for Malamud slyly only takes us into Rosa's mind at an earlier point, to tell us of her sorrow that the professor won't let her share his troubles with him.

Correspondingly, the precise nature of the mixture of Rosa's sexual vitality and her need for a confidante with whom she can discuss her troubles is left tantalizingly vague. Everything in the story—from the character's appearances and daily habits to the revelations of Rosa's various entanglements and Krantz's blend of sympathy and repulsion—is narrated with extraordinary authority. As Theodore Solotaroff wrote in his review of the collection, the style he preferred of the several that surface in the collection "is for the vein of controlled vibrant writing that runs through 'The Maid's Shoes'—a story that seems almost Tolstoyan in its calm moral intelligence.[105]

Like "A Choice of Profession," "Life Is Better Than Death" turns upon the consequences of a spouse's sexual betrayal. When Armando, Etta Oliva's husband of nearly a decade, left her to resume his affair with an eighteen-year-old cousin, Etta fell to her knees and prayed for his death. Her murderous prayers seemed to have been immediately answered: the sleeping Armando rolled out of the back of the truck bringing him back to the cousin in Perugia and "was dead before he stopped rolling" (*IF*, 94). Believing that she caused his death, Etta is—as the story opens, about fifteen months after Armando's death—still consumed with guilt. Consequently her life revolves around visiting his grave almost daily, attending confession, taking communion, lighting candles, and offering masses whenever her low-paying job in a drapery shop permits it. One wonders what the priest at confession could be telling her, for though "still a young woman and at that not bad looking" (*IF*, 96), she often prays that Armando "would move over and let her lie down with him so that her heart might be eased" (*IF*, 89). She is reminded of her advantages by Cesare Montaldi, a free-lance journalist whom Etta meets in the cemetery one drizzly day. Cesare is also mourning at the grave of his spouse who was killed while hurrying to meet a lover. But he has made his way back to life enough to want an involvement with Etta. Intelligent and tactful, he discreetly argues in different ways that she was not the cause of Armando's death, that her obligation is to her own life, not to wasting it in guilt, sorrow, and the acts of penitence that she hopes will speed Armando's way out of purgatory.

During their third meeting, about six weeks after their first conversation, Cesare presents his clinching argument: "if Our Lord Himself this minute let Armando rise from the dead to take up his life on earth, tonight—he would be lying in his cousin's bed" (*IF*, 99). Though Etta cries, she recognizes the truth of Cesare's remark and, her sexual desire reawakened, sleeps with him the next time they meet. Gradually Etta separates her life and her husband's death and begins to feel that "she was not committing adultery. She was a lonely woman and had a lover, a widower, a gentle and affectionate man." And when Etta tells Cesare that she is pregnant, her lover gently and affectionately reassures her that the creation of life is not to be regretted, that he will take responsibility for the child. But a man's actions might show less moral intelligence than his statements. Cesare disappears the next day and Etta both mourns the loss of Cesare and "even with the life in her belly" (*IF*, 100) returns to thinking of herself as an adultress, but this time one who no longer has the right to return to Armando's grave.

Read one way the ending is so grim that it belies the assertion of the title. Having been cynically used by Cesare, Etta has regressed back into her earlier torment over her husband's death but now no longer has even the temporary relief her tears and acts of penitence gave her.

But one can also argue that though Etta again considers herself married to a dead man, so that the sex with Cesare was adulterous, the affect she had toward one or both men has been displaced toward the organism growing within her. This difficult issue comes upon us too suddenly. Although I tend to applaud the ambiguity in Malamud's endings, I wish in this case that we had been given a bit more about Etta's ways so that we could judge how much force to attribute to her commitment to life, and how much to death.

Pictures of Fidelman: An Exhibition

In 1974 Malamud told Daniel Stern that "after I wrote ["The Last Mohican"] in Rome I jotted down ideas for several incidents in the form of a picaresque novel. I was out to loosen up—experiment a little—with narrative structure. And I wanted to see, if I wrote it at intervals—as I did from 1957 to 1968—whether the passing of time and mores would influence [Fidelman's] life. I did not think of the narrative as merely a series of related stories because almost at once I had the structure of a novel in mind and each part had to fit that form."[106]

The first five stories of *Pictures of Fidelman* were published in periodicals between 1958 and 1968, and it was only with the release of the sixth story ("Glass Blower of Venice") with the 1969 publication of the novel that one could discern the controlling form Malamud decided upon back in 1958. In its simplest sense, *Pictures* is about the causes and consequences of Fidelman's vocational failings, first as an art critic, then as a painter and sculptor. In four of the last five stories his aesthetic and erotic identities complexly interpenetrate with the surprising consequence—after two hundred pages of pratfalls, humiliations, and increasing self-degradation—that Malamud brings him to what seems to be the most benignly integrated life of any character in his fiction. The rifts in and between his erotic and vocational lives almost magically healed, Fidelman ends his sojourn of more than a decade in Italy and returns to America.

The life of Fidelman the limited artist, as opposed to Fidelman the limited art historian, is under way by the second story or picture, "Still Life." Malamud seemed to have decided, either before or during its composition, to make possible Fidelman's picaresque career by making him a somewhat different character from the Fidelman of "The Last Mohican." It is not just that Malamud continues in the later stories to strip defenses from the tight, fussy fellow who arrives in Rome to write on Giotto; he gives the character a past more in keeping with the love-sick fool or cynical opportunist we see in the later stories. For example, we're told that the defenseless romantic of the later stories was "ever a sucker for strange beauty and all sorts of experiences."[107] But the

90

sucker never appears in "The Last Mohican." That Fidelman would not sleep with prostitutes "he desired mightily" (*TMB*, 173) because he feared for his health.

To varying degrees, "Still Life" and the four succeeding stories ("Naked Nude," "A Pimp's Revenge," "Pictures of the Artist," and "Glass Blower of Venice") constitute Malamud's Italian holiday from his usual moral broodings, as well as from the tighter forms of the earlier fiction, while "Mohican" is in good part about Fidelman's acceptance of the moral consequences of his being a Jew. In this sense, it's a characteristic *Magic Barrel* story. In contrast, Fidelman's morality or immorality is never an issue in "Still Life," and Jewishness as a metaphor for humanity surfaces in only one of the remaining stories—the penultimate "Pictures of the Artist"—and then in parodic forms. The strange version of Annamaria Oliovini's Catholicism is an important ingredient of "Still Life," but her attractiveness to Fidelman does not particularly follow from her being a gentile, as it probably would have were the story written a few years earlier.

The degree to which "The Last Mohican" and the five later stories belong to different fictional worlds is the most substantial discontinuity in *Pictures*. Lacunae created by Malamud's refusal to follow up in any way such climaxes as Fidelman's fleeing to Switzerland or driving a knife into his stomach, as well as the the unexplained surfacing or disappearance or quest for a number of art objects,[108] were some of the privileges permitted him by the relatively loose form he adopted.

The meshing of Fidelman's aesthetic and erotic lives is under way by the end of the first paragraph of "Still Life," for his search for a place to work brings him to Annamaria's studio, where she is renting space. By the end of the next paragraph he is helplessly infatuated with the *pittrice* (painter) with the violet mouth, piercing breasts, and tormented inner life. Malamud several times protested against critics calling Fidelman a schlemiel, but he bore some responsibility for all the times this admittedly reductive term was dropped upon his comic hero. The new Fidelman, such a prisoner of first impressions that he bargains his way into paying doubled rent for the space, might prove that he is more than a schlemiel, but schlemiel he is.

The Fidelman of "Mohican" who rushed with suit in arms to Susskind, the Leo Finkle of "The Magic Barrel" who rushed with flowers to Stella, might have been holy fools for virtue or for virtuous love. But this Fidelman—driven by sexual desire to slavish generosity toward someone whom he realizes from the beginning is "as a woman, indifferent to him or his type" (*PF*, 40)—is merely a fool whose bouts of self-pity over his unrequited love only add to his foolishness. Buying her meals and giving her gifts bought with money his sister has sent him earn no less contempt from the *pittrice* than his childish running about the studio to pick up tubes of paint and brushes she has dropped. Thinking that she's bored by his presence, Fidelman takes to passing his days in the cold streets, museums, and libraries of Rome and painting at night by lightbulb. La Belle Dame Sans Merci responds by removing the light bulbs before she goes to bed. "Don't waste my electricity, this isn't America" (*PF*, 52) is her sweet admonition.

Yet she does seem to show mercy when Fidelman paints a *Virgin and Child* with Annamaria as the virgin, "saintly beautiful," holding in her arms an infant that resembles a nephew of Fidelman's. "You have seen my soul" (*PF*, 55), the overwhelmed *pittrice* sobs, and after dutifully serving Fidelman supper she takes him to bed. Here Malamud arranges sexual schlemielhood for Fidelman with three interruptions that bring our overwrought hero to premature ejaculation and, "although he mightily willed resurrection, his wilted flower bit the dust." This earns banishment from Annamaria's bedroom with accompanying cries of "pig, beast, onanist" (*PF*, 58), intensified insults, and Annamaria's public display of her rendition of Fidelman, executed during a portrait competition at a party, as a "gigantic funereal phallus that resembled a broken-backed snake" (*PF*, 63).

When Fidelman attempts a self-portrait while in priest's vestments, we find out why Annamaria responds so violently to his impotence; why she's afraid to cross bridges; what goes on with Augusto, the elderly vistor who comes to plead with her once a week; and why she makes Fidelman touch his testicles three times after they pass a nun (whose presence causes the *pittrice* to mutter "Jettatura! Porca miseria!" (Bird of ill omen! Sow of woe!) (*PF*, 45). Somewhat more deranged than usual, Annamaria treats Fidelman as if he were a true priest and finally confesses the agony that has been tearing her apart. Her drowning in the Tiber the child she had by Augusto has both paralyzed her with guilt and caused him to lose his potency. During his weekly visits he begged her to confess so that he might regain his powers. "But every time I step into the confessional my tongue turns to bone. The priest can't tear a word out of me. That's how it's been all my life, don't ask me why." Demanding penances beyond the hundred "Our Fathers and Hail Marys" the dazed Fidelman prescribes, she burrows her head into his lap and our hero feels "the surprised beginnings of an erection." At this point we see the beginnings of the sexual opportunist more fully developed in the fourth story, "A Pimp's Revenge": Fidelman feels the vestiges of conventional morality enough to shudder but still demands that the disturbed woman undress. To her demand that he keep his clothes on he compromises and so it is that, in the final lines of the story, he is wearing a biretta or priest's hat "as she [clasps] his buttocks, he [cups] hers. Pumping slowly he [nails] her to her cross" (*PF*, 67–68).

Malamud's 1974 claim that he wanted, back in 1958, to see if "the passing of time and mores would influence [Fidelman's] life" skips over the crucial link between society and character: the shifts and emergences within the author. Retrospective appraisals of his work have shown it to be deceptively contemporaneous, both thematically and formally. Morris Dickstein has interestingly and persuasively argued that the emphases in Malamud's writing of the fifties on salvation by suffering, on the schlemiel character, and on imprisonment were "one kind of response to the frozen and quietly fear-ridden political atmosphere of the McCarthy and Eisenhower years.[109] Responding to Ihab Hassan's claim that Malamud was in no way a postmodernist writer, Jackson Benson wrote "I wonder if Malamud does not better fit Hassan's description of postmodernism than he thinks. When he speaks of a trend from 'closed' to 'open' forms, from 'realism' to 'surrealism,' from 'myth' to 'parody,' and from 'ironic tragedy' to 'self-ironic comedy,' I think . . . that this is really a rather good description of Malamud's progress from the earliest novels, *The Natural* and *The Assistant*, to the later, *The Tenants* and *Pictures of Fidelman*."[110]

A year after Malamud wrote "The Last Mohican," Norman Mailer wrote in *Advertisements for Myself* of the sexual revolution that was right around the corner. The corner was turned with the federal court decisions of 1959, 1964, and 1966 that overturned the bannings of lower courts and permitted the publishing of the unexpurgated *Lady Chatterley's Lover*, *Tropic of Cancer*, *Naked Lunch*, and *Memoirs of a Woman of Pleasure*. The last text, better known as *Fanny Hill*, had been banned in the United States since 1821.

The publication of "Still Life" in the *Partisan Review* of Winter 1962 signalled the emergence in print of that part of Malamud which is strongly sexual without being particularly moral, and kept pace with the falling of literary and social taboos around him. The value placed in sexual restraint in all three novels Malamud worked on in the fifties is nowhere present in *Pictures*, and the explicitness of the sexual descriptions in "Still Life" goes far beyond anything in his earlier work. Some of the passages in *A New Life,* published a year earlier, come close, but S. Levin pays dearly for his sex life, as the pre-Fidelman males tend to. No mutterings of either the narrator's or Fidelman's vengeful superego darken the final scene, lit by Annamaria's glowing flesh, and the narrator in no way blames Fidelman for the nailing. (Then again, how much "Jewish" restraint should we expect from someone in a priest costume?) Indeed, the very overstatement of the closing metaphor wittily reminds the reader that Annamaria is not being crucified at all; she's getting what she wants. Her wants might be a little crazy, and she might still regard Fidelman as a mortifying presence, but this bit of hypocrisy need not intrude on his pleasure.

If Malamud is still a teacher in this story the lesson seems to be a very breezy assertion of the need to make the best of an imperfect situation. What the two make of their interaction qualifies as happiness in the Aristotelian, functional sense of the word. The lovers' fit is a happy one, both sexually and psychically: the rocks in his head fit the holes in hers, however temporarily. Of course, a feminist critic might not accept as easily as I do Malamud's new stance as a tolerant man of the sexual world. And, after one absorbs the rest of *Pictures,* it is possible to interpret the ending as the first example of the amoral opportunism that takes Fidelman further and further off a moral course as the stories unfold. But "Still Life," judged within its own frame, without reference to the succeeding stories, just doesn't read that way.

The social sinking that began in "Still Life" when Fidelman moved into the "attic-like atelier on a cobblestone street in the Trastevere, strung high with sheets and underwear" (*PF,* 39) accelerates in "Naked Nude." Between "Still Life" and this story, the checks from Bessie have stopped, and Fidelman has made his way from Rome to Milan. The art student of the preceding story becomes "the former art student" (*PF,* 71) either before or after he picks an American traveler's pocket, and the open door that offers him refuge from the two policemen who are chasing him leads him into a brothel. There Angelo, the padrone, relieves him of his passport, the money from the stolen wallet, and "warned that if he ratted to anybody, he would report him to the Questura where his brother presided, as a dangerous alien thief" (*PF,* 71–72). Fidelman's two attempts to escape earn him two beatings (one with a rubber hose), a week chained to his bed, and an appointment as master of the latrine, a title that qualifies him to clean thirty toilets a day. At night he weeps in his sleep, thinks about suicide, and loses the little he earns during the day to Angelo and Scarpio, the padrone's lover and major domo.

His art work is the doodling of despair: Susskind hanged, the head of the artist bouncing down the steps of a guillotine platform. He recalls—in a wonderfully ironic contrast to the philosophical psychopath of Mailer's "The White Negro" (who supposedly reforges his psyche through dangerous, successful acts)—his disastrous career as a pickpocket with an image of himself as "a starving white Negro pursued by a hooting mob of cowboys on horses" (*PF*, 70). But his doodlings give Angelo the idea of having Fidelman make a copy of Titian's *Venus of Urbino,* hanging in a nearby castle on Bella Isola in Lake Maggiore. If Angelo can switch paintings he can sell the original back to the insurance company for $300,000. For this Angelo will give Fidelman his freedom, his passport, and $350 for plane fare. Having convinced Angelo to let him see the painting, Fidelman falls as idiotically in love with it as he had with Annamaria, and with roughly the same buffo effects. His murmurings of his love and his kisses of her hands, thighs, and breasts are interrupted by a guard who "strikes him hard on the head with both fists" (*PF*, 80).

Since his first sallies at the reproduction are grotesque failures, Scarpio, in one of the story's many fine comic scenes, tries to free Fidelman of his painter's block. Psychoanalysis text in hand and knife in his trousers, he asks the American if he had ever spied on his mother:

> "She died young," Fidelman says, on the verge of tears. "I was raised by my sister Bessie."
> "Go on, I'm listening," says Scarpio.
> "I can't. My mind goes blank." (*PF*, 86)

But Fidelman's unconscious rises to fill his blank mind as he dreams that night of spying on his naked sister in her bath. After looking at her hefty young body "with longing that amounts to anguish" (*PF*, 86), the fourteen-year-old of the dream robs fifty cents from Bessie's purse and is slipping out the door when he awakens in Milan. Writing out his dream as Scarpio had told him to, Fidelman suddenly remembers Angelo's telling him that everyone steals, including the artists from each other. Amending the padrone's "We're only human" (*PF*, 78) to "We're all human" (*PF*, 87), Fidelman is then overwhelmed by the thought that he personally steal the painting. To do this he must first paint one. Why he is then to have such a relatively easy, even rapturous, time as he paints what seems to be a very good version demands some explanation.

In "Still Life," Fidelman's aesthetic goals quickly shift from painting well to using his canvases as springboards into Annamaria's bed, and we don't get much sense of his strengths and weaknesses as a painter. Still, the first description of the art student at work pinpoints his central, finally crushing inadequacy:

> Fidelman's work, despite the effort and despair he gave it, was going poorly. Every time he looked at unpainted canvases he saw harlequins, whores, tragic kings, fragmented musicians, the sick and the dread. Still, tradition was tradition and what if he wanted to make more? Since he had always loved art history he considered embarking on a "Mother and Child," but was afraid her image would come out too much Bessie—after all, a dozen years between them. Or maybe a moving "Pietà," the dead son's body held like a broken wave in mama's frail arms? A curse on art history—he fought the fully prefigured pictures though some of his former best paintings had jumped in every detail to the mind. Yet if so where's true engagement? Sometimes I'd like to forget every picture I've seen, Fidelman thought. Almost in panic he sketched in charcoal a coattailed "Figure of a Jew Fleeing" and quickly hid it away. After that, ideas, prefigured or not, were scarce. (*PF*, 47–48)

A fair number of the great painters of the past hang in the massively weighted frames of their greatness throughout *Pictures*. In particular, each of the six parts is connected in some way with a particular master—Giotto, Rembrandt, Titian, Picasso, Modigliani, and Tintoretto, in turn. In his discussion of the novel, Tony Tanner wrote: "References to art works ranging from Sicilian mosaics to the productions of Pop Art contribute to the overall texture, and also help to make us realize the hopeless plethora of styles Fidelman as artistic aspirant is confronted with. Faced with such a gallery, what can originality mean, what indeed can creation mean?"[111]

Originality and successful creation can still mean adopting or modifying or rejecting the forms, subject matters, and techniques of the past or the present to render the artist's own visionary way of seeing. Genius always finds a way. As T. S. Eliot said, "Shakespeare acquired more essential history from Plutarch than most men could from the whole British Museum."[112] Fidelman is so overwhelmed by what others have done because he is in good part ignorant of the value of his own experience. Why not a mother and child starring Bessie and himself if this is the most powerful image of the subject that presents itself? To refuse to paint a fleeing Jew—both Susskind and an aspect of himself—is both to deny the value of his own experience and to flee the kinds of self-confrontation out of which his art must come. The final confrontation must be with the implacable fact that he does not have the talent, the vision, to be a truly successful artist and there is no way he can obtain this vision. Still, small triumphs are possible, and each of the three or four moderately successful paintings Fidelman gets off as he makes his painful way to the renunciation of painting immediately follows a confrontation with his identity.

The first occurs in "Still Life" as Fidelman looks down upon Rome and self-pityingly reflects that because he is unloved in this city of love he is "still straniero," an alien who cannot possess its spirit. But then an aesthetic alternative to the preferences of others occurs to him:

> if you could paint this sight, give it its quality in yours, the spirit belonged to you. History become aesthetic! . . . A wild rush of things he might paint swept sweetly through him: saints in good and bad health, whole or maimed, in gold and red; nude gray rabbis at Auschwitz, black or white Negroes—what not when *any* color dripped from your brush? And if these, so also ANNAMARIA ES PULCHRA. He all but cheered. What more intimate possession of a woman! (*PF*, 53–54).

Malamud has several times proclaimed his right as a human, as a writer, to create gentiles, blacks, talking animals, or cultures he has never lived in. I think that this is part of what he meant when he offered thanks for the privileges of form. Here, Fidelman sufficiently overcomes his anxiety of influence to assert that his experience, lived or imagined, as a Jew or as a saint, might be worth something. As a painter in the most minimal sense, someone whose brush drips paint, he has a right to attempt whatever he wants. From this comes his aesthetic appropriation of Annamaria—in the Madonna and Child. The self-portrait of himself as a priest asserts his right to paint himself any way he chooses. Paradoxically, both aesthetic assertions get him the experiential goal he seeks—admission to Annamaria's bed. We have no way of knowing how good these two paintings were, but they certainly seem to be the best things he achieves in "Still Life.'

For all his childishness, the Fidelman of this story gains enough emotional adulthood to assert his right to function as a painter. In "Naked Nude" Fidelman's early inability to copy Titian's *Venus* successfully is the consequence of a regression to the emotional impasse of a boy frozen in early adolescence. In his regression Fidelman suffers a blurring of his experiential and artistic father-figures that seems a perfect example of Harold Bloom's theories about the anxiety of influence. It does not matter whether or not the sleeping Fidelman imagined or remembered his fourteen-year-old identity as the thief both of money and his mother figure's glowing nudity. The dream reveals the oedipal guilt that has been blocking the "stealing" of the beloved of Father Titian.

The convincing variousness of the underworld characters in "Naked Nude" is perhaps the best thing in the story. Though Scarpio is a brute with a knife, he is also a voracious reader and a vulnerable man who is hurt by a harsh comment of Fidelman's. Angelo is extremely intelligent and possesses a solid knowledge of art history. It is appropriate that in spite of knife, fists, rubber hose, and death threats, Scarpio and Angelo function as improbably nourishing, alternative father figures, who both encourage the dreamer's confrontation with his "sexual theft" and forgive the transgression in advance.

Malamud slyly takes Fidelman's acceptance of himself as a thief further than the Italians or the reader suspects. I'm sure that when I first read the story I never suspected that his "stupendous thought" (*PF*, 87) of personally stealing the painting meant that he would steal his copy away from Angelo, instead of merely helping remove the original from the castle. One can still interpret his insight in this way and conjecture that Fidelman falls more deeply in love with the painting as he creates it. Critics have tended to interpret the theft of the copy as a sign of his inadequacy as an artist—of his limiting narcissism or his willingness to settle for an inferior version.[113] This might be, but I also suggest that just as Borges's Pierre Menard wrote *his Don Quixote* even though each of his sentences was the same as Cervantes's, so, to a relatively important degree, is Fidelman's *Venus of Urbino his*. In creating his version he goes beyond remembering all of the representations of nudes he has ever seen; he enters the paintings of others in the most imaginative way:

Fidelman satyr, with Silenus beard and goatlegs, piping and peeking at backside, frontside, or both, at the "Rokeby Venus," "Bathsheba," "Suzanna," "Venus Anadyomene" . . . at picnickers in dress or undress, bathers ditto . . . hausfrau or whore, amorous ladies modest or brazen, single or in crowds at the Turkish bath, in every conceivable shape or position, while he sports and disports until a trio of maenads pull his tail and he gallops after them through the dusky woods. He is at the same time choked by remembered lust for all the women he had ever desired, from Bessie to Annamaria Oliovino, and for their garters, underpants, slips or half-slips, brassieres and stockings.

But his fantasies have the practical limits of a functioning artist: "He would have prayed her alive if he were not certain she would fall in love, not with her famished creator, but surely the first Apollo Belvedere she lays eyes on. . . . Still, she is his as he paints, so he goes on, planning never to finish, to be happy in loving her, thus forever happy" (*PF,* 88–89).

We can regard the Fidelman of the story's final image, adoring his handiwork by matchlight, as a lovable or unlovable fool. But we can also see him as someone who is consolidating his hold on adulthood. First, in the act of painting, he asserts himself as someone with a right to take symbolic possession of the feminine image. Then he knocks unconscious a truly dangerous adversary. These interpretive possibilities are of course bounded by the parodic aspect of Fidelman's escape. When we compare his flight to safety up Lake Maggiore to Brissago, Switzerland, with that of the romantic predecessors Malamud is obviously alluding to—Frederic Henry and Catherine Barkley in *A Farewell to Arms*—Fidelman could as easily have a plastic, inflatable Venus, with whom he tries to have intimate relations, as his painting.

Whitman's *Song of Myself,* the greatest poetic treatment of the comic variousness of an American self, can most easily be approached as a series of dilations and contractions of the narrator's protean self. We could do worse than regard *Pictures of Fidelman* in the same way. Within Fidelman's movement to his renunciation of art there are two dilating movements and one contracting one. "The Last Mohican," "Still Life," and "Naked Nude" constitute the first dilation, with the tight American who began "Mohican" steadily moving out into more extreme possibilities of behavior until he assumes the guise of the giddily triumphant romantic admiring his hard-won love object in the middle of Lake Maggiore. The first letter of "A Pimp's Revenge," with the protagonist's name compressed from Fidelman to F, alerts us to the contracting movement. In "Pictures of the Artist" the contraction so affects the narrative that, locating itself as it does in Fidelman's unconscious, the effect is of an implosion, with the painter's psyche blown into parts. He is then ready for the reintegration of the self in the book's second and more successful movement out into the world in "Glass Blower of Venice."

The vagueness of the passage of time is a part of the picaresque looseness of *Pictures*. We don't know how long the interval is between any of the stories, but since the Fidelman of "A Pimp's Revenge" has been working on a painting of his mother and himself for five years, it seems that at least this much time has passed since we left him on Lake Maggiore. Now over forty, the painter has changed his behavior a good deal in the interim. Though he weeps with unhappiness at the beginning of the story, a thoughtful practicality has by and large replaced the often melodramatic style of the past. Since there is too much cheap competition for the Madonnas he carves, he is not able to drive very hard bargains in his attempts to sell them. But, as with all of his attempted or completed financial transactions in the story, there is a weary shrewdness that is new. The canniness is backed by a certain functional insensitivity; Fidelman is absolutely untouched by his landlord's pleas for the months of rent the painter owes him. And though he has earlier in the story told Ludovico Belvedere, the former pimp for the girl Fidelman is living with, that "living off the proceeds of a girl's body . . . isn't much of a moral thing to do" (*PF*, 110) he ends up pimping for the girl, Esmeralda, himself. By this time we're quite ready to believe that the lovesick fool Annamaria called Fatso has evolved or contracted into F or Arturo, the efficient pimp who uses the sword in his cane to bully a balky customer into paying, and who begins the story so ravaged that he's told his gauntness is probably hereditary.

Financial pressure drives Fidelman to his new vocation. He had been able to support his painting and a minimal existence by carving and painting wooden Madonnas for five thousand lire each. But, as with one of Malamud's tales of struggling New York shopkeepers, hard times set in. Inexpensive, machine-made Madonnas drive his payment down to two thousand lire—not worth the time it takes to carve the statuettes. A shopkeeper offers a good price for statues of "Marilyn Monroe, nude if possible" or "John the Baptist in shaggy skins" (*PF*, 133), but Fidelman won't even consider carving them. Obsessed with capturing in the painting the face of his mother that has been resisting him for five years, he will, in a strange compromise with necessity, carve only Madonnas. Early in the story he refuses to add a child to a Madonna statue for an extra five hundred lire but does make a minute concession to market conditions when he tries to cadge a living by chalking Madonnas with Child on the sidewalk. This attempt gains him only a few coins and near-arrest, and later jobs at a woodworker's shop and in a laundry leave him little time to paint. Though he refuses to ask Esmeralda to return to whoring, she correctly perceives that his "no"

> "sounds like yes."
> . . . In fact he had been thinking of asking her to go to work, whatever she might do. It's circumstances, he thought. (*PF*, 137)

Since Fidelman feels that he's nothing, not even a man, if he's not painting, his immediate need is to find a way to complete successfully the "Mother and Son," which might justify his life as nothing else has. The pimping is a means to this end, which comes quickly and unexpectedly. After trying for five years to paint his mother's face from a photograph, a thousand times scraping off her features, he had, a few weeks before he took up pimping, decided to change the "Mother and Son" to "Brother and Sister," with Esmeralda modeling as his sister Bessie. Then came the hiatus from painting caused by his jobs at the woodworker's shop and the laundry. When the pimp resumed painting the picture it

> changed from "Brother and Sister" . . . to let's face it, "Prostitute and Procurer." . . . Though he considered sandpapering his own face off and substituting Ludovico as pimp, the magnificent thing was that in the end he kept himself in. This is my most honest piece of work. Esmeralda was the now nineteen-year-old prostitute; and he, with a stroke here and there aging himself a bit, a fifteen-year-old procurer. This was the surprise that made the painting. And what it means, I suppose, is I am what I became from a young age. Then he thought, it has no meaning, a painting's a painting.
> . . . the picture was, one day, done. It assumed a completion: This woman and man together, prostitute and procurer. She was a girl with fear in both black eyes, a vulnerable if stately neck, and a steely small mouth; he was a boy with tight insides on the verge of crying. The presence of each protected the other. A Holy Sacrament. The form leaped to the eye. (*PF*, 142–43)

So far, the blend of painting and pimping seems to come to an even happier end than the mix of portraiture and intercourse in "Still Life": what's even a rapturous tumble with a neurotic compared to the completion of a good work of art? But Malamud is not about to permit an aesthetic end to justify immoral means. Annamaria enjoyed being nailed to her sexual cross; Esmeralda hates whoring. Her preferences matter. Intelligent and attractive, the nineteen-year-old's values are in the right place. Having fled an abusive father whom she blames for her minimal abilities to read and write, she first took up whoring because, with no education, it was the only alternative to being a maid. Like so many of Malamud's yearners, she wants a better life and originally counted on Fidelman, an artist who is more than twice her age, to help her find it. As she tells the painter, "The reason I stayed here is I thought you'd be kind to me. Besides, if a man is an artist I figured he must know about life. If he does maybe he can teach me something. So far all I've learned is you're like everybody else, shivering in your drawers. That's how it goes, when you think you have nothing there's somebody with less" (*PF,* 121).

Fidelman has contracted into a manipulator with considerably less decency than Esmeralda. He attacks her for having been a whore when he thinks she questions his talent, and he is quite willing to subcontract the pimping to Ludovico—for a measly eight percent of what Esmeralda brings in—though she hates the man. Given the direction in which Fidelman is going, Ludovico, who has about him "a quality of having experienced everything, if not more, that gave F the momentary shivers" (*PF,* 107), functions in the story as the embodiment of the painter's future. Past fifty—or about ten years older than Fidelman—the seedy pimp is also thin and mustachioed, was formerly in the art business and has no shortage of eloquent justifications for his pimping. Just as Fidelman confesses to himself that he has always been a manipulator of women, Ludovico freely admits his vanity, selfishness, and tendency to petty evil.

The title of the story follows from the petty evil of his paying Fidelman back for replacing the older man as the recipient of Esmeralda's services. Though he praises the completed painting lavishly, Ludovico suggests that a few strokes of lemon and red would brighten the painting. One of the maxims Fidelman has stenciled on the wall is Whistler's "A masterpiece is finished from the beginning." Since Fidelman lacks a master's uncanny intuition of the best possible painting, his few touches turn into hours of work during which he ruins the painting. Ludovico and a dealer he has brought along laugh at the new version and, thinking "five long years down the drain," Fidelman squeezes black paint over both faces. When Esmeralda, who expected to marry Fidelman now that the painting was finally completed, rushes at him with a bread knife for murdering both her future and the image of herself in the portrait

> F twisted it out her grasp, and in anguish lifted the blade into his gut.
> "This serves me right."
> "A moral act," Ludovico agreed. (*PF*, 147)

Is Fidelman punishing the man who has treated Esmeralda badly in a half dozen ways as well the schlemiel of an imperfect artist who ruined the painting? Ludovico's comment refers back to an earlier disagreement he had with Fidelman in which the older man claimed that only acts, not feelings, are moral or immoral. But it could also mean that he feels the painter should be so punished for robbing him of his mealticket, or for destroying the painting or for wronging Esmeralda. The multiple ambiguities of the ending tend more toward the unconvincing, toward confusion, than toward the beautifully poised, closing tensions of "The Last Mohican" or "The Magic Barrel."

A good deal of the confusion of the ending follows from the quarrel over the interrelatedness of life and art going on through the story. Seven years after Malamud published the story he refused to assert that art was unequivocally moral. Instead it "tends toward morality." The kind of art he preferred was in some way moral, but he conceded that some art was not. When asked if art changes the world, Malamud's response was similarly qualified:

Malamud: It changes me. It affirms me.

Stern: Really?

Malamud: *(laughs)* It helps.[114]

I read his response to say that creating art makes him more moral, but he knows, as does Ludovico, that it doesn't always work this way, that "some of the greatest pricks . . . have been great painters" (*PF*, 129). Since Fidelman is not as good a man as he might be, critics have attacked the aesthetic positions he articulates in Ludovico's very funny interview without considering that many of the positions Fidelman articulates—about how he is shaped by his art, about the moral potential of form or order, about the possibilities of tradition—are also positions Malamud has articulated.[115] Malamud believed, all other things being equal, the more moral an artist, the better an artist he or she was likely to be, but each case had to be studied separately. Fidelman's ability to capture his amorality in paint is a paradoxically moral act, but this does not make him moral enough to consider Esmeralda's vested interest and leave his painting alone.

The story would have been much more successful had Malamud ended with the completed painting, which silently asserts the paradox of Fidelman's moral assertion of his immorality. But if Fidelman turns inward to confront the manipulative presence within him, Malamud backs away from seeming to endorse pimping as a means to an artistic end and brings his punitive conclusion down upon the miscreant with the same excessive vehemence he brought to Levin-Freeman in "The Lady of the Lake." It is fortunate, though, that the vehemence comes as late in the story as it does. The Malamud on moral holiday in the last two stories, who let Fidelman copulate with impunity and was able to consider positively the possibilities of stealing, is still on holiday when, in this story, he presents Florence through Fidelman's observing painter's eye and thus gains a convincing immediacy of local detail that the preceding two stories lacked. Correspondingly, the descriptions of Fidelman painting, and of his and Esmeralda's lives after he becomes her pimp, are matter-of-fact and authoritative. The reporter of the imagined in Malamud considers the whoring and pimpery with laconic detachment, and as far as we know Esmeralda suffers no loathsome experiences in her work: she seems to experience boredom and weariness, not horror or self-loathing. All of this makes the destruction of the painting and Fidelman's self-immolation seem forced by the sudden reassertion of the artist's conscience.

The protagonist's name expands from F into Fidelman in the fifth story, "Pictures of the Artist," but his world contracts into the solipsism, disconnectedness, and jagged conflicts of the unconscious. With the story's first sentence—"Fidelman pissing in muddy water discovers water over his head"—the narration registers the felt realities of the dreaming more than the waking world. The next sentence locates the engulfment in the canal in Livorno, the hometown of Modigliani who, also submerged and the dominant painter of "Pictures," wanders past, searching for statues he had dropped in the water. This is the first of the story's many allusions to painters. Two important literary allusions also surface among the opening paragraph's discordant data: "If we wake we drown, says Fidelman. *Chant de Maldoror*" (*PF*, 149). The first five words are a recasting of the closing line of Eliot's "The Love Song of J. Alfred Prufrock." Unable to maintain his imaginative or literal quest for love against his milieu's opposition, Prufrock retreats into solipsistic gratifications, imagining lovely, vital images like "sea-girls wreathed with seaweed red and brown . . . Combing the white hair of the waves blown back."[116] Until the last pages of the section Fidelman also drowns in his imagination, but his fantasies are relieved by humor, never by lyrical, lifting imagery. Mostly the images are horrific, for Fidelman is counting himself among the *artistes maudits,* the artists damned to miserable existences like Modigliani and Lautreaumont, the author of the hypnotic hallucinations, the strange and cruel prose poems, of his 1869 book, *Les Chants de Maldoror.*

A crucial difference is that if Modigliani had a miserable life, suffering from pleurisy, typhus, alcoholism, and drug addiction before he died of tubercular meningitis at the age of thirty-five, he also created great art. This Fidelman has not done, and his bitterness turns his survey of religious art into what might at first seem an unrelieved gallery of horrors: "S. Agatha, breasts shorn clean, running enflamed. Painted carrying both bloody breasts in white salver. . . . S. Catherine, broken apart on spiked wheel. Pictured married to wheel." But the horror is leavened by humor, whether of Fidelman laughing at himself or of the narrator laughing at his character's morbidness. The list continues

> "S. Lawrence, roasted on slow grill. *I am roasted on one side. Now turn me over and eat.* Shown cooked but uneaten. . . . S. Genet in prison, pictured with boys. S. Fidel Uomo, stuffing his ass with flowers.
> Still Life with Herrings. S. Soutine.
> He divideth the gefilte fish and matzos. (*PF*, 150)

Ruth Wisse has observed that this section's "frenetic, staccato pace gives the uncomfortable impression that Fidelman's time has run out, like a wound-up doll that is stumbling to a halt after a lengthy dance."[117] Fidelman might speedily spin inward upon his own torment and moral emptiness, but Malamud's stylistic acceleration is anything but counterproductive. In "A Pimp's Revenge" he was often able to have the painter's inquiring eye bring great vividness to the page even while he emphasized Fidelman's limitations:

> The painter blew his nose at the open window and gazed for a reflective hour at the Tuscan hills in September haze. Otherwise, sunlight on the terraced silver-trunked olive trees, and San Miniato, sparkling in the distance by black cypresses. Make an interesting impressionist oil, green and gold mosaics and those black trees of death, but that's been done. Not to mention Van Gogh's tormented cypresses. That's my trouble, everything's been done or is otherwise out of style—cubism, surrealism, action painting. If I could only guess what's next. (*PF*, 96)

In "Pictures" the notation of images and paintings wildly speeds up and so does the rate at which the tone changes. With this chapter Malamud took his place among the writers publishing between 1960 and 1975 whom Roger Sale has designated as the imperial novelists. Citing such examples of bravura style as Pynchon's *V.*, Heller's *Catch-22*, Mailer's *An American Dream*, Bellow's *Herzog*, Roth's *Portnoy's Complaint*, and Doctorow's *Ragtime*, Sale wrote: "I call them 'imperial' because their demeanor is individual and commanding: 'I call the shots here,' says the imperial novelist in every sentence. . . . Underlying it all is a huge assertion of personal power, which leads to aggressive showmanship, plots used as feats of narrative skill, marvelous flights of fancy—in other words, style used as a badge of personal authority, and personal authority having the ability to invent and master whole worlds."[118]

By creating in the world of Fidelman's unconscious the hell in which he must die before he can begin the reintegration he will complete in the novel's final story, Malamud accommodated his moral and playful urges with unusual success. It's true enough that in the second of the three main narratives of the story Susskind returns as the new Christ, lecturing Fidelman on the importance of life over art, content over form. It's also true that this is the way an updated Christ might come off in a Mel Brooks movie, as he does in this segment of a dialogue between Judas-Fidelman and Christ-Susskind: "Tell me, Master, art thou the Living God? Art thou at least the Son of God? / So we will see, its not impossible. / Art thou the Redeemer? / This could be also, Im not sure myself. Depends what happens. / Is thy fate ordained? / I act like I Am. Who knows my fate? All I know is somebody will betray me. Dont ask how I know, I know. You dont but I do. This is the difference" (*PF*, 163). Of course the expressive assertions of the Jewish performing artists of the sixties were sometimes far more discordant, more abrasive than Brooks's comedy routines or movies. With all its shticks and wildness, "Pictures of the Artist" often has a good deal in common with one of Lenny Bruce's surrealistic monologues.

Having obeyed Susskind and foresworn choosing things over people by dropping paint and brushes in the Dead Sea—a part of which then fades—Fidelman betrays his lord first by sketching him and then by accepting not forty but thirty-nine pieces of silver. With this, in one of the story's many mock archaisms, the painter "runneth out to buy paints, brushes, canvas" (*PF*, 166). The rendering of the Crucifixion, which has somehow resulted from the betrayal, has more than a touch of the kind of outrageousness a 1960s reader might have associated with Bruce. A line of twenty number 12s is followed by a line of fourteen number 369s, which is followed by a line of seven *veyizmirs* (woe is me), followed by eleven number 12369s. One can play lots of games with the paragraph, some of them spiced by the belittling quality of the *veyizmirs* and sexual suggestions generated by the frequent use of the number 69.

Fidelman particularly needed the spiritual rebirth Susskind offered him because in the preceding fantasy he was killed. Told in a mocking version of the reverential tone Vasari employed in his *Lives of the Painters*, this section has Fidelman literally scratching out a living by holding sculpture exhibitions of the holes he has just dug. The following gives some sense of the easy cheekiness he has acquired: "To the one or two who rudely questioned him, saying, Why do you pass off on us as a sculpture an empty hole or two? the artist, with the greatest tact and courtesy, replied, It were well if you relaxed before my sculptures, if you mean to enjoy them, and yield yourself to the pleasure they evoke in the surprise of their forms" (*PF*, 154). To a peasant who wants "the sculptor" to return his ten lire so he can buy bread for his family Fidelman moves into more heightened folderol—for example, "There is also a metaphysic in relation of down to up, and vice versa[;] . . . I do not in advance choose the exact form and position of the hole; it chooses me." His closing argument brings the hatefulness behind the emptiness out in the open: "Tough Titty if you can't comprehend Art[;] . . . Fuck off now" (*PF*, 156–57).

Shortly after the peasant leaves a stranger, whose "iron eyes in a leather face [cause] the flesh on Fidelman's neck to prickle and thicken," arrives and drives the con man to defend the empty holes as perfectly realized forms that "may be and often [are] the content of art" (*PF*, 158–59). but as Malamud wrote two years before *Pictures* came out, "After what one lives through, who runs from content?"[119] The rhetorical question followed a two-paragraph listing of some of the horrors of the twentieth century, from World War I to the ongoing war in Vietnam. Malamud's implicit position was that his complex responses to these events were appropriate and crucial parts of his ongoing experience. One of his tasks as an artist was to find the forms to these responses, this experience. The Fidelman of this fantasy has lost all sense of the value of his experience and, consequently, his sense of a place in the human community.

If the dialogue between Fidelman and the leather-faced stranger is reminiscent of colloquies between the protagonist and the devil in Mann's *Doctor Faustus*, it is because the stranger is the devil, "also that youth that he is now dead in the Bay of Naples, that you would not give him back his poor ten lire so he could buy bread for his babies." With this the stranger hits Fidelman on the head, and after the sculptor falls into one of holes he has dug, its waiting emptiness echoing his own,

> He-who-Fidelman-did-not-know then proceeded to shovel in earth until the sculpture and its creator were extinguished.
> So it's a grave, the stranger is said to have muttered. So now we got form but we also got content. (*PF*, 160)

In the third and final of the story's main fantasies, Fidelman's abstraction from experience takes the form of devoting years to playing (in Ruth Wisse's words) "an artistic Plato, trying to capture pure ideas in geometric designs."[120] In this section Malamud turns the allegory of the cave from the *Republic* inside out. The denizens of Plato's cave could never perceive the perfect forms behind them, only the forms' imperfect shadows on the wall before them. Malamud would have argued that the experiencing of the shadows *was* the denizens' primary reality, the abstracted, "perfect" forms behind them a derivative one. What Fidelman paints on his cave wall is, for Malamud, as serious an error as mistaking the shadows for the realities was for Plato.

In this case the reality from which Fidelman is hiding is that of his sister Bessie, alone, sick, and dying in the house above the cave. As Wisse has observed,

> Susskind reappears in the cave of shadows as the source of light—a one-hundred-watt light bulb. The bulb is the Hebraic light giving out its moral message to the Hellenized painter, telling him to go upstairs to "say hello to your poor sister who hasn't seen you in years." . . . At first Fidelman insists on staying put and painting out his perfect truths on the walls of the cave, but eventually he gives up his "graven images" long enough to fulfill his obligation, to go upstairs and say his last goodbye. "Bessie died and rose to heaven, holding in her heart her brother's hello." The standard bedside leave-taking, although here in a parodistic form, does not entirely cancel out the underlying seriousness of Fidelman's decision.[121]

Fidelman's fantasy reconciliation with Bessie accomplishes more than bringing him back to a realm of minimal humane gesture, for she is also one of the two mother figures he has had in his life. There are a great many ways of explaining why Fidelman could not capture his mother's image in the painting of "A Pimp's Revenge," but the ones that work best for me follow from Fidelman's sense that to settle upon her appearance is "to paint a Kaddish" (*PF*, 113). To offer his pictorial equivalent of the prayers for the dead is to conclusively admit that she is dead, that he is an orphan, that his generation is the next to die. His inability to cry at her funeral or to say the prayers for the dead silently speak of all this, as well as of the coldness that is the product of his flight from these realities. In Sophocles' *Antigone*, Creon stains the hearts and altars of Thebes by burying the living Antigone instead of her dead brother Polyneices. In trying to keep his mother alive in the wrong way and in treating his living sister as if she were dead, Fidelman has also failed to meet his obligations to the living and the dead.

A Jungian might say that the heroes of Malamud's fiction who make the movement from man to mensch, who transcend their damaging pasts to become ethical men, symbolically become their own fathers. One of the dominant processes in *Pictures* is of Fidelman's gradual coming to terms with his own feminine component—of, in a sense, becoming his own mother. After noting the protagonist's inability to capture his mother's image, and that "one of the first objects that Fidelman notices on his arrival in Italy is a statue of the 'heavy dugged Etruscan wolf suckling the infants Romulus and Remus,'" Tony Tanner observed that "Fidelman has to find out just which is his real mother, or where the source of true nourishment is to be found. He has to learn to distinguish between what suckles life and what negates it."[122]

The dreamworld reconciliation with Bessie begins the integration into Fidelman's psyche of that which is life-giving, feminine, both within his mind and without. The movement is completed in the waking world of "Glass Blower of Venice" by Beppo Fassoli, the handsome, strongly built husband of Fidelman's mistress. Although Beppo never admits that he knows of the affair, he seems to bless it by telling the ex-painter, as Fidelman is now called, that he rarely sleeps with his wife. Relieved of his guilt at cuckolding this increasingly likable and profound man, Fidelman invites Beppo to a private exhibition of the fifteen or so paintings and sculptures he has not destroyed. After a cerebral explanation that belies the sterility of his first painting—it's organized by "'the broad lavender band bisecting the black field'" and thus "'achieves, partly through color, a quality of linear universality' . . . it occurred to the ex-painter that he looked in his handsome way much like his mother. . . . He had then and there an urge to paint Beppo to his core, so much like a seizure he thought of it as sexual, and to his surprise found himself desiring Margherita [Beppo's wife] so strongly he had to restrain himself from rushing out to jump into bed with her" (*PF,* 194–95).

Painting and heterosexual sex have become, or perhaps always were, ways of fleeing from the feminine, life-giving part of Fidelman that wants to love. Thus, though he feels he is truly in love with Margherita when they are first about to go to bed, Fidelman refuses to obey her wish that he join her only after she has undressed and gotten into bed. Instead he hurries into the bedroom and turns on the light, explaining that "Painters love nudes, also ex-painters." The idealizing lover who pursued Margherita is dispatched by the painter who gets to see how

> her shapely legs were veined, splotched purple here and there . . .
> the stomach streaked with lesions of her pregnancies. She was forty
> if she was a day.
> "Well, caro, are you disenchanted?"
> "No more than usual," Fidelman confessed. (*PF,* 187).

When Margherita first mentioned Beppo, she told Fidelman that he'd like her husband, for he was wise about life. Beppo proves his wisdom when he ends the exhibit by telling Fidelman that his work "lacks authority and originality," that he must "show who's master of your fate—bad art or you" and by destroying the pieces. Having closed off the escape route from loving that creating bad art had offered to Fidelman, Beppo interrupts his quarry's next tryst with Margherita to mount the ex-painter himself. Instead of "the spray job" (*PF*, 195)—Fidelman's initial description of the second painting he showed—Beppo promises him

> "a cool job, I'm wearing mentholated vaseline. You'll be surprised at the pleasure."
> "Is your mother watching?"
> "At her age she has no curiosity."
> "I suppose I deserve this."
> "Think of love," the glass blower murmured. "You've run from it all your life."

And so all of the anticipations of homosexual sex in the preceding four stories are finally realized.[123]

Loving—instead of being in love—for the first time in his life, Fidelman thinks, "If that's the way it works, that's the way it works. Better love than no love" (*PF*, 199). His new tolerance for love in whatever form it takes would also seem to match his creator's, who in 1958 had suggested that fiction about homosexuality was "underselling Man," was a refusal to write with "imagination and hope."[124] What a difference a decade can make. After an odyssey that is vocational, sexual, emotional, and geographical in nature, the book's final sentence brings its hero to a port where he seems wondrously able to satisfy his fundamental needs: "In America he worked as a craftsman in glass and loved men and women" (*PF*, 208). Possibly his ability to reconcile his diverse parts followed from Malamud's calm acceptance of his own quite unexceptional bisexual potential. That Fidelman's mother (like Malamud's) died young, that her married name was the same as the maiden name of the author's mother, and that the protagonist's sexual identity is profoundly related to his quest for his lost mother encourage conjectures that posit Fidelman as an alter ego of the author.

In a posthumously published statement, Malamud said that while he did not regret the years he put into his work, "perhaps I regret the fact that I was not two men, one who could live a full life apart from writing; and one who lived in art, exploring all he had to experience and know how to make his art right."[125] For Fidelman's last year or so in Italy, Malamud gave him a life that seems a wish fulfillment in its blending of craft and human interaction, *ananke* (material need) and eros, for Beppo, "who was teaching him the rites of love, also taught him to blow glass." Fidelman learns a trade that will sustain him vocationally and itself "excites him sexually. He felt creative, his heart in his pants." The craft is inherently a sexually charged one in its orality as well as in its androgynous plasticity. As Beppo puts it, "with a snip or two of the scissors . . . you can change the male organ into the female." And if Freud's use of the word *erotic* widened until it included all life-giving instincts, so do the possibilities of liquid glass: "Fidelman . . . loved dipping the tapered blowpipe into the flaming opening of the noisy furnace—like poking into the living substance of the sun for a pudding of glowing fire—Prometheus Fidelman" Moreover, all of this occurs in the presence of his lover: "Every move they made was in essence sexual, a marvelous interaction because among other things, it saved time and trouble: you worked and loved at once" (*PF*, 201–2).

The other male helpers in Malamud's fiction—Morris Bober, Mr. Cattanzara, Susskind, Salzman—bring the protagonist to much more compromised improvements than the ones Beppo almost magically brings to Fidelman. Malamud's willingness to suspend conventional morality in this story renders Beppo blameless for apparently using his wife, mother, even the image of his swimming sons, "their young asses flashing in sunlight" (*PF*, 191) to possess Fidelman sexually. If that's the way it must be for Fidelman to gain happiness, that's the way it must be. It's as if someone so magnificently secure in his mother's love as Beppo can do no wrong.

His last service is to bring Fidelman back from a relapse into using glass instead of the material of the past (paint, marble or vinylite) to create bad art. Indeed Fidelman even becomes enough of a functional romantic to transform his grief at the inevitable parting from Beppo into creating two objects—a bowl and a horse—that could only have been created by a good craftsman, not a bad artist.

Fidelman's benign transformation is rendered in a wonderfully palpable Venice, which slowly drowns in the cold rains, mists, and the rising waters of the winter but which in spring amply rewards inhabitant and reader alike: "Young jewel-like leaves of myrtles and laurels rose above ancient brick walls in back alleys. Subtle pinks, apricots, lavenders streaked an underwater architecture of floating Gothic and Moorish palazzi. Mosaics glittered, golden and black, on the faces of churches. Sandali sailed under bridges, heaped high with eggplants, green peppers, mounds of string beans. . . . A sense of sea enlivened the air, lagoon and Adriatic under high blue sky above the outer islands" (*PF*, 182). Having headed east to create a wonderful life for himself, Frank Alpine in *The Assistant* at one point feels that the self he so valued is in reality a dead rat. Having headed much farther east to begin "Glass Blower of Venice" fishing "with a net out of the canals dead rats" (*PF*, 177)—nice correlatives of his inner life—Fidelman stays on in Venice and Murano to become such a doting lover that he seems an improbable Venus who, in his fifteen or so months in the city, rises reborn from its wondrously changing waters. The story provides a luminous ending to a splendid book.

Later Stories

Apart from the three new Fidelman tales, Malamud published fifteen new stories between the release of *Idiots First* and his death in March 1986. Eight of these he collected in 1973 in *Rembrandt's Hat*, his third and last gathering of previously uncollected stories: "The Silver Crown," "Man in the Drawer," "The Letter," "In Retirement," "Rembrandt's Hat," "Notes From a Lady at a Dinner Party," "My Son the Murderer," and "Talking Horse." Two stories published a bit earlier— "An Exorcism" (1968) and "God's Wrath" (1972)—lost out in the competition for inclusion in *Rembrandt's Hat*, although Malamud did include "God's Wrath" among the twenty-five stories of *The Stories of Bernard Malamud* (1983). No stories were published for the rest of the seventies, for Malamud was absorbed with *Dubin's Lives*, the 1979 novel he considered his most ambitious, but "A Wig" appeared in 1980. Then came "The Model," which was first published in August 1983 and reappeared later that year in *The Stories*. In 1984 two stories were published that dealt with actual artists: Alma Mahler and her lovers in "Alma Redeemed," and Virginia Woolf in "In Kew Gardens." His last published story, "A Lost Grave," appeared in May 1985. According to his agent, Tim Seldes, Malamud did not at the time of his death regard the four uncollected stories of the past seventeen years as being strong enough to serve as the nucleus of a subsequent collection.[126]

His evaluation was accurate: neither "The Model" nor the four uncollected stories have the resonance of the best stories of the preceding collections. But Malamud's ability to define character sharply in two or three sentences, and to blend it perfectly with the story's thematic concerns, persisted to the end. In "A Lost Grave," when Hecht, a sixty-five-year-old widower who had not thought of his dead wife "in too many years to feel comfortable about,"[127] seeks her grave but cannot find it, he is ushered into the office of Mr. Goodman, the cemetery's director. After pouring orange juice in a glass, Goodman—with just the right arresting sententiousness for a man in his profession— asks Hecht "Will you join me in a sweet mouthful? . . . I usually take refreshment this time of the morning. It keeps me balanced." A few minutes later, the reader—with Hecht—sees Goodman anew and perceives that the grandiloquence both goes with the vocational territory and brings a verbal stature to what is missing physically: "Goodman rose at his desk, a short man, five feet tall. 'I will institute a careful research.'" When he later calls Hecht with the news that his wife is buried with her lover, who convinced a judge that he had more claim to her than her husband, his sententiousness becomes thematically appropriate: "Are you prepared for an insight?" (205). The humor is characteristically tempered by the grimness of the insight brought to Hecht with Goodman's last few sweet mouthfuls: because he had not loved his wife as he should have, he has lost even the sense that he is a widower, and all he has left is the empty grave waiting for him.

Malamud's willingness to experiment with new techniques to register the alarming vicissitudes of the inner life also persisted to the end. Although "In Kew Gardens" ends with an account of Woolf's suicide, the story is unified more by the repeating and recombining of a number of motifs than by the more conventional modes of narrative development Malamud had almost always employed. If he tried to make "In Kew Gardens" approach the condition of music, the story's disjointed melodies and strident harmonies are ones we might normally expect to find in a characteristically upsetting work by Schoenberg or Webern. Malamud tried to capture only negative states, like Woolf's frigidity, hallucinations, and depressions, or negative acts, like her suicide attempts or her being obscenely pawed by George Duckworth, the half-brother who was her elder by fourteen years. As far as I can tell, all that Malamud did not invent came from Quentin Bell's biography, *Virginia Woolf*, and what he did with what he used is curious. For example, Bell writes:

> From the first she was felt to be incalculable, eccentric and prone to accidents. She could say things that made the grown-ups laugh with her; she did things which made the nursery laugh at her. Is it to this, or to a rather later period, that we can ascribe an incident in Kensington Gardens when, not for the last time by any means, she lost, or at least lost control of, her knickers? She retired into a bush and there, in order to divert public attention, she sang *The Last Rose of Summer* at the top of her voice. It was this and similar misadventures which earned her, in the nursery, the title of "The Goat" or more simply "Goat," a name which stuck to her for many years.[128]

The Short Fiction: An Essay

Compare the opening of "In Kew Gardens":

> Once as they walked in the gardens, Virginia felt her knickers come
> loose and slip down her ankles. She grabbed at her maidenhair as
> the garment eluded her frantic grasp and formed a puddle of cloth
> at her feet. Swooping up her underpants, with a cry of dismay she
> plunged into the bushes, shrilly singing "The Last Rose of Sum-
> mer." As she stood up, the elastic knot she had tied, snapped, and
> the knickers again lay limp at her feet.
> "Christ, Goddamn!"
> Vanessa listened at the bushes.
> "Don't be hysterical. No one will see through your dress."
> "How can you be certain?"
> "No one would want to."
> She shrieked slowly.
> "Forgive me, dear goat," Vanessa told her. "I meant no harm."
> "Oh, never, no, never."
> Insofar as I was ever in love I loved Vanessa[129]

For some reason, Malamud turned Kensington Gardens, quite close
to Woolf's childhood home, into Kew Gardens—the title of a Woolf
story but one that has little to do with this incident. More important,
he turned the high-spirited little girl who comically called attention to
herself by trying not to call attention to herself into an adolescent or
postadolescent hysteric. The historical Vanessa's basic stance toward
her younger sister was not at all the cruel one we see here, and the last
line of the passage suggests that even Woolf's positive feelings toward
people followed from the particular way that they wounded her. Although Bell is not the most fervent Virginia Woolf supporter—his description of Woolf's emotional difficulties as "madness" has been
challenged by other Woolf scholars[130]—Malamud never hints at the behavior, both admirable and sane, that Bell describes in large parts of
his book. The behavior of Malamud's Woolf is much more eccentric
than Bell's; indeed, the fiction writer makes every occurrence, every
association, a symptom of Woolf's pathology.

For example, the broken elastic surfaces again in the biography
when Woolf was about eighteen, at a time when George Duckworth
was trying to introduce her into high society. Woolf was embarrassed
when "her drawers fell down while she was in the very act of saying

goodbye to her hostess," but she drew some satisfaction from her perception that the gaffe "was even more painful to George. . . . Finding George at home she came into the drawing-room and flourished the errant garments in his face. George was speechless with indignation."[131] In the story the second mention of the underpants ("Virginia lost her underpants and wondered where she had been") appears between the conclusion of an account of George's pawings and the narrator's comment that "Her erotic life rarely interested her. It seemed unimportant compared with what went on in the world" (537). The underpants are associated not with Woolf's social awkwardness, as they are in Bell, but with the molestations that began when she was six or seven and continued into her twenties, with the consequent frigidity, and finally with her death. In Malamud's account, though not in Bell's, Woolf removes "shoes, stockings, underpants" (540) before she drowns.

But the motifs that Malamud most often returned to in the story follow from Bell's account of Woolf's second breakdown. This began in May 1904 when she was twenty-two, less than ten weeks after her father died. Convalescing at a friend's house, Woolf threw herself from a window too low to cause her any serious harm and lay in bed "listening to the birds singing in Greek and imagining that King Edward VII lurked in the azaleas, using the foulest possible language."[132] Though Woolf's mother had died in 1895, Malamud made the recent death hers, and different combinations of the king, the birds, things Greek, the leaping from a window, and Julia Stephens's death occur ten times in this story of just more than four pages. The king might curse Woolf quite generically, calling her "filthy names." Two pages later he's quite explicit: "'Maiden, there's turd in your blood,' King Edward chanted" (539). Sometimes his identity coalesces with those of the birds, as he sings or—through the association of the birds with Greece or Greek—strums a lyre or "chants in Ancient Greece." The king also blurs into the critics Woolf feared so much when he reads aloud "dreadful reviews of books she had yet to write" (537). At one point the birds screech in Greek; at another Malamud fuses bird, king, orange flowers, and the conflagration inside Woolf's head:

> Her scream blew the bird off its one legged perch and it flapped into the burning wood.
> An old king strode among the orange azaleas. (539)

All old men become Woolf's father, desolate after his wife's death, and adding his own tortured motifs to the painful music: "The father moaned, 'Why won't my whiskers grow?'"(536); "'I shall never grow my whiskers again'" (539). Several times the motif of Woolf's ineffectual leaping from the window is associated with the successful effort of Septimus Warren Smith (Malamud curiously calls the character Warren Septimus Smith), who took his life in this way in *Mrs. Dalloway.*

The last line of the story, "I don't think two people could have been happier than we have been" (540), was the last line of Woolf's suicide note to her husband Leonard Woolf, and, as far as we know, the last one she ever wrote. Since the story works to belittle the relationship with Leonard, who became "her Jewish mother" (537) instead of her sexual companion, the closing of the story emphasizes the inadequacy of her sexual life more than the pathos of her death.

In all, "In Kew Gardens" inspires curiosity over Malamud's emotions during its composition. He was of course writing a work of fiction and aesthetically free to invent and to transform what he read about Woolf in any way he chose. But I have heard from a former student of Malamud's at Bennington of the sympathy and sensitivity with which he taught Woolf's novels. Moreover, there is no shortage of admirable women in Malamud's fiction—though I suppose a feminist might describe as inverse sexism the frequent use in his earlier fiction of women as sources of salvation—and Malamud attributed the sympathetic characterization of the often unfaithful Fanny Bick in *Dubin's Lives* to the consciousness raising he received from his daughter. In fact he suggests in the novel's last sentence that as masterful a biographer of men as Dubin was, he could only hope to enjoy comparable success with a female subject if a woman assisted him. In "The Wig," the first story he published after the novel, he continued to try to think his way into women's psyches in new, sympathetic ways. But the strangely canted snapshots of Woolf and those she loved[133] seem to follow from much different attitudes. The sentences of "In Kew Gardens" that best reveal these attitudes are "Her erotic life rarely interested her" and "In fact, I dislike the quality of masculinity. I always have" (537). Masculinity for Woolf was primarily the analytic, bullying, dissecting mind but it was also unpleasant and unwelcome male sexual desire. "In Kew Gardens" reads as if Malamud was determined to punish Woolf for this rejection of the masculine, and one can only speculate how much the poor health of his last years contributed to the severity of the punishment.

Published a few months earlier, "Alma Redeemed" also has its experimental aspects. With its quick cuts and revelations of the quirks of the famous, the story is stylistically reminiscent of E. L. Doctorow's *Ragtime*—which is to say that its narrative developments are much less fragmented and tangled than those of "In Kew Gardens." Malamud's stance toward his protagonist, and toward her attitudes about masculinity, is correspondingly amiable. No genius like Virginia Woolf, Alma was instead a woman who "loved men of genius."[134] The wife of Gustav Mahler, Walter Gropius, and Franz Werfel and the mistress of Oskar Kokoschka, Alma wonders throughout her eventful life when she will realize her talent. Mahler, who told her on their wedding day "You must give yourself to me unconditionally and desire nothing except my love" (31), was more concerned that she like his music better than Wagner's than he was about her own fulfillment. A half-century after his death, the composer's ghost returns to ask Alma if she is not "yet moved by my classically beautiful music. One can hear eternity in it" (34). Earl Rovit once criticized Malamud's Jews for not maintaining their own ways before God as Job did.[135] Alma's great talent is to maintain her own ways before all the powerful male intellects that might have imprisoned her, and she will not surrender her preference for Wagner. Having outlived all of the talented men that she loved, she was, in the story's penultimate sentence, "eighty-five when she died in 1964, older than King Lear"—another frustrated tyrant of the female psyche. It is thus a part of Alma's independence that she regarded "Hitler as a genuine German idealist, something that is unthinkable to the Jews"—and Mahler could certainly be thought of as a Jewish idealist who wanted to be thought of as German. Unless I have misread the story, the author who had recently savaged Virginia Woolf offered some approval in the last sentence of the story (which is also its title) for an admirer of Hitler.

The protagonist of "A Wig" also earned more of Malamud's sympathies than did Virginia Woolf. Ida is "an energetic, competent woman of fifty, healthy, still attractive. Thinking of herself, she touched her short hair. What's fifty? One more than forty-nine?[136] But neither the assistance of doctors nor home remedies have kept that hair from falling out. Martin, her easygoing husband, was not bothered by the hair loss, but he died a few weeks before the unspecified dramatized span of the story. Ida's painful apprehension of the fate of her hair is bound up with her apprehension of the future, particularly the manless future she fears her potential baldness will create.

Malamud subtly superimposed upon this tension an interestingly ambiguous relationship with Amy, her daughter, who is in her mid-twenties. Either Martin's death has not ended the sexual competition between them now that Ida is so concerned about her ability to attract men, or Ida now hopes to experience men vicariously, through Amy's involvements. For example, after looking into a wigmaker's shop for the first time but rejecting going in (because "If I buy a wig, people will know why"), Ida instead buys "a wide-brimmed felt hat with a narrow, bright green ribbon. Amy had green eyes" (34). But by the final twenty-four hours of the story, Ida is looking at wigs in the same shop for the third time. Her refusal to purchase one results in a quarrel with the wigmaker, and her obvious jealousy, when she learns at home that Amy is moving from their apartment to her boyfriend's, causes another quarrel.

During Ida's apology she notices that Amy's hair is thinning. What are we to make of the story's concluding sentence: "In the morning she left the house early and bought herself an attractive wig" (36)? Has a reconciliation been effected by Ida's perception that a woman with thinning hair can still attract men and she will no longer attempt to enjoy them vicariously through her daughter's adventures? Or is it that Ida feels that she can still compete effectively with a daughter who is showing the signs of age herself, so that the story closes with the sense of the irresolvable nature of their struggle?

The second reading of the ending of "The Wig" is much more consistent with the rest of Malamud's later fiction. In his earlier work, if the central character was a young man, more often than not an older one helped him. But in quite a few of the later stories, and in *Dubin's Lives*, an elderly or middle-aged protagonist, whose sexual yearnings make him vulnerable, is humiliated by a younger character, sometimes the woman he desires. In "The Model" Ephraim Elihu, a seventy-year-old widower, hires a model in her mid-twenties to pose nude for him. By the time Elihu has painted for an hour, the model accuses the old man of hiring her to satisfy needs "that have nothing to do with painting." Elihu confesses his sadness at having no women friends, articulating some of Malamud's familiar poetry of pathos as he explains that he didn't "realize I would be so moved by [your body], and, on reflection, about the way my life has gone. I hoped painting again would refresh my feeling for life." But the model is determined that he pay for the insult of his eyes "crawling over my body" and she demands that he strip. After quickly sketching the nude old man, she disfigures the face of the image, and leaves. Elihu is left to ask himself

> "Is there nothing more to my life than it is now? Is this all that is left to me?"
>
> The answer seemed to be yes, and he wept at how old he had so quickly become."[137]

To turn for a moment to one of the stories that was included in *Rembrandt's Hat,* the much more substantial retired doctor of "In Retirement" feels death draw still closer when he's publicly rejected by the young woman who has become the object of his infatuation. The retired sexton of "God's Wrath" cannot attempt to write off his prostitute daughter as Salzman seems to have done in "The Magic Barrel," but in a sort of marriage of pain he punishes her with his presence as he follows her down the grimy Manhattan streets where she plies her trade. Since he feels that he is somehow responsible for her whoredom "He calls down God's wrath on the prostitute and her father."[138] In "An Exorcism" the young chambermaid with whom the middle-aged Eli Fogel has been sleeping has him locked out in the hall of his hotel while he is naked.

Fogel is a writer whose work comes slowly: having taken six years to write half of his third novel, he completes only seventy more pages in the last two of the three years the story covers. Published before *Pictures* came out, "The Exorcism" signaled that Malamud was still fascinated with the ways in which creating art might collide with the other demands of an artist's existence. In particular, the story is in certain ways a trial run for *The Tenants,* published four years later. Like Fogel, Frank Lesser is a slender talent who has been working on his third novel for too long—nine years. Malamud immensely complicated the life of Lesser by moving a black militant, Willie Spearmint, into the building deserted by all but Lesser. In "An Exorcism" Malamud brings in the manipulative Gary Simmson, who desperately wants to be a writer and slavishly attaches himself to the older man at the summer workshops where they meet. Suffering as he does from a shortened leg and "primal loneliness,"[139] the smallish Fogel envies the ability of Gary—burly, half his age—to attract lovely young women.

The older writer has a great deal more reason to dislike the young man when he reads a thinly veiled account of the humiliation in the hotel hallway that Gary had published as a short story. But Fogel is not able to cut the young writer off until, in his attempt to earn a recommendation for a grant, Gary reads him his newest story—a loathsome effort in which the protagonist, clearly Gary, manages to have sex with three roommates (in separate bouts over a night in his microbus) by lying to two and brutalizing the masochistic third. Although Malamud has Fogel admit in the discussion that follows the reading that a successful artist need not be moral in his life, Gary's unwillingness or inability to transform actual into imagined experience is in keeping with the moral sloth that caused him to betray Fogel and to abuse the three women. Fogel refuses to write the recommendation and, in an act that nicely blends his sexual envy and sympathy for Gary's sexual victims, slashes and lights on fire the frequently used mattress in the microbus.

The discussions between the two writers drag a bit and, for a Malamud story, "An Exorcism" lacks the varieties of tone and the cumulative force he would normally crowd into its considerable length, around nine thousand words. But the tale is an extremely predictive one, for all eight of the stories in *Rembrandt's Hat* cluster in some way around one or more of the main motifs of "An Exorcism": the tension between parent and child or symbolic parent and child; the dangers of sexual competition; problems of communication—whether of an artist's frustrated attempt to relay his transformed experience through his art, or through some other breakdown of the attempt to connect with another human.

At first glance, the collection's most radical example of the agonies of incomplete communication occurs in "The Letter": the blank pages that Teddy, a middle-aged patient in a mental hospital, repeatedly and unsuccessfully tries to get the visiting Newman to mail. But Newman brings his own frustrations to the gate where Teddy waits for him. His psychotic father bitterly rejects everything Newman offers during his weekly visits: food, the reminder that the patient's wife is dead, the request that the inmate let Newman know if he can skip one of his weekly visits. Uncannily paired with the Newmans are Teddy and his father Ralph, also an inmate, who urges Newman to mail the blank pages, for his son "wants to communicate to me"[140] Newman, who insists on playing by the rules of the world outside the hospital gates, demands that something be written on the pages, even if he, Newman, writes it. Malamud implicitly suggests that Newman should mail the pages, that he might have more luck communicating with his father if he would bow to the imperatives of madness by trying to move imaginatively into the psychotic worlds Teddy, Ralph, and Newman's father have created. After all, one of these is a shared world in which Teddy is confident enough of his father's love to try to mail him blank pages and in which his father applauds the effort. And if idiots have first claim to our generosity (as the earlier title insists), shouldn't we at least think twice before we demand that psychotics attempt to follow our perception of sane behavior?

Thus there's a grain of truth in Ralph's telling Newman that he is crazy—for insisting upon the rationality of the outer world—and should "come back here and hang around with the rest of us" (*RH*, 106). In all, the story ingeniously plays on the relativity of "sane" and "insane" behavior; that is, to refuse to concede at all to the wishes of the "insane" is, well, crazy.

The fusing of the need to bow to the irrational with the motif of a son struggling to assist his infirm father is also at the center of "The Silver Crown." The petitioner is Albert Gans, a biology teacher whose father is dying of a disease so diversely and unsuccessfully diagnosed and treated that Gans finally goes to a faith healer, Rabbi Jonas Lifschitz. Although Gans has given up on the rational empiricism of the doctors, he still tells the rabbi that his "cast of mind is naturally empiric and objective—you might say non-mystical" (*RH*, 9). He therefore wants to know just how his father will be saved by either of the two available silver crowns (wonderfully priced at $401 or $986) that the rabbi will have cast and then pray over. Empiricist that he is, Gans demands to see a crown before he pays and later threatens to go to the police if he does not see the one for which he has paid $986.

Although the story is grounded much more in the tradition of realism than of fantasy, it characteristically swerves toward the allegorical. For Lifschitz and Rifkele, his lumpish, retarded daughter, embody the nonrational or irrational that Gans can only partially embrace. The rabbi cannot permit Gans to see a finished crown because "a miracle is a miracle" (*RH*, 27). Most important to him is not whether Gans doubts, "for doubts we all got" (*RH*, 11), but whether he loves his father. Certainly Gans cares enough to have sorrow, to feel frantic over his father's state, and finally to pay $986. But his strongest positive emotion toward his father seems to be gratitude—a good distance from the kind of consuming, suprarational love Manischevitz felt for his wife and Mendel for his son—and self-interest undercuts the gratitude.

Gans will feel guilty if he does not buy the crown and his father dies. All of this is still further undercut when, near the end of the story, Gans cries out to Lifschitz and Rifkele that he "was mesmerized, suckered" with "freaking fake magic, with an idiot girl for a come-on and hypnotic mirrors" (*RH*, 29).

In the two earlier great stories about desperate petitioners, "Angel Levine" and "Idiots First," Manischevitz embraces irrationality, Mendel—with his leap at Ginzburg's throat—violence. The two releases are, as I suggested above, ways of holding fast to the value of the other. "The Silver Crown" also leads to an explosion that is a holding fast, but here the commitment is to love of self, not of other. For it is Gans's concern for his self-image—that he, the rational empiricist, has been tricked—that leads to his cruel accusations. The epiphany comes when Gans responds to the rabbi's pleading "Be kind. . . . Be merciful to an old man. Think of my poor child. Think of your father who loves you" with "He hates me, the son-of-a-bitch, I hope he croaks" (*RH*, 29). The terms of the story are such that we cannot tell whether the elder Gans, who dies an hour later, would have been saved had it not been for his son's curse. But Malamud sharply emphasizes how inappropriate in a situation where love is required is any tangle of feeling less than love. In good part, Gans's final outburst follows from his fury over the situation into which he has been led by what positive filial affection he does possess. Malamud also wryly suggests how impractical practicality or half-measures can be in ultimate situations: Gans loses the $986, his self-esteem, and the chance to see whether the crown will work. Ironically, he finally does receive a crown he can feel—the "massive, spike-laden headache" (*RH*, 29) he wears as he rushes out of Lifschitz's.

But the thematic control is only part of what makes "The Silver Crown" one of Malamud's best stories. The characterizations of the rabbi and his daughter emerge through their interactions with Gans, the story's central intelligence, and memorably vivid ones they are. Everything about Rifkele works to nettle the already tightly strung Gans: "Her skin glowed, face wet, fleshy, the small mouth open and would be forever; eyes set wide apart on the broad unfocused face, either washed-out green or brown, or one of each—he wasn't sure. . . . Her thick hair was braided in two ropelike strands; she wore bulging cloth slippers, burst at seams and soles . . . a heavy brown sweater vest, buttoned over blown breasts, though the weather was still hot September" (*RH*, 4). Her body bumps against the walls as she moves down a corridor; Gans is distracted from one of his efforts to understand how the crowns might heal by the awareness "of Rifkele, standing at the door, eating a slice of bread with lumps of butter on it" (*RH*, 12). The sounds she makes are "impossible" (*RH*, 5), "like two eggs frying" (*RH*, 6), "panting like a cow for a bull" (*RH*, 22).

As for Lifshitz, "it was hard to say whether he resembled his daughter; Rifkele resembled her species" (*RH*, 8). But with his "thickened left eyelid" (*RH*, 6) the old man shares a bit of his daughter's thickened deformity. Moreover, any kind of ocular asymmetry in a Malamud character usually hints that he or she occupies an uncanny terrain, one that baffles another character's attempts to enter it with confidence. Seen in a mirror, the eyes are "sad . . . compelling, inquisitive, weary, perhaps even frightened, as though they had seen more than they cared to but were still looking." But, as a glorious crown appears on the reflection of his head, "the rabbi's eyes glowed like sun-filled clouds" (*RH*, 19). These eyes can mist over with sentimentality when Lifshitz asks the wholly outclassed Gans if he loves his father and, after he tells Gans that Rifkele is made in God's image, is it weakened muscle control or a conman's chutzpah that causes the thickened eyelid to close in a wink? Hawthorne never created a more ambiguous character, and never so successfully blended the commonplace and the mysterious. In particular, Lifshitz's explanations of his operation are beyond praise. He accepted no checks because sometimes there are delays in getting to work on the crown immediately. How do the crowns work? "Like two winds that they meet in the sky. A white and a blue. The blue says 'Not only I am blue but inside I am purple and orange.' So the white goes away" (*TMB*, 17). Is the mystic book from which he reads prayers the Kabbalah? "Like the Kabbalah" (*RH*, 10), Lifshitz "explains." Every detail about the rabbi is fully imagined, perfectly realized—from the fleshy earlobes over which he pulls the ears of his glasses to his "brown eye pouches and [smell] of old age," to the possibly genuine mystic intensity, to the "trousers a week from ragged" (*RH*, 8) before he pockets Gans's money, to the "glad rags" (*RH*, 26) he and Rifkele later wear (religious socialites that they are) as they return to their dingy apartment from a fancy new synagogue on Mosholu Parkway.

In "My Son the Murderer" it is the son who seems near death while the father anguishes over the condition of his offspring. The twenty-two-year-old Harry has graduated from college and returned home to

Brooklyn to watch "a big burning war on a small screen. It rains bombs and the flames go higher. Sometimes I lean over and touch the war with the flat of my hand. I wait for my hand to die" (*RH*, 167). Though he will flee to Canada rather than join the horror in Vietnam, the war seems to Harry only the most dramatic symptom of a larger condition. Toward the end of the story he reflects that "I'm frightened of the world [;] . . . It fills me with fright" (*RH*, 173). By this time he has made his way into the ocean off Coney Island, where he stands with his shoes covered by the icy water.

But even here, at the edge of dissolution, looking out into the annihilating immensity of the ocean in February, Harry is pursued by Leo, his father, who has followed his son by bus and foot from their apartment. Unable or unwilling to communicate his fear, Harry says nothing until Leo rushes off to rescue his windblown hat; nor does he respond when his father returns to plead with him to walk out of the ocean and come home. The son has threatened to murder his father for meddling—Leo had just been caught opening a letter of his son's— but there is nothing trivial about Leo's concern. It is passionate, sometimes lyrical, as when he offers as proof of his love the way, when Harry was small, "I picked you up and lifted you up to the ceiling. You liked to touch it with your small hand" (*RH*, 169). But this is a son whose hand is now pressed not to the ceiling but to the murderous images the television screen offers up to him.

He feels his father's concern only as another oppression, and what is most impressive about the story is the way Malamud uses the point of view to deepen one's sense of the finally dangerous way each has invaded the other's psyche. "My Son the Murderer" begins in this way:

> He wakes feeling his father is in the hallway, listening. He listens to him sleep and dream. Listening to him get up and fumble for his pants. He won't put on his shoes. To him not going to the kitchen to eat. Staring with shut eyes in the mirror. Sitting an hour on the toilet. Flipping the pages of a book he can't read. To his anguish, loneliness. The father stands in the hall. The son hears him listen. (*RH*, 165)

In this, the story's first paragraph, it takes a bit of sorting to perceive that the second sentence describes Harry listening to his father out there trying to invade his son's dreams through listening. The paragraph's many repetitions—for example, the three sentences beginning with "he"; the way the second, fourth, fifth, and sixth sentences begin with present participles—capture both the deadly repetitiveness of Harry's obsessions and Leo's equally compulsive concern.

The drama of an obsessively concerned man whose attentions only drive the sufferer to greater anguish is reminiscent of the grim comedy of "Take Pity." Sanford Pinsker has argued that the "Hell is other people" motif of the earlier story, as well as its setting in an afterworld, were influenced by Jean-Paul Sartre's *No Exit*.[141] This may or may not be; what interests me here is the way the story centers on a conclusive shift in Eva's and Rosen's fates while the central concern in Sartre's play is summarized with the statement of Garcin's that closes the play: "Let's get on with it"[142]—let's run through these agonizing subject-object power games again, as we will for eternity.

Daniel Stern observed that "'My Son the Murderer' is a strange, darkly intense recitation, a brooding in shifting tenses and points of view. It succeeds more as a poem than a tale."[143] By this, I think that Stern suggests that the piece lacks the process we normally expect a short story to have; like Sartre's play, it stands more as an extended image of disastrous entanglement. There is, however, a process of sorts in the course of the story: Harry moves closer to suicide, and Leo's concern and sense of futility deepen. Whether we call "My Son the Murderer" a short story or a sketch or a prose poem matters much less than, for example, the way the choric quality of the recitations bring an overlay of Greek tragedy to Leo's modified Yinglish and help to make the piece vintage Malamud, one of his most lyrical renderings of obsessive involvement.

The presence or absence of letters is a recurrent motif in *Rembrandt's Hat*'s tales of baffled communication. There are the unmailed blank pages in "The Letter" and in "In Retirement" Dr. Morris's letter to a much younger woman—a letter that earns him considerable derision and pain. In "My Son the Murderer" Leo at one point wishes that Harry would send him a letter. In "Notes from a Lady at a Dinner Party" Max Adler is intrigued, sexually inflamed, and then humiliated by the barrage of little letters that Karla Harris, his dinner party hostess, keeps slipping into his pockets. As Malamud stories go, this one is unusually devoid of the idiosyncratic. Far from being the usual yearning or sorrowing Malamud protagonist, Adler is an overweight, successful architect in his early thirties visiting his former mentor,

Clem Harris. More than three decades younger than her husband, Karla has borne him two children. In her final note, she announces to Adler that she cannot meet him at a nearby motel as they planned because she is six months pregnant. We can leave the story wondering if she's lying—surely the pregnancy would be noticeable—but the moral accents are clear enough: she's been playing with the self-satisfied Adler all along, and a man willing to betray a father figure for sex is only getting what he deserves.

The duration of the story is that of the dinner party, and everything in the Harrises' tasteful house—people, objects, conversations—is rendered with the professionalism that is the point of departure for a Malamud story. But the absence of obsessively committed characters makes it hard for Malamud to take the story much beyond the parameters of a suburban dalliance misfired. "Notes" is well done, but Malamud's talent lay in rendering more extreme ranges of experience in more idiosyncratic language than he permitted to enter this story. While Malamud was, in his earlier collections, able to write from an experiential and stylistic midrange such fine stories as "A Summer's Reading" and "The Maid's Shoes," I do not find that faculty present in *Rembrandt's Hat*. The collection's only outstanding stories are one charged with the possibilities of the supernatural ("The Silver Crown"), the stylistically adventurous "My Son the Murderer," and the fantasy "Talking Horse."

If Adler is vocationally fulfilled, the collection's other artists—Feliks Levitansky in "The Man in the Drawer" and Rubin in the title story—share in the embitterment that seems very nearly endemic to Malamud characters. In each case, the stories' protagonists, Howard Harvitz and Arkin, can only alter the painful relationships they've developed with the artists by putting themselves in the respective artists' positions. All four characters are Jewish or half-Jewish—as in the case of Levitansky—but Jewishness only becomes an issue in "The Man in a Drawer," and even here its use is much more muted than it would have been were the story written earlier.

The story begins at the moment that Howard Harvitz, a free-lance writer of forty-seven who is visiting Moscow, hears "a soft shalom" (*RH*, 33) from Levitansky, the driver of the cab that has just picked up the American. This is also the first word that another American tourist, Arthur Fidelman, hears from Susskind, and one awaits the Russian's attempt to manipulate the American's sense of his responsibility to other Jews. And indeed, after Levitansky suggests that he made his life more difficult by registering as his religion on his internal passport the one of his Jewish father and not his gentile mother ("in respect for my father"), Harvitz concedes, "I had not been much of a Jew myself. 'My mother and father were totally assimilated.'" In fact his parents were so assimilated that, as Harvitz confessed a few moments earlier, his father had changed the name to Harris just before the son entered college. Having undergone great sorrow with the recent death of his wife, Harris once again became Harvitz, with the result that "I am closer to my true self" (*RH*, 37).

When Levitansky, a short story writer who claims with some justification "to be in tradition of Chekhov, Gorky, Isaac Babel" (*RH*, 62), and who cannot get his version of social realism published in the Soviet Union, asks Harvitz to smuggle out eighteen of the stories and attempt to publish them in the United States, we expect Levitansky's ultimate appeal to be to Harvitz, the true Jewish self, who mourns his wife and does what he can for other needful humans. But just as Malamud took to bridling at hearing some of his schlemiel characters called schlemiels, so did he seem to have become wary of a reader responding with something like "Ah yes, the metaphorical Jewishness again." Levitansky appears to Harvitz as a writer, as a human being, and as an American, but the Russian never invokes their common Jewishness.

Fearful of being caught and jailed for attempting to smuggle the proscribed writings out of Russia, Harvitz refuses four times to try to rescue the Russian from the fate of writing for his drawer, with mouse droppings the appropriate commentary his stories receive. But during his last night in Russia, Harvitz's defenses—like those of Manischevitz and the Fidelman of "The Last Mohican"—are breached by a dream. In it, a dwarfish Levitansky emerges from the drawer in which he had been living and condemns the American (as he had during some of the disputes of their waking hours) as "Atombombnik! You massacred innocent Japanese people! Americansky bastards!" (*RH*, 79).

But guilt is not enough of an animus for Harvitz to risk his freedom. Dreaming or awake—we cannot tell—he resists identification with this aspect of the American past and instead constructs a scenario of the future in which he denounces in an epic poem an America grown monstrous, a place where his poem cannot be published. "A bearded Levitansky, in better times a Soviet tourist," appears at his door and

kindly offers to sneak the manuscript of the poem out for publication in the Soviet Union.

The Short Fiction: An Essay

> Why? Harvitz suspiciously asks.
> Why not? To give the book its liberty. (*RH*, 80)

Here Malamud pushes beyond a simple categorical imperative ("I'd want Levitansky to do this for me, so I should do this for him") to a sort of political existentialism: one cannot will the freedom of one book without willing the freedom of all. Although Malamud's commitment to freedom of expression was intense—the celebrations of freedom included in part 2 are supported by the fact that he was president of PEN for three years—he was not at his best in his fiction as a fighting liberal. Levin's political awakening is the weakest thing in *A New Life*, and the large political sentiments articulated in *The Fixer* are earned more by the overwhelming authority of the writing in the rest of the novel than by their own clarion call. There's a sense of Malamud being so eager to have the timid Harvitz converted by large political truths that the most obvious reason for smuggling out the manuscript—Levitansky's state is becoming so desperate that his admirable wife is about to make it worse by leaving him—is never considered. And Harvitz's ruminations are so relatively repetitive and frequent that, alone of Malamud's forty-five stories, this one could have benefited from some editing.

But there is no shortage of compressed force in the conclusion. Malamud ended *The Fixer* with Yakov Bok heading toward his trial, and he ends Harvitz's involvement as the cab—which holds the American, his suitcase and the manuscript hidden in the suitcase—approaches Moscow airport. But then, as a sort of envoi, Malamud justifies Levitansky's claims for his fiction by offering scenarios of four stories that might have been written by a Russian Malamud—stories of desperate old men, of Jews persecuted by the police, and writers crushed by their inability to express themselves. The implicit superimposition of Malamud in the guise of a bitter Russian dissident upon the sensibility the reader had induced from the past fiction is a good deal more striking than the conversion of the timid Harvitz.

"Man in the Drawer" accelerates in its last pages; the closing of the intensely interesting and suggestive "Talking Horse" is simultaneously a shaggy dog joke and a profound metaphor of the human condition. The first part of the fantasy is narrated in the present tense by Abramowitz, a sideshow performer who, in the story's opening sentence, is pondering whether he is "a man in a horse or a horse that talks like a man" (*RH*, 177). For a bit more than two-thirds of the twenty-seven-page story, Abramowitz ruminates over his origins and nature and describes his interactions with Goldberg, his brutal deaf-mute master. This first section concludes with Abramowitz's conclusive resisting of Goldberg's definition of him as a talking horse, for the former has decided that his intelligence, best evidenced by this very capacity for questioning, could only belong to a human—though one trapped in a horse. For its final eight pages the fantasy moves into the third-person past, though Abramowitz remains as the reflector, and recounts the horse's attempts to gain his freedom. He succeeds when he finally attacks Goldberg and, in their struggle, "the horse's head and neck, up to an old wound, came off in his [Goldberg's] hands. Amid the stench of blood and bowel a man's pale head popped out of the hole in the horse. . . . Abramowitz, straining to the point of madness, slowly pulled himself out of the horse up to his navel. At that moment Goldberg broke his frantic grip and disappeared" and "departing the circus grounds . . . [Abramowitz] cantered across a grassy soft field into a dark wood, a free centaur" (*RH*, 204).

I recommend a perusal of Paul and Beth Burch's discussion (in part 3) of the different strands of Greek mythology and Hebrew theology that Malamud wove into "Talking Horse." Here I'd like to consider Daniel Stern's perceptive considerations in terms of "what is called in philosophy the mind-body problem . . . via horse-ness and man-ness both of which Abramowitz possesses. He is spirit-locked–in–matter, desperately yearning to be free. . . . If it is speech that separates man [here the deaf-mute Goldberg] from the animals, then who, in this case, is man and who is animal? The Beckett-like image is powerful: a clown-animal-man stuck in his animal-body, in his animal-nature, while forced to perform in the humiliating circus act of daily life by a mute, vengeful and ambiguous God."[144]

The terms of Abramowitz's dilemma are of course changed by the consequences of his final struggle with this God who is so flawed that he exists only through human capitulation. What seems to be the culminating joke in what is perhaps the wittiest of all of Malamud's stories is the suggestion that if only Goldberg had not run away when he did, the human who was suffering the weirdest of the many imprisonments in Malamud's fiction might have pulled himself all the way out and avoided the new organization of man and horse. Beneath this joke lies the pervasive human comedy: something will always come up; our liberations will always be partial; wholeness, perfect unity will always recede before the grasp of creatures whose existence is, in Santayana's words, lyric in essence, tragic in fate, and comic in existence.

But a more benign existential strain, Malamud's fascination with the uses of freedom, is also in the story. It could be said that Abramowitz's justification of his humanity was Cartesian: he thought in certain ways; therefore he was human. But as different existential writers have perceived, man always thinks in a particular context; thought is never fully abstracted from the conditions of one's existence. One of these conditions is that one invariably uses one's freedom within limits, but in ways that either expand or limit the arena in which freedom might function.

The particularities of our existences have a way of distracting us from Cartesian conceptions of ourselves: "Sometimes I think of myself as an idea, yet here I stand in this filthy stall, my hoofs sunk in my yellow balls of dreck" (*RH*, 190). By itself, cogitation will not better his situation, for "once you start asking questions one leads to the next and in the end it's endless" (*RH*, 195). Action would have to be taken to escape his servitude, and some of the story's comedy follows from the consequences of Abramowitz's efforts to escape. (The first one ends with his being caught while he's on a station platform, waiting for a train.)

What we might call the ontological quest—Abramowitz's struggle to discover his being—is necessarily linked to the existential (or in this case political) quest to gain his physical freedom. But freedom is such an expansive force that the rich story is also a parable of the artist's need for freedom of expression. Once Abramowitz decides he is human he insists on introducing his own riddles into his performances, on belittling the boring ones of Goldberg's routine. His moral and aesthetic needs explode the limiting riddle form. Through speeches that celebrate freedom, stories, and poems he tries to humanize an audience that has been further banalized by the fare they've been receiving. Now when Goldberg is depressed, the horse "heehawed at his appearance, brayed at his 'talk,' stupidity, arrogance." He even becomes a sort of equine performance artist of the sixties: "Sometimes he made up little songs of freedom as he danced on his hind legs, exposing his private parts" (*RH*, 199). Whenever possible, he pleads with the audience to help him gain his freedom, but in keeping with Malamud's increasing politicization over the years, he can only escape physical oppression when he is ready to bring force to bear.

I like the idea of leaving Malamud's stories not with the weaker efforts of his last years—particularly the stories of sexual rejection, of shrinking lives unleavened by the startling language and imagery of his earlier work—but with this splendid fantasy. It is such a characteristic effort—with its pain and qualified triumph; imprisonment and release; freedom and limitation; bawdiness and restraint; the fantastic and the quotidian; the balls of dreck and the mythic layerings; the physical and the spiritual; the colloquial and the poetic; humor, complexity, profundity. "Talking Horse" is a most appropriate envoi for a writer about whom Philip Roth wrote "What it is to be human, and to be humane, is his deepest concern,"[145] one who designated freedom as "our most extraordinary invention."[146] One of Malamud's favorite poets wrote, "One could do worse than be a swinger of birches." One could also do worse than swinging with and on Malamud's stories to wherever they take you.

Notes

1. Michiko Kakutani, "Malamud Still Seeks Balance and Solitude," *New York Times*, 15 July 1980, C7.

2. Daniel Stern, "The Art of Fiction: Bernard Malamud," *Paris Review* 61 (Spring 1975):43.

3. Ibid., 44.

4. Ibid., 53.

5. Bernard Malamud, *The Assistant* (New York: Farrar, Straus & Giroux, 1957), 27; hereafter cited in text.

6. Kakutani, "Malamud Still Seeks," C7.

7. "Bernard Malamud," in *World Authors, 1950–1970: A Companion Volume to Twentieth-Century Authors*, ed. John Wakeman (New York: H. H. Wilson, 1975), 917.

8. Ralph Tyler, "A Talk with the Novelist," *New York Times Book Review*, 18 February 1979, 33.

9. Dr. Doris A. Milman, letter to author, 10 March 1988.

10. Philip Roth, "Pictures of Malamud," *New York Times Book Review*, 20 April 1986, 41.

11. *World Authors*, 917.

12. Stern, "Art of Fiction," 44.

13. Dean Cadle, "Bernard Malamud," *Wilson Library Bulletin* 33, no. 4 (December 1958):66.

14. *World Authors*, 917.

15. Stern, "Art of Fiction," 44.

16. Katha Pollit, "Bernard Malamud," *Saturday Review* 8 (February 1981):32.

17. Joseph Wershba, "Not Horror but 'Sadness,'" *New York Post*, 14 September 1958, M2.

18. Miriam Lang, letter to author, 8 March 1988.

19. Curt Leviant, "Bernard Malamud: My Characters Are God Haunted," *Hadassah Magazine* 55, no. 10 (June 1974):18. The title is misleading, for Malamud did not necessarily agree with the claim it makes. In discussing the Jewish qualities of his characters Malamud said, "Someone said recently that my characters are God-haunted" (19). What the critic said was *"Idiots First*, like his earlier collection *The Magic Barrel*, is brutal, thoughtful and baroque, the product of an imagination as haunted by religion, and as perturbing, as any since Kafka's" (Robert Taubman, "People of the Law," *New Statesman* 67 [5 June 1964]:883).

20. Curt Supplee. "God, Bernard Malamud, and the Rebirth of Man." *Washington Post*, 27 August 1982, F8.

21. Stern, "Art of Fiction," 43.

22. Miriam Lang, letter to author, 6 April 1988.

23. Wershba, "Not Horror," M2.

24. Lang letter of 8 March 1988.

25. Burt Rush, telephone conversation with author, 22 February 1988.

26. Milner letter of 10 March 1988.

27. Wershba, "Not Horror," M2.

28. "Long Work, Short Life," *Michigan Quarterly Review* 26, no. 4 (Fall 1987):603.

29. Lang letter of 8 March 1988.

30. Pinner's wife took her life at the same time in their Jackson Heights apartment. Rush telephone conversation of 22 February 1988.

31. "Long Work," 604.

32. Lang letter of 8 March 1998.

33. "Long Work," 604.

34. Lang letter of 8 March 1988.

35. Richard Astro, "In the Heart of the Valley: Bernard Malamud's *A New Life*," in *Bernard Malamud*, ed. Leslie and Joyce Field (Englewood Cliffs, N.J.: Prentice-Hall, 1974), 143–44.

36. Wershba, "Not Horror," M2.

37. Israel Shenker, "For Malamud It's Story," *New York Times Book Review*, 3 October 1971, 20.

38. Roth, "Pictures of Malamud," 41.

39. Quoted in Supplee, "God, Bernard Malamud," F2.

40. Ann Malamud, letter to author, 25 November 1986.

41. "The Place Is Different Now," *American Preface* 8, no. 3 (Spring 1943):232; hereafter cited in text.

42. "Benefit Performance," *Threshold* 3, no. 3 (February 1943): 20; hereafter cited in text.

43. Ann Malamud letter of 25 November 1986.

44. "The First Seven Years," in *The Magic Barrel* (New York: Farrar, Straus & Cudahy, 1952) 3–4; hereafter cited in text.

45. Daniel Stern, "Commonplace Things and the Essence of Art," *Nation* 217 (3 September 1973): 181.

46. Mikhail Bakhtin, *Problems of Dostoevsky's Poetics*, trans. R. W. Rotsel (Ann Arbor, Mich.: Ardis, 1973), 12.

47. Herman Melville, *Billy Budd*, in *Herman Melville: Selected Tales and Poems*, ed. Richard Chase (New York: Holt, Rinehart & Winston, 1948), 324–25.

48. "Under Forty: A Symposium on American Literature and the Younger Generation," *Contemporary Jewish Record* 4 (February 1944):15–16.

49. Alfred Kazin, "The Alone Generation," *Harper's* 219 (October 1959):131.

50. "Under Forty," 35.

51. "The Writer's Task," in *Writing in America*, ed. John Fischer and Robert B. Silvers (New Brunswick, N.J.: Rutgers University Press, 1960), 173.

52. Saul Bellow, *Seize the Day* (Greenwich, Conn.: Fawcett Publications, 1956), 92.

53. Joseph C. Landis, "Reflections on Jewish American Writers," *Jewish Book Annual* (New York: Jewish Book Council of America, 1967), 141.

54. Robert Alter, "Sentimentalizing Jews," in *After the Tradition* (New York: E. P. Dutton & Co., 1969), 42.

55. Philip Roth, "Imagining Jews," in *Reading Myself and Others* (New York: Farrar, Straus & Giroux, 1976), 229.

56. Leviant, "Bernard Malamud," 19.

57. Quoted in the introduction to *Bernard Malamud: A Collection of Critical Essays*, ed. Leslie Field and Joyce Field (Englewood Cliffs, N.J.: Prentice-Hall, 1975), 7.

58. "Idiots First," in *Idiots First* (Farrar, Straus & Giroux, 1963), 14; hereafter cited in text.

59. Marcia B. Gealy, "Malamud's Short Stories: A Reshaping of Hasidic Tradition," *Judaism* 28 (Winter 1979):51. In particular, Gealy points out that "Malamud's father came from 'Zbrish in or around Kamentz Podolsk,' a city in the western Ukraine and a former capital of Podolia. Podolia is the legendary birthplace of the Baal Shem Tov (the founder of Hasidism) and was an important early center of Hasidic influence."

60. Ann Malamud, letter to author, 23 January 1986.

61. Shenker, "For Malamud It's Story," 20.

62. Stern, "Art of Fiction," 56.

63. Roth, "Writing American Fiction," in *Reading Myself and Others*, 127.

64. Earl Rovit, "The Jewish Literary Tradition," *Critique* 3, no. 2 (Winter–Spring 1960):5.

65. Supplee, "God, Bernard Malamud," F8.

66. Kakutani, "Malamud Still Seeks," C7.

67. Irving Howe, "Mass Society and Post-Modern Fiction," in *The American Novel Since World War II*, ed. Marcus Klein (Greenwich, Conn. Fawcett Publications, 1970), 133.

68. Roth, "Writing American Fiction," 120.

69. *A Treasury of Yiddish Stories*, ed. Irving Howe and Eliezer Greenburg (New York: Viking Press, 1965), 38.

70. Joseph Featherstone, "Bernard Malamud," *Atlantic Monthly* 219 (March 1967):95.

71. Howe and Greenburg, *A Treasury*, 7.

72. Marcus Klein, "The Sadness of Goodness," in *After Alienation* (Cleveland: World Publishing Co., 1965), 248.

73. Ruth Wisse, *The Schlemiel as Modern Hero* (Chicago: University of Chicago Press, 1971), 47.

74. Leslie Field and Joyce Field, "An Interview with Bernard Malamud, in *Bernard Malamud: A Collection of Critical Essays*, 10–11.

75. *The Fixer* (New York: Dell Books, 1972), 142.

76. For example, after his first meeting with Salzman, Leo "ran around in the woods" (*TMB*, 199). One is reminded of the way the people of Israel wandered in the wilderness after denying the necessity of the Lord's spirit (Exod. 15:24). While Leo is walking with Lily, he senses Salzman "hiding perhaps high in a tree" (*TMB*, 202); Zacchaeus stood in a tree to view Christ (Luke 19:1–4). After Salzman miraculously beats Leo home, the student fixes him a sardine sandwich. In Matthew 14:19–21 Christ fed the five thousand with fish and bread. To turn to later folklore, Gealy identifies Stella as "a combination Lilith-*Shekhinah* or destroyer-preserver figure who tests the hero and offers pain, judgment and ultimate insight. The female in that role, as demon and godly presence, is an interesting aspect of Jewish mysticism and Hasidic folklore" (Gealy, "Malamud's Short Stories," 55). Then there's the use of Greek mythology with the image of Salzman as "a cloven-hoofed Pan, piping nuptial ditties as he danced his invisible way before them" (*TMB*, 202).

77. Saul Bellow, *Henderson the Rain King* (New York: Viking Press, 1959), 214.

78. Charles May, "The Bread of Tears: Malamud's 'The Loan,'" *Studies in Short Fiction* 7, no. 4 (Fall 1970):652.

79. "Writer's Task," 173.

80. Roth, "Pictures of Malamud," 40

81. Theodore Solotaroff, "Bernard Malamud's Fiction: The Old Life and the New," *Commentary* 33, no. 3 (March 1962):200.

82. Here is Morris offering his sense of the law: "This means to do what is right, to be honest, to be good. This means to other people. Our life is hard enough. Why should we hurt somebody else? For everybody should be the best, not only for you or me. We ain't animals. This is why we need the Law. This is what a Jew believes" (*TA*, 124).

83. F. Scott Fitzgerald, *The Great Gatsby* (New York: Charles Scribner's Sons, 1953), 15.

84. Roth, "Pictures of Malamud," 1.

85. Sidney Richman, *Bernard Malamud* (New York: Twayne Publishers, 1966), 118. Probably Malamud was, with the Italian name *Panessa*, ironically punning upon the Yiddish word *parnusseh* (livelihood). Thus Morris Bober's wife laments moving away from friends and other Jews to the neighborhood of their prison of a store "for parnusseh unrealized" (*TA*, 8).

86. Gealy, "Malamud's Short Stories," 53.

87. Ibid.

88. Ernest Hemingway, *The Sun Also Rises* (New York: Charles Scribner's Sons, 1970), 247.

89. Edwin Eigner, "Malamud's Use of the Quest Romance," *Genre* 1, no. 1 (January 1968):58.

90. Rita Kosofsy, *Bernard Malamud: An Annotated Checklist* (Akron: Kent State University Press, 1969), viii.

91. "An Apology," *Commentary* 12 (November 1951):460–61; hereafter cited in text.

92. *A New Life* (New York: Dell Publishing Co., 1970), 211.

93. For example, see Herbert Leibowitz, "Malamud and the Anthropomorphic Business," *New Republic* 153, no. 2 (21 December 1965):21–25; Helen Weinberg, *The New Novel in America: The Kafkan Mode in Contemporary Fiction* (Ithaca, N.Y.: Cornell University Press, 1970).

94. Franz Kafka, "Reflections on Sin, Pain, Hope, and the True Way," in *Dearest Father: Stories and Other Writings* (New York: Schocken Books, 1954), 39.

95. When Mendel and Isaac enter a park, they confront "a leafless two-branched tree," which has a raised thick right branch and a thin left one that hangs down. After Ginzburg appears and the father and son flee from the park, Mendel turns and notices that "the dead tree had its thin arm raised, the thick one down. He moaned" (*IF*, 9). Earle V. Bryant ("The Tree-Clock in Bernard Malamud's 'Idiots First,'" *Studies in Short Fiction* 20, no. 1 [1983]:52–54) has conjectured that the reversed branches are a clock, indicating that it is now close to 10:20 P.M. Since Mendel heard a clock chime ten times only a few minutes earlier, Bryant interprets the temporal disparity as a way of emphasizing Mendel's race with time. There's also the possibility that the natural world is collaborating with Ginzburg to cheat Mendel of some of the little time he has.

96. Thus the three stories that Malamud published during his "break-through year" of 1950 lay out three fictional ways he might go with his knowledge of the life of Jewish shopkeepers: transplant it into a gentile setting (as with "The Prison"), write a Kafkaesque tale with one of his little Jews over-powered by nameless adversaries (as in "The Cost of Living"), or create a tale in which two Jews are obsessively intertwined (as in "The First Seven Years"). The third road was the one most traveled.

97. Sigmund Freud, *Civilization and Its Discontents* (New York: W. W. Norton, 1961), 61.

98. *God's Grace* (New York: Farrar, Straus & Giroux, 1982), 194.

99. Melville, "Bartleby the Scrivener," in *Herman Melville: Selected Tales and Poems*, 116.

100. Ibid., 129.

101. Letter to Whit Burnet in *This Is My Best in the Third Quarter of the Twentieth Century*, ed. Whit Burnet (Garden City, N.Y.: Doubleday & Co., 1970), 505.

102. Merrill Maguire Skaggs, "A Complex Black-and-White Matter," in *The Process of Fiction*, ed. Barbara McKenzie (New York: Harcourt, Brace & World, 1969), 388.

103. Ibid., 389.

104. Shenker, "For Malamud It's Story," 20.

105. Theodore Solotaroff, "Showing Us 'What It Means Human,'" *Washington Post and Times Herald Book Week*, 13 October 1963, 12.

106. Stern, "Art of Fiction," 58–59.

107. *Pictures of Fidelman: An Exhibition* (New York: Farrar, Straus & Giroux, 1969), 40; hereafter cited in text.

108. Although in "Still Life" Fidelman is referred to as "the student," a sculptor mentions having seen exhibited "some symmetric hard-edge biomorphic forms" (*PF*, 62) of Fidelman's; there's the portrait of Esmeralda that Ludovico takes off, claiming he can get Fidelman a million lire for it; in Venice "he sought an object of art nobody would recognize but Fidelman" (*PF*, 178); then there's the missing red bowl of "Glass Blower of Venice."

109. Morris Dickstein, "Cold War Blues," *Partisan Review* 41, no. 1 (Winter 1974):43.

110. Jackson Benson, "An Introduction: Bernard Malamud and the Haunting of America," in *The Fiction of Bernard Malamud*, ed. Richard Astro and Jackson J. Benson (Corvallis: Oregon State University Press, 1977), 16.

111. Tony Tanner, *City of Words* (New York: Harper & Row, 1971), 340.

112. T. S. Eliot, "Tradition and the Individual Talent," in *Selected Essays* (New York: Harcourt, Brace & Company, 1950), 6.

113. For example, Iska Alter calls the theft "Solipsism triumphant! . . . For while Fidelman is free in the physical sense, he is still imprisoned in a

closed psychic structure, isolated by self-love, trapped by the notion of art as autoeroticism" (*The Good Man's Dilemma* [New York: AMS Press, 1981], 136).

114. Stern, "Art of Fiction," 51–52.

115. See the selections in part 2 from Malamud's "Theme, Content and the 'New Novel'" and "Long Work, Short Life," as well as the interviews with Field and Field and Daniel Stern.

116. T. S. Eliot, "The Love Song of J. Alfred Prufrock," in *T. S. Eliot: The Complete Poems and Plays* (New York: Harcourt, Brace & World, 1971).

117. Wisse, *Schlemiel*, 115.

118. Roger Sale, "The Golden Age of the American Novel," in *On Not Being Good Enough* (New York: Oxford University Press, 1979), 112.

119. "Theme, Content and the 'New Novel,'" *New York Times Book Review*, 8 October 1967, 2.

120. Ibid.

121. Wisse, *Schlemiel*, 116.

122. Tanner, *City of Words*, 341

123. At the party in "Still Life" a sculptor with "bleached blond hair" approaches Fidelman and suggestively asks "Haven't we met before, caro?" When Fidelman tells him that he admits that Annamaria's art "is bad but I find her irresistible," the sculptor replies "Peccato [what a pity]" (*PF*, 61–62), shrugs, and drifts away. In "Naked Nude" Fidelman has to reject Scarpio's physical advances. During his stint as a pimp in "A Pimp's Revenge" Fidelman "sometimes finds himself drawing dirty pictures: men and women, women and women, men and men" (*PF*, 138). An early image in "Pictures of the Artist," one that salutes the homosexual writings of Jean Genet, is of "S. Fidel Uomo, stuffing his ass with flowers" (*PF*, 150). Fidel-*man*, "loyal man" or "Fidel Uomo," is here being loyal to his own homosexual component. Thus Fidelman's conversion to bisexuality is not as unprepared as Philip Roth would have it. Roth is certainly right though about Malamud's refusal to have any of the residual taboos about homosexuality tested. I see the ease of Fidelman's conversion to homosexual love as only a part of the dreamlike unity Malamud gave to his character. See Roth's "Imagining Jews," 237–42.

124. Wershba, "Not Horror," M2.

125. "Long Work, Short Life," 611.

126. Tim Seldes, telephone conversation with author, 16 April 1988.

127. "A Lost Grave," *Esquire* 103 (May 1985):204; hereafter cited in text.

128. Quentin Bell, *Virginia Woolf* (New York: Harcourt Brace & Jovanovich, 1972), 24.

129. "In Kew Gardens," *Partisan Review* 51, no. 4 (1984), 52, no. 1 (1985):536

130. For example, in *The Unknown Virginia Woolf* (Highlands, N.J.: Humanities Press, 1982) Roger Poole argues that Woolf was never mad and that

in 1941, fearing death by German shrapnel, she quite sanely chose death by water—which "represented for her two things[:] . . . the kind of intellection which was not abrupt, logical, male, hacking, dominant, fractious and pseudo-logical; but smooth flowing, integrating, harmonious. Second, it represented the possibility of the resolution of intolerable conflicts in death" (260). Poole argues that the explanation in the suicide note to Leonard—she knew she was sinking into a madness from which she would never recover—was a lie, made to ease his conscience.

131. Bell, *Virginia Woolf*, 79.

132. Ibid., 90.

133. For example, Malamud wrongly claims that Vanessa "loved Duncan Grant until he loved her" and offered as proof for his claim that Lytton Strachey had no use for the quality of masculinity the fact he asked 'Semen?' . . . when he saw a stain on Vanessa's dress" (537). This was the response to Strachey's question, which Bell took from Woolf's diary: "Can one really say it? I thought & we burst out laughing. With that one word all barriers of reticence and reserve went down. A flood of the sacred fluid seemed to overwhelm us. Sex permeated our conversation. . . . It is strange to think how reticent, how reserved we had been and for how long" (Bell, *Virginia Woolf*, 124).

134. "Alma Redeemed—a Story," *Commentary* 78, no. 1 (July 1984):33; hereafter cited in text.

135. Rovit, "Jewish Literary Tradition," 8.

136. "A Wig," *Atlantic Monthly* 241, no. 1 (January 1980):33; hereafter cited in text.

137. "The Model," *Atlantic Monthly* 252, no. 1 (August 1983):81.

138. "God's Wrath," *Atlantic Monthly* 225, no. 1 (February 1972):62.

139. "An Exorcism" *Harper's* 237, no. 1423 (December 1968):76.

140. *Rembrandt's Hat* (New York: Farrar, Straus & Giroux, 1973), 105; hereafter cited in text.

141. Sanford Pinsker, "A Note on Bernard Malamud's 'Take Pity,'" *Studies in Short Fiction* 6, no. 2 (Winter 1969):212.

142. Jean-Paul Sartre, *No Exit*, in *No Exit and Three Other Plays* (New York: Vintage Books, 1953), 47.

143. Stern, "Commonplace Things," 181.

144. Ibid., 182.

145. Roth, "Writing American Fiction," 127.

146. Field and Field, "An Interview," 12.

Part 2

THE WRITER

Malamud on Life and Art

Some of the interviews with Bernard Malamud begin with comments about how seldom this author who so much wanted his works to speak for him granted interviews. Still, Joel Salzberg lists twenty-seven different interviews—two of them in Italian, one in Serbo-Croatian, and one in Japanese—in *Bernard Malamud: A Reference Guide*. The following extracts were selected from ten of these interviews, from four of Malamud's writings, and the book and article in which appeared two different parts of the author's acceptance speech for the 1959 National Book Award. The extracts were chosen with the particular hope of deepening the reader's sense of Malamud's values and principles—whether aesthetic or immediately experiential—and, for all Malamud's reticence on this issue, of the experiences that helped to shape his stories. The articulations range from 1958, when *The Magic Barrel* appeared—one year after *The Assistant*—to solidify Malamud's position as one of his country's leading writers, to October 1984, when Malamud first presented "Long Work, Short Life" as a lecture.

Excerpts from Joseph Wershba's 1958 interview-article. (Wershba's comments are in brackets.)

The work comes first[;] . . . The artist is secondary. There is much to be said for the old admonition, "never meet the artist." . . .

I write about Jews because I know them. But more important, I write about them because the Jews are absolutely the very *stuff* of drama. . . .

[Malamud is consumed with the drama of personality fulfilling itself. This should be the chief business of the writer, he says.]

The sell-out of personality is just tremendous. Our most important natural resource is Man. The times cry out for men of imagination and hope. Instead, our fiction is loaded with sickness, homosexuality, fragmented man, "other-directed" man. It should be filled with love and beauty and hope. We are underselling Man. And American fiction is at its weakest when we go in for journalistic case studies, instead of rich character development. . . .

[Making Frank Alpine in "The Assistant" an Italian was a careful calculation.] Italians and Jews are closely related in their consciousness of the importance of personality . . . in their emphasis on the richness of life, in their tremendous sense of past and tradition. . . .

The suffering of the Jews is a distinct thing for me. I for one believe that not enough has been made of the tragedy of the destruction of 6,000,000 Jews.

And I felt exactly the same in 1936 when the Yellow River flooded and six to ten million Chinese were drowned. Not enough has been made of such tragedies.

Somebody has to cry—even if it's just a writer, 20 years later. . . .

The purpose of the writer . . . is to keep civilization from destroying itself. But without preachment. Artists cannot be ministers. As soon as they attempt it, they destroy the artistry. . . .

[Asked about "influences," he begins to enumerate, then gives up. In the short story he has deep debts to Anderson, Hemingway, Joyce, Chekhov, and Katherine Mansfield. In the novel, his influences are the Bible, Shakespeare, Dostoyevsky, Tolstoy, Flaubert, Hardy, Hemingway, and Faulkner.]

And in the new book [A New Life]—Stendahl.

[He has also been influenced by painters.] Remember what Hemingway has said, how painting teaches us to write? Painters, of necessity, have to abstract, they have to highlight, they have to compress. . . .

My premise is that we will not destroy each other. My premise is that we will live on. We will seek a better life. We may not become better, but at least we will seek betterment.

My premise . . . is for humanism—and against nihilism. And that is what I try to put in my writings.[1]

Excerpt from Malamud's acceptance speech for the 1959 National Book Award for Fiction, which he received for The Magic Barrel.

It seems to me that [the writer's] most important task, no matter what the current theory of man, or his prevailing mood, is to recapture his image as human being as each of us in his secret heart knows it to be, and as history and literature have from the beginning revealed it. At the same time the writer must imagine a better world for men the while he shows us, in all its ugliness and beauty, the possibilities of this. In recreating the humanity of man, in reality his greatness, he will, among other things, hold up the mirror to the mystery of him, in which poetry and possibility live, though he has endlessly betrayed them. In a sense, the writer in his art, without directly stating it—though *he* may preach, his *work* must not—must remind man that he has, in his human striving, invented nothing less than freedom; and if he will devoutly remember this, he will understand the best way to preserve it, and his own highest value.

I've had something such as this in mind, as I wrote, however imperfectly, my sad and comic tales.[2]

Another excerpt from the acceptance speech for the 1959 National Book Award.

I am quite tired of the colossally deceitful valuation of man in this day for whatever explanation: that life is cheap amid a prevalence of wars; or because we are drugged by totalitarian successes into a sneaking belief in their dehumanizing processes; or tricked beyond self-respect by the values of the creators of our own thing-ridden society; . . . or because, having invented the means of his extinction, man values himself less for it and lives in daily dread that he will in a fit of passion, or pique or absent-mindedness, achieve his end. Whatever the reason, his fall from grace in his eyes is betrayed in the words he has invented to describe himself as he is now: fragmented, abbreviated, other-directed, organizational, atonymous man, a victim in the words that are used to describe him of a kind of synecdochic irony, the part for the whole. The devaluation exists because he accepts it without protest.

Excerpts from an anonymous 1963 interview-article. (The interviewer's comments are in brackets.)

. . . one lives on premises, a kind of experimental optimism. One has to. And there is the test-ban treaty. But beyond this, there is intuition: No, the worst won't happen. . . . You can get mad, but how mad can you get? There are unseen victories all around us—it's a matter of plucking them down. It takes effort, the kind of courage that causes man constantly to fabricate the means of his preservation. . . .

[Is he involved with social problems outside writing?] No: the writer's involvement in writing *is* involvement with social problems; he doesn't need political involvement. A writer must say something worthwhile, but it must be art; his problem is to handle social issues so imaginatively and uniquely that they become art. Otherwise I'm not interested. . . .

[One of Malamud's most famous early stories is "The Last Mohican." Its protagonist, Arthur Fidelman, an artist living in Rome, reappears in two stories in *Idiots First.*] Oh, yes, he's a favorite, . . . and I'm still involved with him—the problem of the artist manque, the man who wants to find himself in art. I hope that by the seventh story he may find himself both in art and self-knowledge. . . . there will be a collection about him. I am moved by him, and can only write about him when I am so moved. I have great affection for these stories; you know, they bring real belly laughs when read aloud.[3]

A comment by Malamud from Haskell Frankel's 1966 interview-article.

My work, all of it, is an idea of dedication to the human. That's basic to every book. If you don't respect man, you cannot respect my work. I'm in defense of the human.[4]

Excerpts from Malamud's 1967 article, "Theme, Content and the 'New Novel.'"

What the matter boils down to, I think, is that a "mighty theme" is useful only when it inspires a good writer to an unusual response; when it proliferates possibilities in every thought. If a writer is, as an individual, moved by themes that may be called "mighty," obviously it will pay him to involve himself with one, a task that isn't so simple, because the mighty themes have been used again and again, and he must struggle to discover how they can be presented in such a way as to seem new. Since times change but not, essentially, man, the old themes have the force of both the contemporary and the eternal. . . .

Theme discovered—one doesn't clip it out of a book or newspaper and paste it on the page—may lead to understanding essence, hence to crystallizing style, and form. If the theme, inartistically handled, hardens to exoskeleton, or drips like printer's ink from the center of the fiction—if, in other words, it has become "message"—then the failure is of the art. The existence of theme, contrary to the thinking of some who want fiction refined almost to pure form, does not contaminate the work. Theme achieves the formal value in art that only an artist can give it. It is evolved from understanding, knowledge, evaluation of experience, though the mind that invents theme is not necessarily present as the inventor. . . .

The purpose of the "new novel," according to Robbe-Grillet, . . . is "to construct a world more solid and more immediate" rather than "a universe of signification"—to present, in other words, what is there, without interpretation, hence to invent a form "capable of expressing (or of creating) new relations between man and the world." As a writer I welcome the invention of new forms that may bring the novel to greater power, but I cannot welcome a theory of the novel that ultimately diminishes the value of a writer's experience, historical and personal, by limiting its use in fiction. . . .

I welcome, as I said before, the seeking for new forms in fiction. However, no form dies; they are all eternally available to the artist to use in a manner original to him. He reinvents them as he uses them. A 19th-century form used by a 20th-century writer becomes a 20th-century form. Nothing is outdated if it creates art. The best form for an artist is that which compels him to use his greatest strength.[5]

Excerpts from Israel Shenker's 1971 interview-article. (Shenker's comments are in brackets.)

[He has a hunger to achieve order for the day.] What would throw me would be a day when I had planned to write and couldn't. So it isn't "O God, I'm writing!" but "O God, I'm not writing."

[An average day ends with half a page, a page, occasionally two.] Sometimes you hit it big and knock off five pages . . . usually dialogue.

[For Malamud, fiction is an effort of the imagination to create a world, not simply recall it.]

Sometimes I'll start a first draft to see if it'll go anywhere. If, after a short journey, it looks meager, I won't go on. I don't, as a rule, start a novel without a body of prior experience—a richness of notes that gives me enough to work with and enrich further.

With me it's story, story, story. Writers who can't invent stories often pursue other strategies, even substituting style for narrative. I feel that story is the basic element of fiction—though the idea is not popular with disciples of the "new novel." They remind me of the painter who couldn't paint people, so he painted chairs.

The story will be with us as long as man is. You know that, in part, because of its effect on children. It's through story they realize that mystery won't kill them. Through story they learn they have a future. . . .

A Malamud character is someone who fears his fate, is caught up in it, yet manages to outrun it. He's the subject and object of laughter and pity.[6]

Some comments by Malamud in Joyce and Leslie Field's 1973 interview-essay.

I don't believe in the supernatural except as I can invent it. Nor do I look for a "neutral ground" for my fiction. I write fantasy because when I do I am imaginative and funny and having a good time. . . .

[Kafka] writes well. He moves me. He makes me want to write well and move my readers. Other writers have had a similar effect. I guess what I'm trying to say is that I'm influenced by literature. . . .

I think I said "All men are Jews except they don't know it." I doubt I expected anyone to take the statement literally. But I think it's an understandable statement and a metaphoric way of indicating how history, sooner or later, treats all men. . . .

I did make use of what might be called Chagallean imagery in "The Magic Barrel." I did so intentionally in that story, but I've not done it again in any other piece of fiction, and I feel that some critics make too much of Chagall as an image maker in my work. Chagall, as a painter, doesn't mean as much to me as Matisse, for instance. Painting helps me to see with greater clarity the multifarious world and to depict it simply. . . .

It's [the prison motif] a metaphor for the dilemma of all men throughout history. Necessity is the primary prison, though the bars are not visible to all. Then there are the man-made prisons of social injustice, apathy, ignorance. There are others, tight or loose, visible or invisible, according to one's predilection of vulnerability. Therefore our most extraordinary invention is human freedom. . . .

It [the life versus art theme] isn't life versus art necessarily; it's life *and* art. On Fidelman's tombstone read: "I kept my finger in art." The point is I don't have any large thoughts of life versus art; I try to deepen any given situation. . . .

Right after I wrote "The Last Mohican" in Rome in 1957, I worked out an outline of other Fidelman stories, the whole to develop one theme in the form of a picaresque novel. Why do it the same way all the time?

I used my mother's maiden name because I needed a name I liked. . . .

I would never deliberately flatten a character to create a stereotype. . . . Most of all I'm out to create real and passionate human beings. I do as much as I can with a character. I may not show him in full blast every moment, but before the end of a fiction he has had a chance to dance his dance. . . .

They're [the stories of *Rembrandt's Hat*] the stories of an older man than the one who wrote *The Magic Barrel* and *Idiots First,* possibly a man who knows more than he did ten or fifteen years ago. . . .

There is comedy in my vision of life. To live sanely one must discover—or invent it. Consider the lilies of the field; consider the Jewish lily that toils and spins.[7]

Excerpts from Curt Leviant's 1974 interview-essay.

Leviant: What role does the Jewish tradition play in your work? . . .

Malamud: I would say that my subject matter mixes the universal and the particularly Jewish. Some borderline figures in my work act under the influence of their Jewish background. I write about Jews because I know them. I'm comfortable with them. The interest in ethicality by the Jews has always excited me. The struggle against self is a basic struggle. Almost anything one reads touches on this. Also, the history of the Jews is a great drama. Obviously, it's not one of pure darkness. I also like Jewish history as a metaphor for the fate of all men. . . .

Leviant: What besides their names and milieu makes your characters Jewish?

Malamud: Their Jewish qualities, the breadth of their vision, their kind of fate, their morality, their life; their awareness, responsibility, intellectuality, and ethicality. Their love of people and God. Someone said recently that my characters are God-haunted.

Leviant: God-haunted? I had supposed man-haunted was more accurate.

Malamud: There are some characters who believe strongly in God. And let me add that I don't feel inhibited in inventing God-haunted characters, which has nothing to do with whether or not I am or am not religious.

Leviant: Would you like to speak on how one of your stories came to be written? . . .

Malamud: I don't like to explain my stories, and as a rule I won't comment on interpretations of my fiction, so that students will feel free to interpret it as they please. I like imaginative interpretations of my books whether I agree with them or not, so long as they are consistent and make sense.

Leviant: If the characters in "Talking Horse" had had general American or, let's say, Irish names, would you have had a different tale?

Malamud: Yes, but I still might have had a Jewish story. Richard Fein, the critic, once wrote that there are three ingredients to a Jewish story. It has to have a horse, a victim, and loose technique. Since "Talking Horse" has all of these, I suppose it may be defined as a Jewish story. However, I don't think that's very important.

Leviant: Why, then, did you choose to make the heroes of "Talking Horse" Jews?

Malamud: Because I write easily of Jews. Of course, "Talking Horse" has some relation with the Book of Jonah, and also to the Old Testament beyond the Book of Jonah. Incidentally, "Jewbird" . . . led to "Talking Horse," and I plan to do a third story with a talking animal, probably a short story.

Leviant: Could you categorize your stories as falling into any of these groups: stories from real life, stories spurred by other fiction, stories purely imaginative?

Malamud: A combination of these. . . .

Leviant: Wasn't ["The Silver Crown"] based on a news item, late in 1972, that two hasidic faith healers had been arrested in the Bronx for conning Jews out of their money with false promises of miracles?

Malamud: Yes, it was taken from the *New York Times*. However, all the characters are mine.

Leviant: In one of Hawthorne's prefaces, he defines romance as "a neutral territory somewhere between the real world and the fairyland, where the actual and the imaginary meet." Elsewhere, he states that romance is a piece of writing "wherein the author mingles the marvelous rather as a slight delicate evanescent flavor . . . in which there is some legendary mist which the reader may either disregard . . . or allow to float imperceptibly for the sake of picturesque effect." Can this version of romance as a genre of fiction be applied to your stories?

Malamud: I believe that the line with Hawthorne exists, and so does one with Henry James which critics recently commented upon. . . .

Leviant: Some of your magnificent endlines sound as though they might have been the spurs to the entire story. (For example, the first epigraph in *Rembrandt's Hat*, "And an old white horse galloped away in the meadow," is by T. S. Eliot.) Have you ever constructed a story from an endline?

Malamud: Yes, I have had experiences of this sort. However, I re-read the line from Eliot's "Journey of the Magi" after "Talking Horse" had been written. . . .

Leviant: Do you see an inner cohesiveness, a miniature world, in your works? . . .

Malamud: I like to be told that I've created a world.[8]

Excerpts from Daniel Stern's 1975 interview-essay.

Malamud: The movies tickled my imagination. As a writer I learned from Charlie Chaplin.

Stern: What in particular?

Malamud: Let's say the rhythm, the snap of comedy; the reserved comic presence—that beautiful distancing; the funny with sad; the surprise of surprise.

Stern: Please go on about your life.

Malamud: . . . In sum, once I was twenty and not so young, now I'm sixty inclined on the young side.

Stern: Which means?

Malamud: Largely the life of imagination, and doing pretty much what I set out to do. I made my mistakes, took my lumps, learned. I've resisted ignorance, limitations, obsessions. I'm freer than I was. I'd rather write it than talk. I love the privileges of form. . . .

Sometimes I have to tell [student writers] their talents are thin—not to waste their lives writing third-rate fiction.

Stern: Fidelman as a painter? The doubtful talent?

Malamud: Yes. Among other things it is a book about finding a vocation. . . .

Stern: In *Fidelman* and *The Tenants* you deal with artists who can't produce, or produce badly. Why does the subject interest you so much? Have you ever been blocked?

Malamud: Never. Even in anxiety I've written, though anxiety, because it is monochromatic, may limit effects. I like the drama of non-productivity, especially where there may be talent. It's an interesting ambiguity: the force of the creative life versus the paralysis caused by the insults, the confusions of life. . . .

Genius, after it has got itself together, may give out with a *Ulysses* or *Remembrance of Things Past*. One doesn't have to imitate the devices of Joyce or Proust, but if you're not a genius, imitate the daring. If you are a genius, assert yourself, in art and humanity.

Stern: Humanity? Are you suggesting art is moral?

Malamud: It tends toward morality. It values life. Even when it doesn't it tends to. My former colleague, Stanley Edgar Hyman, used to say that even the act of creating a form is a moral act. That leaves out something, but I understand and like what he was driving at. It's close to Frost's definition of a poem as "a momentary stay against confusion." Morality begins with an awareness of the sanctity of one's life, hence the lives of others—even Hitler's to begin with—the sheer privilege of being, in this miraculous cosmos, and trying to figure out why. Art, in essence, celebrates life and gives us our measure.

Stern: It changes the world?

Malamud: It changes me. It affirms me.

Stern: Really?

Malamud: (*laughs*) It helps. . . .

Perhaps I use it [the prison motif] as a metaphor for the dilemma of all men: necessity, whose bars we look through and try not to see. Social injustice, apathy, ignorance. The personal prison of entrapment in past experience, guilt, obsession—the somewhat blind or blinded self, in other words. A man has to construct, invent, his freedom. Imagination helps. A truly great man or woman extends it for others in the process of creating his or her own.

Stern: Does this idea or theme, as you call it, come out of your experience as a Jew?

Malamud: That's probably in it—a heightened sense of prisoner of history, but there's more to it than that. I conceive this as the major battle of life, to transcend the self—extend one's realm of freedom.

Stern: Not all your characters do.

Malamud: Obviously. But they're all more or less engaged in the enterprise.

Stern: Humor is so much a part of your work. Is this an easy quality to deal with? Is one problem that the response to humor is so much a question of individual taste?

Malamud: The funny bone is universal. I doubt humorists think of individual taste when they're enticing the laugh. With me humor comes unexpectedly, usually in defense of a character, sometimes because I need cheering up. When something starts funny I can feel my imagination eating and running. I love the distancing—the guise of invention—that humor gives fiction. Comedy, I imagine, is harder to do consistently than tragedy, but I like it spiced in the wine of sadness.

Stern: What about suffering? It's a subject much in your early work.

Malamud: I'm against it but when it occurs why waste the experience?

Stern: Are you a Jewish writer? . . .

Malamud: I'm an American, I'm a Jew, and I write for all men. A novelist has to be or he's built himself a cage. I write about Jews, when I write about Jews, because they set my imagination going. I know something about their history, the quality of their experience and belief, and of their literature, though not as much as I would like. Like many writers I'm influenced especially by the Bible, both Testaments. I respond in particular to the East European immigrants of my father's and mother's generation; many of them were Jews of the Pale as described by the classic Yiddish writers. And of course I've been deeply moved by the Jews of the concentration camps, and the refugees wandering from nowhere to nowhere. I'm concerned about Israel. Nevertheless, Jews like Rabbis Kahane and Korff set my teeth on edge. Sometimes I make characters Jewish because I think I will understand them better as people, not because I am out to prove anything. That's a qualification. Still another is that I know that, as a writer, I've been influenced by Hawthorne, James, Mark Twain, Hemingway, more than I have been by Sholem Aleichem and I. L. Peretz, whom I read with pleasure. Of course I admire and have been moved by other writers, Dostoyevsky and Chekhov, for instance, but the point I'm making is that I was born in America and respond, in American life, to more than Jewish experience. . . .

Stern: Do characters ever run away from you and take on identities you hadn't expected?

Malamud: My characters run away but not far. Their guise is surprises.

Stern: Let's go to Fidelman. You seem to like to write about painters.

Malamud: I know a few. I love painting.

Stern: Rembrandt and who else?

Malamud: Too many to name, but Cézanne, Monet, and Matisse, very much, among Modernists.

Stern: Chagall?

Malamud: Not that much. He rides his nostalgic nag to death. . . .

After I wrote ["The Last Mohican"] in Rome I jotted down ideas for several incidents in the form of a picaresque novel. I was out to loosen up—experiment a little—with narrative structure. And I wanted to see, if I wrote it at intervals—as I did from 1957 to 1968—whether the passing of time and mores would influence his life. I did not think of the narrative as merely a series of related stories because almost at once I had the structure of a novel in mind and each part had to fit that form. Robert Scholes in the *Saturday Review* has best explained what I was up to in Fidelman.

Stern: Did you use all the incidents you jotted down?

Malamud: No.

Stern: Can you give me an example of one you left out?

Stern: Yes, Fidelman administering to the dying Keats in Rome—doing Severn's job, one of the few times in his life that our boy is engaged in a purely unselfish act, or acts. But I felt I had no need to predict a change in him, especially in a sort of dream sequence, so I dropped the idea. The painting element was to come in via some feverish watercolors of John Keats, dying.

Stern: Fidelman is characterized by some critics as a schlemiel.

Malamud: Not accurately. Peter Schlemiel lost his shadow and suffered the consequences for all time. Not Fidelman. He does better. He escapes his worse fate. I dislike the schlemiel characterization as a taxonomical device. I said somewhere that it reduces to stereotypes people of complex motivations and fates. One can often behave like a schlemiel without being one. . . .

Stern: You've done two short stories and a novel about blacks. Where do you get your material?

Malamud: Experience and books. I lived on the edge of a black neighborhood in Brooklyn when I was a boy. I played with blacks in the Flatbush Boys Club. I had a friend—Buster; we used to go to his house every so often. I swiped dimes so we could go to the movies together on a couple of Saturday afternoons. After I was married I taught for a year in a black evening high school in Harlem. The short stories derive from that period. I also read black fiction and history. . . .

Stern: Will you predict how it will be between blacks and Jews in the future?

Malamud: How can one? All I know is that American blacks have been badly treated. We, as a society, have to redress the balance. Those who want for others must expect to give up something. What we get in return is the affirmation of what we believe in.

Stern: You give a sense in your fiction that you try not to repeat yourself?

Malamud: Good. In my books I go along the same paths in different worlds.

Stern: What's the path—theme?

Malamud: Derived from one's sense of values, it's a vision of life, a feeling for people—real qualities in imaginary worlds.

Stern: Do you like writing short stories more than you do novels?

Malamud: Just as much, though the short story has its own pleasures. I like packing a self or two into a few pages, predicating lifetimes. The drama is terse, happens faster, and is often outlandish. A short story is a way of indicating the complexity of life in a few pages, producing the surprise and effect of a profound knowledge in a short time. There's, among other things, a drama, a resonance of the reconciliation of opposites: much to say, little time to say it, something like the effect of a poem.

Stern: You write them between novels?

Malamud: Yes, to breathe, and give myself time to think what's in the next book. Sometimes I'll try a character or situation similar to that in a new novel.[9]

A comment from a short autobiography Malamud contributed to the 1975 World Authors article about him.

I had written a few stories in college but after graduation began to write again. The rise of totalitarianism, the Second World War, and the situation of the Jews in Europe helped me to come to what I wanted to say as a writer.[10]

A comment by Malamud from Mary Long's 1976 interview-article.

Narrative tries to find the way from one condition into another more blessed.[11]

Excerpts from Ralph Tyler's 1979 interview-article. (Unquoted text is Tyler.)

Dubin's Lives is dedicated to Max and Bertha Malamud, the author's parents, and to Anna Fidelman, the widow of an uncle[;] . . . Asked what his parents were like, Malamud at first replied that this was too complex to deal with, but after a long pause said they were "simple, feelingful, troubled, human." . . . In his view, some people have over-emphasized the impact of Yiddish on his prose. "What I actually do best is what I would call immigrant English." He concedes, however, that he salts his dialogue with idioms that have the quality of Yiddish. As for his word order, which sometimes varies from the traditional, he says that this anomaly might derive as much from Latin or German as from Yiddish. And he believes it is to Hemingway more than Yiddish that he owes his ability to compress. . . .

Mr. Malamud was taken aback by one final question: Does literature do any good? He started by saying: "It elevates, enriches, changes and, in some cases, reveals the meaning of life. In some cases, it makes you want to change your life."[12]

A Comment by Malamud from Michiko Kakutani's 1982 interview-article.

The writer does not have to be defeated by events and losses as time goes by. It's possible to dig within the self and find something new. . . . In other words, you gain new ways of saying old things. What you may lose in complexity, you may make up for in the force of simplicity. What you may lose in terms of words, you make up in understanding.[13]

Excerpts from Malamud's introduction to his 1983 The Stories of Bernard Malamud.

One day I began to write seriously: my writing had begun to impress me. Years of all sorts had gone by. The annunciation had long since tolled and the response was slow awakening. Much remained to do and become, if there was time. Some are born whole; others must seek this blessed state in a struggle to achieve order. That is no loss to speak of; ultimately such seeking becomes the subject matter of fiction. Observing, reading, thinking, one invents himself. A familiar voice asks: Who am I, and how can I say what I have to? He reads his sentences to see if the words answer the question. Thus the writer may tell his fortune. His imagination impels him to speak in several tongues though one is sufficient. At this point he, or she, may begin to write a story, a daring endeavor. . . .

New York had lost much of its charm during World War II, and my wife and I and our infant son took off for the Pacific Northwest when I was offered a job in Corvallis, Oregon. Once there, it was a while before I had my bearings. I was overwhelmed by the beauty of Oregon, its vast skies, forests, coastal beaches; and the new life it offered, which I lived as best I could as I reflected on the old. My almost daily writing—I taught three days a week and wrote the other four—helped me to make reasonable choices: what to zero in on and what to omit. On the whole I was learning much about America and holding fast to the discipline of the writing life.

Yet, almost without understanding why, I was thinking about my father's immigrant life—how he earned his meager living and what he paid for it, and about my mother's, diminished by fear and suffering—as perhaps matter for my fiction. In other words, I had them in mind as I invented the characters who became their fictional counterparts. . . .

At this time I was sharing an office with a colleague who often wished aloud that he were a Jew. I understood the sentiment. I was glad I was, although my father had his doubts about that. He had sat in mourning when I married my gentile wife, but I had thought it through and felt I knew what I was doing. After the birth of our son my father came gently to greet my wife and touch his grandchild. I thought of him as I began *The Assistant* and felt I would often be writing about Jews, in celebration and expiation, though perhaps that was having it both ways. I wanted it both ways. I conceived of myself as a cosmopolitan man enjoying his freedom. . . .

Almost from the beginning of my career as a writer I have more or less alternated writing novels with periods of work on short stories. I like the change of pace and form. I've enjoyed working in both forms—prose makes specific demands—although I confess having been longer in love with short fiction. If one begins early in life to make up and tell stories he has a better chance to be heard out if he keeps them short. *"Vus hoks du mir a chinik?"* (What tune are you banging on your pot?) my father once asked me when I went into a long tale about my mother's cousin.

Writing the short story, if one has that gift, is a good way to begin writing seriously. It demands form as it teaches it, although I've met some who would rather not be taught. They say that the demands of form interfere with their freedom to express themselves. But no good writer writes only as he pleases. He writes for a purpose, an idea, an effect; he writes to make himself understood and felt. I'm for freedom of thought, but one must recognize that it doesn't necessarily lead to art. Free thought may come close to self-deceit. One pays for free thought in the wrong cause if it intrudes, interferes with the logic of language and construction—if it falls like a hammer blow on the head as one is attempting to work out his fiction. Standards diluted at the start may exact a mean toll. Not many "make it" as serious writers of fiction, especially those who think of form as a catchword. Elitism in a just cause has its merits. Some in art have, by definition, to be best. There are standards in literature that a would-be writer must become familiar with—must uphold: as in the work of the finest writers of the past. The best endures in the accomplishment of the masters. One will be convinced, if he or she reads conscientiously and widely, that form as ultimate necessity is the basis of literature. . . .

Some writers don't need the short story to launch them into fiction, but I think it is a loss not to attempt to find out whether one can write them. I love the pleasures of the short story. One of them is the fast payoff. Whatever happens happens quickly. The writer mounts his personal Pegasus, even if it is an absent-minded nag who never made it on the race track; an ascension occurs and the ride begins. The scenery often surprises, and so do some of the people one meets. Somewhere I've said that a short story packs a self into a few pages predicating a lifetime. The drama is tense, happens fast, and is more often than not outlandish. In a few pages a good story portrays the complexity of a life while producing the surprise and effect of knowledge—not a bad payoff.

Then the writer is into the story for more than the ride. He stays with it as the terrain opens and events occur; he takes pleasure in the evolving fiction and tries to foresee its just resolution. As soon as his characters sense his confidence they show him their tricks. Before he knows it he becomes a figure in a circus with a boom-boom band. This puts him in high spirits and good form. If he's lucky, serious things may seem funny.

Much occurs in the writing that isn't expected, including some types you meet and become attached to. Before you know it you've collected two or three strangers swearing eternal love and friendship before they begin to make demands that divide and multiply. García Márquez will start a fiction with someone pushing a dream around, or running from one, and before you know it he has peopled a small country. Working alone to create stories, despite serious inconveniences, is not a bad way to live our human loneliness.

And let me say this: Literature, since it values man by describing him, tends toward morality in the same way that Robert Frost's poem is "a momentary stay against confusion." Art celebrates life and gives us our measure.

I've lived long among those I've invented.

"Good morning, professor. Are you by chance looking for a bride, I offer only the best quality."

"I've got one, Salzman, but if she should come with other plans I'll let you know. In the meantime, I'm hard at work on a new story."

"So enjoy," said Salzman.[14]

Selections from a public lecture Malamud gave at Bennington College in 1984.

And though I was often lonely [in Washington, in 1940], I stayed in the rooming house night after night trying to invent stories I needn't be ashamed of.

One night, after laboring in vain for hours attempting to bring a short story to life, I sat up in bed at an open window looking at the stars after a rainfall. Then I experienced a wave of feeling, of heartfelt emotion bespeaking commitment to life and art, so deeply it brought tears to my eyes. For the hundredth time I promised myself that I would someday be a very good writer. This renewal, and others like it, kept me alive in art years from fulfillment. I must have been about twenty-five then, and was still waiting in my fashion, for the true writing life to begin. I'm reminded of Kafka's remark in his mid-twenties: "God doesn't want me to write, but I must write." . . .

We left in late August 1956 for Italy. On board the S.S. *Constitution* I spent hours studying the horizon, enjoying the sight of ocean as the beginning of a more profound adventure, amid thoughts of new writing. One night we passed our sister ship, the S.S. *America*, steaming along in the mid-Atlantic, all decks alight. I felt I was on the verge of a long celebration.

I was ready for a broader kind of living with as much range in writing as I could manage. Before leaving Oregon to go abroad, I had completed *The Assistant*, and had begun to develop several of the stories that became *The Magic Barrel*, some of which I wrote in Rome.

Italy unrolled like a foreign film; what was going on before my eyes seemed close to unreality. An ancient city seemed to be alive in present time. It was larger than life, yet defined itself as our new life. I felt the need to live in a world that was more than my world to live in. I walked all over the city. I walked in the ghetto. I met Italian Jews who had been tortured by the Nazis; one man held up his hand to show his finger-shorn fist. I felt I was too much an innocent American. I wandered along Roman streets and studied Roman faces, hoping to see what they saw when they looked; I wanted to know more of what they seemed to know. On All Soul's, I walked in the Campo Verano cemetery. I visited the Ardeatine Caves where the Nazis had slaughtered Italians and Jews. Rome had its own sad way of sharing Jewish experience.

Mornings I walked my eight-year-old son to Piazza Bologna where he took his bus to the American school. At noon, after finishing my morning's work, I picked up my four-year-old daughter at her kindergarten. She would hand me her drawings as we walked home. Home was 88 Via Michelo Di Lando, not far from where Mussolini had lived with Clara Petacci, his mistress. We had made friends of our landlords. Mr. Gianolla was an old Socialist who had been forced to swallow castor oil by Mussolini's Fascist thugs. His wife, thin and energetic, talkative, courteous, was one of the rare women university graduates of her time. . . .

I have written almost all my life. My writing has drawn, out of a reluctant soul, a measure of astonishment at the nature of life. And the more I wrote well, the better I felt I had to write.

In writing I had to say what had happened to me, yet present it as though it had been magically revealed. I began to write seriously when I had taught myself the discipline necessary to achieve what I wanted. When I touched that time, my words announced themselves to me. I have given my life to writing, without regret, except when I consider what might have been done better. I wanted my writing to be as good as it must be, and on the whole I think it is. I would write a book, or a short story, at least three times—once to understand, the second time to improve the prose, and a third to compel it to say what it still must say.

Somewhere I put it this way: first drafts are for learning what one's fiction wants him to say. Revision works with that knowledge to enlarge and enhance an idea, to re-form it. Revision is one of the exquisite pleasures of writing: "The men and things of today are wont to lie fairer and truer in tomorrow's meadow," Henry Thoreau said.

I don't regret the years I put into my work. Perhaps I regret the fact that I was not two men, one who could live a full life apart from writing; and one who lived in art, exploring all he had to experience and know how to make his work right; yet not regretting that he had put his life into the art of perfecting the work.[15]

Notes

1. Joseph Wershba, "Not Horror but 'Sadness,'" *New York Post*, 14 September 1958, M2.

2. "The Writer's Task," in *Writing in America*, ed. John Fischer and Robert B. Silvers (New Brunswick, N.J.: Rutgers University Press, 1960), 173.

3. "Interview with Bernard Malamud," *New York Times Book Review*, 13 October 1963, 5.

4. Haskell Frankell, "Bernard Malamud,' '*Saturday Review* 49 (10 September 1966):40.

5. "Theme Content and the 'New Novel,'" *New York Times Book Review*, 8 October 1967, 2.

6. Israel Shenker, "For Malamud It's Story," *New York Times Book Review*, 3 October 1971, 20.

7. Leslie Field and Joyce Field, "An Interview with Bernard Malamud," in *Bernard Malamud: A Collection of Critical Essays* (Englewood Cliffs, N.J.: Prentice-Hall, 1975), 10–16.

8. Curt Leviant, "Bernard Malamud: My Characters Are God Haunted," *Hadassah Magazine* 55, no. 10 (June 1974):19.

9. Daniel Stern, "The Art of Fiction: Bernard Malamud," *Paris Review* 61 (Spring 1975):44–62.

10. In *World Authors, 1950–1970: A Companion Volume to Twentieth-Century Authors*, ed. John Wakeman (New York: H. H. Wilson, 1975), 917.

11. Mary Long, "Interview: Bernard Malamud," *Mademoiselle* 82 (August 1976): 235.

12. Ralph Tyler, "A Talk with the Novelist," *New York Times Book Review*, 18 February 1979, 33–34.

13. Michiko Kakutani, "As the Author Grows Up," *New York Times Book Review*, 25 July 1982, 24.

14. *The Stories of Bernard Malamud* (New York: Farrar, Straus & Giroux, 1983), vii–xiii.

15. "Long Work, Short Life," *Michigan Quarterly Review* 26, no. 4 (Fall 1987): 602–11.

Part 3

THE CRITICS

Introduction

The urgency and originality of Malamud's fiction has excited an immense critical response. In his *Bernard Malamud: A Reference Guide,* Joel Salzberg annotates 857 reviews, interviews, articles, sections of books, and whole books (including theses and dissertations) published between 1952 and 1983 that deal in one way or another with Malamud's stories and novels. If perhaps forty of the listings are reprints, more critical efforts than this have appeared since 1983, and I have come across a few interviews and articles that Salzberg missed. Quite a bit of the criticism is acute, particularly so since a fair number of our best interpreters of fiction have written repeatedly on Malamud's work. Out of this embarrassment of riches I've chosen reminiscences by two of our leading fiction writers, Philip Roth and Cynthia Ozick, both of whom have a good deal to say about Malamud's fiction achievement and the man himself. I've also chosen parts of studies by Theodore Solotaroff and Mark Shechner, selections that argue in turn for the rocklike solidity of Malamud's moral vision, and for the way that the passage of years has revealed how the vision was compromised by the warring tensions within the author. To these four differing appraisals of Malamud's significance, I've added Charles Angoff's eccentric and provocative dismissal. Then there are helpful close readings of "The Bill" and "Talking Horse"—two of the best representatives of Malamud's early and late short fiction.

Bernard Malamud's Fiction: The Old Life and the New

*Theodore Solotaroff**

I would say that Bernard Malamud has been a writer almost unique in our time. He has found the objects and idiom and viewpoint that allow him to see the will directly and portray its commitment to moral struggle. While the work of other contemporary novelists has been seriously affected by the forces of fragmentation and cynicism that demoralize our lives and efforts, the best of Malamud's has stood against these forces by resolutely ignoring them. Most often, and in his most characteristic fiction, he has created a type of half-legendary world in the middle of New York City—the Malamud province of moral comedy and affirmation. In this spectral province, with its familiar streets and strange interiors, live a few lost souls with Jewish names, their figures deeply etched by their creator's fantasy. But their needs are so simple and so complete that fundamental human feelings and values can be insistently expressed and defined. This original folk poetry has been obviously inspired by the Jewish immigrant experience and the ghetto sensibility. Yet its main significance has not been in its Jewishness. Malamud's creation has signified, as Norman Podhoretz so well said when he reviewed *The Magic Barrel*, "an act of spiritual autonomy perfect enough to persuade us that the possibility of freedom from the determinings of history and sociology still exists."

The province in which Malamud's characters live is not a simple place. Morris Bober, the moral exemplar in *The Assistant*, goes to his death with the realization that "I gave my life away for nothing. It was the thunderous truth." Nor is there anything very reassuring about the fate of the two characters in "Take Pity" who both are eventually driven to suicide by the difficulties of extending and accepting charity. And in "The Magic Barrel," love finally comes to the careful Rabbi Finkle in the person of a whore. Malamud's figures have, or gain, an expert knowledge of suffering, whether in the flesh from poverty and illness, or in the mind from frustration and remorse. Character is almost invariably formed by hunger, and at twenty-three a pretty girl already

*Reprinted by permission from *Commentary* 33, no. 3 (March 1962): 197–201.

fights "a sense of mourning to a practiced draw." Malamud's Jews (and his Gentiles) are connected to each other not by religious and social ties but by a common fate of error and ill luck and sorrow, of having lost much by their mistakes and recovered little by their virtues. The back streets of life become a kind of timeless depressed area, where dying men go begging for money to send idiot sons to California and bakers weep in their bread; when their children manage to escape to the modern world, they carry the ghetto's aches with them.

It is an implacably comic world of absurd reversals and last straws and of uncertain stairs that lead seemingly nowhere. But this antic world is shaped by a tough and subtle intelligence in the service of an embattled ethic. Its people are not charming or vigorous; they are usually too impoverished to represent any real range of contemporary human possibilities. But their lives are suffused with a directing earnestness that we miss in ours and are formed from assurances that ours are increasingly without—the assurances that principles matter, that the "soft" facts of life are more important than the "hard," that there are ways men can change themselves and become free, if not rich.

From where do these assurances come? Most of the figures who contain them are unassimilated Jews, which is less to the point than one sometimes likes to think. The truth is that Malamud's Jews are creatures of a particular moral vision which is as accessible to Christians as to Jews. To be sure, one can make (as Malamud sometimes explicitly does) a correlation between the nature of their lives and of Jewish experience and values, particularly of the East European Pale where history preserved the extremities of deprivation, irony, and idealism in a virtually pure and congruous form. Yet Jewishness is a source of Malamud's sensibility rather than the object: just as his characters are almost entirely detached from any real Jewish community—of the past or of the present—so are the causes and purposes of their suffering. There are times when Malamud's feelings for the immigrant Jewish melancholy and ethos, and for its idiom and wit, produce an objectification such as the story of "The Magic Barrel." But, in general, the sense of the ghetto experience is abstracted from the communal life in which its social and religious meanings were embedded. Malamud's Jewishness is a type of metaphor—for anyone's life—both for the tragic dimension of anyone's life and for a code of personal morality and salvation that is more psychological than religious. To the extent that the Jew and his problems become a way of envisaging the human condition, he becomes more symbol than fact, fashioned to the service of an abstraction. Hence, when, at the end of *The Assistant*, Frank Alpine gets circumcised and becomes a Jew, the whole point is not that he will now *daven* or move into a neighborhood that has a synagogue but that he has confirmed his investiture of a set of moral attitudes. In effect, the Malamud Jew is partly Jew and partly construct—a way of viewing the relation of the conscience to deprivation and love, of exploring the resources and process by which, as Ihab Hassan phrases it, "a man can become a *mensch.*"

Which is to say that for all the homely trappings and Yiddishisms of his fiction, Malamud is nevertheless a modern American writer—detached, introspective, preoccupied with the problems of contactlessness and self-integration, for which each man's experience is his own gospel, *"Each in his prison / Thinking of the key each confirms a prison"*: the lines from Eliot suggest the burden of Malamud's vision, the consistency with which his chief figures are confronted less by the world than by themselves. . . .

Most modern literature has conditioned us to accept the idea that a man's limitations are the main truth about him. The technique of modern fiction, stemming from Flaubert and Joyce, has been designed to discover these limitations. If *The Assistant* came as a revelation as it did for me, partly the reason was that it restored a sense of the dynamics of character and of the older intention of fiction to show the ways men change. Despite its small compass and thinness of social reference, *The Assistant* could thus take on some of the power and clarity of the great 19th-century novels by the graphic depiction of Alpine's development from a bum to a man of principle.

That Malamud's fiction has been able to support its heavy moral interests is due to other resources as well. He has a particular gift for portraying the obsessive kinds of relationship that lead his characters into themselves, or otherwise dramatize the ambiguities of their hearts. The resonance of such brief tales as "The Loan," "The Bill," and "Take Pity" result mainly from Malamud's uncanny sense of what types of people belong in the same story, of the subtle and unexpected ways in which relations bind and influence. His sense of character, like his sense of episode and place, is rooted in a strong feeling for the bizarre—the kind of spiritual inventiveness and wit that creates a Negro *shul* and a debauched Negro angel named Levine. His imagination, in fact, seems most highly charged before the extremes of personal confrontation and crisis, and succeeds in authenticating by macabre comedy. Out of these situations come his semi-hallucinatory demons such as the *macher* in *The Assistant*, or Susskind in "The Last Mohican" or Salzman in "The Magic Barrel," who provide the electrifying quality of the Malamudian vision and allow the tone to fill out to the dimensions of the theme. Similarly the moments to which one assents in *The Natural* are usually those in which Malamud gives up the horseplay abut baseball and produces the tortured and truly wacky images of Hobb's inner life.

In general, the special achievement of Malamud's technique has been the movement back and forth between the grimly plain and the fantastic, the joining of the natural to the supernatural, and endowing his abstracted version of the commonplace with the entanglements of a dream. His most impressive prose has been a similar mixture of hard common speech, twisted by Yiddishisms or by his own syntax so that it vibrates, and lit here and there by a sudden lyrical image. The solidity of his best work has come from an obsessive mood and vision which from moment to moment seems to take the place of the realist's eye for physical detail. The slow, grueling development of Frank Alpine unfolds against the mood of the vacuous, mean neighborhood and of the mixed atmosphere of suffering and aspiration, discipline and defeat within the Bobers' milieu. Similarly, in his religious stories Malamud manages—as much by abstraction as by detail—to create a vividly spiritualized reality. A dying man in search of money for his idiot son, the *malach-ha-moves* [angel of death] who pursues and frustrates him, the bitter city streets, and the iron gates of Pennsylvania Station all come to belong, through the sustained unity of writing, to the same order of things.

The Bread of Tears: Malamud's "The Loan"

*Charles E. May**

The key to understanding the meaning and structure of Bernard Malamud's "The Loan" is embodied in Lieb's explanation of his prosperity: "One day, out of misery, he had wept into the dough. Thereafter his bread was such it brought customers in from everywhere." This microcosmic myth of the bread suggests the broad Jewish experience within which one must read the story. It echoes the Psalmist crying out in Psalm 80:5 about the misery of the Jews: "Thou feedest them with the bread of tears; and givest them tears to drink in great measure." The obvious irony of Lieb's crying into his bread to make it sell reflects the broader irony of the traditional Jewish experience of misery—an historical misery that instead of defeating one makes one strong.

Malamud suggests the power of misery in a different way by the arrival of Kobotsky. "If suffering had marked him, he no longer sought to conceal the sign; the shining was his own—him—now. So he frightened Bessie." Kobotsky frightens Bessie precisely because he is showing forth his misery. She knows from the instinct of her own Jewish experience of suffering that such a man is a threat because of the irresistibility of his sorrow. Lieb, covered with flour, is fleshy and jovial—in contrast to the gaunt Kobotsky. Although he resembles a "paunchy ghost," the real ghost through his flour-covered glasses is "Kobotsky, not he." And indeed Kobotsky is the ghost of Lieb's distant past "when they were at least young, and circumstances were—ah, different." As such, Kobotsky, "enthroned" in his superior position of present misery, places Lieb (Love) under the obligation of his name.

When Kobotsky finally asks Lieb for the two hundred dollar loan, Lieb recalls the "memoried outrage" of the lost and bitter hundred fifteen years ago and waits a "cruelly long time." But when he stares at Kobotsky's crippled hands and thinks of his own eyes cloudy with cataracts, he is united with Kobotsky's sickness and old age in the present just as he is united with him through their carefree youth in the past. Bessie, however, is not so united with Kobotsky's past. A second wife, she is not even united with Lieb's past. And jealous of

*Reprinted by permission from *Studies in Short Fiction* 7, no. 4 (Fall 1970):652–54.

the first wife's prerogatives within the framework of that past, she is suspicious and spiteful. Her face "like the inside of a loaf," she firmly refuses to allow the loan.

After Bessie and Lieb have argued bitterly about the loan—Bessie worrying about her own future security, and Lieb saying his money is worth nothing if he cannot share it with a friend—Kobotsky prepares to leave; but not before he can make his shining misery manifest. Revealing that he wants the loan to buy a tombstone for his dead wife, he recounts his five years of misery: first an operation, the second year imprisoned by arthritis, the third a widowed sister to support, the fourth incapacitated by boils, and now only making enough money to eat and sleep. Even Bessie is affected and Lieb thinks he has won and they will all sit down at the table and eat together. But Bessie, with an abrupt bit of one-upmanship, recites her own tale of affliction, that, coming as it does on the heels of Kobotsky's story, is almost comic in the extreme way it surpasses it: how the Bolsheviki killed her father, how her husband died of typhus, how her brother sacrificed himself and his family in one of Hitler's incinerators so that she could come to America. With this, the game is over. Both Lieb and Kobotsky realize it as Kobotsky holds his hands over his ears, and Lieb, having heard the story many times before, munches resignedly on a piece of bread. However, at this moment, Bessie, the mock tears streaming down her face, screeches and runs to throw open the oven door; and the mood of the story changes with a significant metaphor: "A cloud of smoke billowed out at her. The loaves in the trays were blackened bricks— charred corpses."

The effect of this powerful image on the reader is to remind him of several elements in the story at once. It is, of course, the culmination of all the references to the bread throughout the story. The bread of tears that became the bread of life for Lieb has now become the bread of death for Kobotsky—the death of his hope for the loan. But it is also an extension of the broad Jewish experience of misery—the gas ovens of the Nazi persecution and the charred corpses of millions of Jews. It recalls part of Bessie's story, that her brother sacrificed himself and his family in Hitler's incinerators to allow her to come to America and have a new life. Finally, it recalls the image of Kobotsky himself—the ghost or corpse searching for the money to buy a stone for the corpse of his wife.

All these implications of the "charred corpses" create a moral dilemma for the reader that reflects the moral dilemma of the characters within the story. It is true that Kobotsky's misery has given him the power to come and ask for the loan, just as it is true that Lieb's past misery has made him prosperous. But it is also true that it is Bessie's misery that has made her stronger than both men, that enables her to overcome both of them and deny the loan. For although misery can give one the capacity to understand and sympathize with the sorrow of others as it does Lieb, it can also make one burned out and hard like Bessie—can turn one into the brick-hard corpse she has become. However, even as the reader is tempted to judge Bessie harshly for her lack of compassion, he finds it difficult to do so; for what her choice amounts to is a decision to refuse the money for the sake of the dead wife and keep it for the sake of the living one. Recognizing this unresolvable moral situation—a situation that remembrance of their youthful and happy past cannot obviate—the two men can do nothing more. "Kobotsky and the baker embraced and sighed over their lost youth. They pressed mouths together and parted forever."

How "Jewish" Are Jewish Writers in America?

*Charles Angoff**

The three customary Jewish-American writers who are generally grouped together—because of their relative popularity among the reading public and because of their quondam favorable acceptance by a small section of the critics who happen to have an in with the influential media—are Bernard Malamud, Philip Roth and Saul Bellow. Not one of them has produced a single full-bodied authentic Jewish character, and not one of them has contributed much illumination on a single important Jewish issue or situation. Malamud has written some fairly good short stories, especially in his collection *The Magic Barrel and Other Stories*. And he has written three-quarters of a good novel, *The Assistant*, dealing with a *schlimazel* [born loser] of a Jewish grocer who has a wayward daughter on his hands. The grocer is depicted well, but the treatment of his troubles with his offspring, who compounds

*Reprinted from *Tradition* 16, no. 2 (1976): 31–32.

Mark Shechner

her problem by falling in love with a Christian, leaves much to be desired. The chief problem with Malamud seems to be that in depicting Jewish life he is pretty much of a *kalte neshome* (cold fish). He misses almost entirely the Jewish spirit, that marvelous combination of ebullience, transcendent morality, spiritual anarchism, the cosmic daring, the deep all-enveloping warmth of heart that is Jewishness. And he misses the laughter, the special Jewish *meshugas* [craziness], Jewish *ta'am* [zest, flavor]. These are all largely alien to him, it seems. . . .

Jewish Writers
*Mark Shechner**

Over the years, Malamud's staunch adherence to a claustral and depressive vision has tended to shift our focus from the common sentiments for which he once seemed to speak to those personal struggles his books now apparently express. True, novels such as *The Natural* and *The Assistant* and the stories in *The Magic Barrel* (1958) and *Idiots First* (1963) did speak for a certain mid-century climate of opinion and did appeal to principles of reading that have since passed out of vogue. Their persistent tone of admonition, their apolitical appeals to the individual best self, their blending of Yiddish dialect into medieval fertility myth in celebration of Judeo-Christian solidarity, and their wealth of reference to T. S. Eliot, Jessie Weston, Wagner, *Parzifal,* and the Bible now look like habits of thought peculiarly suited to an era that placed a premium on symbolism and orthodoxy. It is signficant that the start of the Kennedy era in 1961 saw the publication of *A New Life,* in which Malamud announced his readiness to cast off stodginess and to mount a critique of intellectual and political reaction[;] . . . By 1966, *The Fixer* was all for revolution—in czarist Russia, at any rate—and though its hero, Yakov Bok, is less a revolutionary than a conscientious objector, bombs nevertheless fly through the air on his behalf.

But in later years, though Malamud has tried to maintain an air of currency in *The Tenants* (1971), which is ostensibly about the black-white *Kulturkampf* in New York City, his voice has become increasingly

*Reprinted by permission from *Harvard Guide to Contemporary American Literature,* ed. Daniel Hoffman (Cambridge: Harvard University Press, 1979), 207–12.

private. In the wake of *Pictures of Fidelman* (1969), *The Tenants, Rembrandt's Hat* (1973), and *Dubin's Lives* (1979) Malamud sounds less than ever like a moral Everyman and more and more like a driven and eccentric writer. At times the civilized skin of his writing, its campaign for the whole checklist of humanist virtues for which Morris Bober had once been the spokesman, wears thin, and conflicts and anxieties that had previously been held in solution by the skillful application of narrative techniques and mythic frameworks come forward as open violence that quite overwhelms all moral implications and literary meanings. Earlier antagonists like Seymour Levin and Gerald Gilley (*A New Life*) or Frank Alpine and Morris Bober, may have wished to do away with each other but always wound up striking civilized, if bitter, *modi vivendi*, substituting mannered hostility for physical assault. But the main characters in *The Tenants* . . . just smash each other to bits, and Malamud apparently wants us to conclude that both get what they richly deserve.

The Tenants, whose ostensible message is mercy but whose innermost emotion is pure rage, highlights a long-standing discrepancy in Malamud's books between their didactic lessons and their deeper emotional ground rules: those dialectics of transgression and retribution that put his characters through their paces. . . .

"The Lady of the Lake" is a particularly straightforward rendition of a basic Malamudian story: sex denied and the denial moralized. Levin/Freeman, like Roy Hobbs, Frank Alpine, and numerous figures in the short stories, yearns for what he may not have or, since this dilemma is instructional, what might have been his had he played his cards right. But it need not be moral dereliction that intercepts pleasure: when fulfillment threatens, any intervention will do: the hero may have second thoughts and lose his appetite, or succumb to irruption of conscience or disgust, or find himself outmaneuvered by some rival on the road to release. To be tricked into self-betrayal by a Jewish princess, or shot down in a hotel by a maniacal temptress (*The Natural*), or put down by Helen Bober as an "uncircumcised dog" (*The Assistant*), or put off by a nubile temptress who at the point of consummation suddenly loses control of her bowels (*Dubin's Lives*) are only some of the more spectacular possibilities.

These tales of prurience and responsibility derive their power and interest from their underlying sense of sexual deadlock, out of which come those stunning, final tableaux in which the ambiguities of the story are framed and held fast. One thinks of Freeman clutching his moonlit stone, or Leo Finkle ("The Magic Barrel") rushing forward, bouquet in hand, to meet the girl of *his* dreams[;] . . . Indeed, where emotional symmetries are not meticulously adjusted and artistically controlled, we get mayhem instead of epiphany, as we do in *The Tenants*. But in the novels, generally the stalemate is grudgingly lifted and the hero released into a future that looks like an even more insidious entrapment. . . .

What is best about Malamud when he is at the top of his form are his intuitions about the unfulfilled life and his epiphanies of disappointment and loss; his frozen moments of the sinking heart. He is par excellence the writer of the half-life, the shabby region of mediocre attainment between pure wish fulfillment and total disaster, and he has perfect pitch for the language of poignancy and loss. He is also most spokesmanlike when drawing that life of quiet desperation which he sometimes places in the thirties but which is really a permanent feature of our national existence and the emotional underside of our prosperity. But poignancy is a small note on which to found a literature; it does not lend itself readily to sustained effects. As a result, Malamud's stories are generally more moving than his novels, and the novels more convincing in their momentary touches than in their sustained architecture.

Malamud's reluctance to serve up happy endings could be taken for moral realism of a sort, the sober assessment that life is tough, especially for a Jew, and moral compromise the essence of maturity. What removes their sobriety from realism but places it in the mainstream of Jewish sentiment is its puritan bias, which attaches personal fate to sexual conduct. Those Malamud heroes who suffer from history commonly encounter it through a woman, and their new lives are characteristically erotic quests that lead them to keyholes, transoms, and other furtive blinds for the ogling of their dream women. But the gap between their arousal and their fulfillment is never closed, leaving a space between hope and attainment in which their strange destinies can unfold. Sexual agony is Malamud's stock in trade. It is not, however, the standoff between the pleasure and reality principles that sets the moral curve of his fiction but the ambivalences of appetite itself; his characters are disappointed *because* they desire, and where they fail they do so because their desire either sabotages itself or is undercut by Malamud's own distaste for achievement. . . .

Malamud is a leading figure among the Jewish writers who specialize in ambivalence, and his conflicting cultural perspectives have led to the creation of improbable words. He has drawn heavily upon folkloric sources for his characters and situations while at the same time keeping an eye on modern life. He is both an inventor of sexual romances and a gloomy interpreter of modern experiences. The same dialectic may be found in Saul Bellow's writing, though there it seems the product of skillfully effected mergers that make it appear to arise neither out of the exigencies of culture nor out of the primal interior world of conflicts and anxieties, but out of his sensibility—the negotiating agency of his talent. But with Malamud we feel ourselves in the company of two writers: one who is responsible for the textures, the local realities, the English Departments and grocery stores that he portrays so well, and another who supplies the plots, the predicaments, the titillations, the fables, the moral ferocity, and, not incidentally, the dramatic tension. Little wonder, then, that his books seem so ambiguous, like real ghettoes with imaginary Jews in them.

Myth on Myth: Bernard Malamud's "The Talking Horse"

*Beth Burch and Paul W. Burch**

Bernard Malamud's "The Talking Horse" is a fantasy story permeated with ambiguity. "Am I a man in a horse or a horse that talks like a man?" muses Abramowitz in the opening sentence, introducing a perplexing duality that is never resolved. Throughout this unusual and sometimes bizarre story, Malamud meshes Greek myth and Judaic theology in the characters of Goldberg and Abramowitz, creating a crosshatching of mythologies and allusions which are as confounding as they are enlightening. . . . In this story, Goldberg is a Poseidon-God figure ruling over a freakish world of absurdities, and Abramowitz is a curious combination of horse-beast and dutiful son, as his name suggests.

Goldberg is remarkably similar to the Greek god of the sea, Poseidon. As the sea god's power is symbolized by his trident, so too is Goldberg characterized by a three-pronged spear which hangs on the

---

*Reprinted by permission from *Studies in Short Fiction* 16, no. 4 (Fall 1979); 350–53.

wall over a stuffed pony's head. Goldberg's trident is "mildewed," suggesting decay and stagnation[;] . . . Poseidon, thought to be responsible for earthquakes, was called "Earth-Shaker," but the vibrations that Goldberg creates are of lesser magnitude; as he taps out Morse code messages on Abramowitz's head, the horse can "feel the vibrations run through his bones to the tip of [his] tail." Bad tempered, vindictive, and dangerous may describe both Poseidon and Goldberg: as sea-ruler, Poseidon represents the might of the sea storm as well as its destructive power;[1] as trainer and master, Goldberg is moody and impatient with Abramowitz, wielding his cane like a "zing-zong of lightning," then later guiltily painting the horse's back to conceal the wounds.

Like the Greek god who sometimes behaves like man, Goldberg is a combination of human and divine aspects. Sometimes he is solicitous toward Abramowitz, caring about his physical welfare; just as often he curses him ("You bastard horse") and flays him viciously with his cane, displaying an arbitrary, omnipotent nature. Goldberg, godlike, "stares in awe at the universe on the [television] screen" and steadily refuses to accommodate complaints, pleas and protests. Clearly he has the power to solve Abramowitz's dilemma; Abramowitz pleads for identity as either a man or a horse: "It's in your power, Goldberg," yet Goldberg, who "has his mysteries" as does any other god, merely deflects the request: "You got the wrong party, my friend." Goldberg also omnisciently warns Abramowitz of the classical source of man's downfall: "Watch out for hubris, Abramowitz."

One of the most significant intimations of Poseidon in the character of Goldberg is his link with the horse. Poseidon, known as a god of horses (Hippios),[2] is generally credited with giving the horse to man. The father of horse-creatures, he begot the winged horse Pegasus upon the Gorgon and also took Demeter in the form of a horse since she had assumed the shape of a horse to avoid him.[3] Goldberg too is intimately associated with the horse-man Abramowitz; though he did not sire Abramowitz (although that would explain his man-horse being), his command of the horse's speech is reminiscent of creation: "TALK, he knocked on my head after he told me about the act. 'You're a talking horse.' 'Yes, Master.' What else can you say?" During a performance Goldberg beams at Abramowitz "as if he were his only child"; after the horse has butted his head in frustration against the stall gate, Goldberg bandages his nose and talks to him in "a fatherly fashion." Goldberg is indeed the vehicle by which the man emerges from the horse, the source of the centaur's being. Abramowitz holds on to Goldberg "for dear life," and in a scene replete with struggling, tugging and straining is reborn—at least partially.

Goldberg's role as creator of the centaur links him to the Judaic concept of God as creator, as do the motifs of father of the universe. Like God, Goldberg possesses the secrets of the universe—at least the ones that Abramowitz wants to know—and the power to reveal or conceal them. With "no visible friends," he is alone, as befits the concept of God. One of his favorite amusements is doing card tricks; this suggests his manipulative ability, another Godlike power. Goldberg illustrates deific vengeance when Abramowitz fails to obey his commands and tries to run away on the train. And Goldberg does not communicate in an ordinary fashion but speaks in elusive four-letter words—geee, gooo, gaaa—suggesting the unspoken name of God. He intones Biblical wording in response to Abramowitz's perennial question about his parentage: "In the beginning was the Word." Thus Goldberg embodies aspects of both Greek and Judaic systems of mythology.

Abramowitz also exemplifies the dual myth. He is a man in a horse's body. In classical mythology the horse, sacred to the sun, is associated with the "light" and the intellect.[4] Four horses draw the chariot of the sun, bearing Apollo across the sky. Because Apollo represents truth, light, and peace, Abramowitz's embodiment as a horse is appropriate to his quest for answers and his love for truth and freedom: "the true pain, at least to me, is when you don't know what you have to know." The unicorn introduces another horse motif; for performances Goldberg ties an upside-down feather duster on Abramowitz's head to create the illusion of a slightly wilted unicorn. The unicorn has traditionally symbolized purity, stength, and virtue—"The emblem of perfect good."[5] But the impostor unicorn, Ambramowitz, though obsessed with his search for truth, does not act consistently with the positive Apollo-unicorn concept of the horse. As his discontent increases, so does his derision; he disrupts the act and ridicules Goldberg increasingly. Twice he attacks his master: once in a flourish of anger during a performance and again as Goldberg stares at the television. At the end of the story Abramowitz becomes a centaur after an abortive attempt to emerge as a man. Mythological centaurs are the grandchildren of Apollo but have apparently failed to inherit any of his virtues (Chiron is an exception). Centaurs feed on meat and are brutal and lascivious creatures; obviously uncivilized, they are given to such amusements as rape and fighting.[6] Thus Abramowitz's transmutation to a centaur does not bode well.

Equally important in a consideration of "Talking House" is the tie between Abramowitz and Abraham, patriarch of Judaism. "Abraham," meaning "father of a multitude,"[7] is the name give to Abram after he accepts the covenant. Additional simiarities between Abramowitz and Abraham exist. Abraham questions God (Gen. 18:23–24) as Abramowitz persistently queries Goldberg, and Abraham laughs at God (Gen. 17:17) as Abramowitz snickers at Goldberg during performances, which to Abramowitz's mode of thinking are sacrificial acts. But Abraham represents . . . a beginning, the seed of a great nation, whereas Abramowitz is always searching for his beginnings: "Where did you get me, master? Did you buy me from somebody else? Maybe in some kind of auction?"

Goldberg and Abramowitz live in a world of freaks, an absurd world that Goldberg refuses to leave. He dresses as a clown in balloony red-and-white polka-dot suit, puts a feather duster on Abramowitz's head and performs in a dialogue of corny jokes via answer-question techniques. And the audience laughs. They laugh, paradoxically, not at the answers, but at the questions, which is the way Goldberg has it planned. The master is in control: "it's the only way he works. At the end of the story Abramowitz in an act of desperation attacks Goldberg but is not entirely successful in his attempt to escape his horse's body. Instead he becomes a free centaur, cantering toward the dark wood. Here the myth-on-myth becomes especially confusing. Does Malamud imply the dominance of the ethics of the centaur, a creature of dubious intentions, heading for the ominous dark woods? Or does he intimate the metaphor of the dutiful Abraham bearing the ark of the covenant toward the oaks of Mamre? Perhaps through the fusion of the myths, he indicates the futility of man's relationship with God; the prospect of man's fulfilling the covenant is a ludicrous one, especially since he lives in a dark world where the mores of the centaur prevail.

    1. Michael Grant and John Hazel, *Gods and Mortals in Classical Mythology* (Springfield, Mass.: G. and C. Merriam, 1973) 341.

    2. Grant and Hazel, 344.

    3. Grant and Hazel, 341.

    4. Elizabeth E. Goldsmith, *Life Symbols as Related to Sex Syumbolism* (New York: G. P. Putnam, 1924), 424.

5. Goldsmith, 441
6. Grant and Hazel, 107.
7. *The New Combined Bible Dictionary and Concordance* (Grand Rapids: Baker, 1961), 20.

Pictures of Malamud

*Philip Roth**

In the early fifties I was reading Malamud's stories, later collected in *The Magic Barrel*, as they appeared—the very moment they appeared— in *Partisan Review* and the old *Commentary*. He seemed to me then to be doing no less for his lonely Jews and their peculiarly immigrant, Jewish forms of failure—for those Malamudian men "who never stopped hurting"—than was Samuel Beckett, in his longer fiction, for misery-ridden Molloy and Malone. Both writers, while bound inextricably to the common life of the clan, severed their racial memories from the larger social and historical setting, and then, focusing as narrowly as they could upon the dismal, daily round of resistance borne by the most helpless of their *landsmen*, created, improbably, parables of frustration charged with the gravity of the grimmest philosophers.

Not unlike Beckett, Malamud wrote of a meager world of pain in a language all his own: in this case, an English that often appeared, even outside the idiosyncratic dialogue, to have in large part been clipped together from out of what one might have thought to be the least promising stockpile, most unmagical barrel, around—the locutions, inversions and diction of Jewish immigrant speech, a heap of broken verbal bones that looked, until he came along in those early stories to make them dance to his sad tune, to be no longer of use to anyone other than the Borscht Belt comic and the professional nostalgia-monger. Even when he pushed his parable prose to its limits, Malamud's metaphors retained a proverbial ring. In his most consciously original moments, when he sensed in his grimly-told, impassioned tales the need to sound his deepest note, he remained true to what seemed old and homely, matter-of-factly emitting the most touchingly unadorned poetry to

*Reprinted by permission from the *New York Times Book Review*, 20 April 1986, 1,40.

make things even sadder than they already were: "He tried to say some sweet thing but his tongue in his mouth hung in his mouth like dead fruit on a tree, and his heart was a black-painted window."

The forty-six-year-old man that I met at the Bakers' little house in Monmouth, Oregon in 1961 never let on that he could have written such a line, neither then nor in all the years I knew him. At first glance Bern looked to someone who'd grown up among such people like nothing so much as an insurance agent—he could have passed for a colleague of my father's, employed, as he was during the thirties and forties, by the downtown Newark district office of the Metropolitan Life. When Malamud entered the Bakers' hallway after having attended my lecture, and stood there on the welcome mat removing his wet overshoes, I saw a conscientious, courteous, pinochle-playing working man of the kind whose kibbitzing and conversation had been the background music of my childhood, a stubborn, seasoned, life insurance salesman who does not flee the snarling dog or alarm the children when he appears after dark at the top of the tenement stairwell—soberly reassuring in dark fedora and black overcoat, and carrying beneath his arm one of Metropolitan Life's large, black, oblong ledgers, the collection book which to me, as a boy, looked like a scaled-down portent of the coffin—to try to pry out of the poor breadwinner the half a buck that will prevent his policy from lapsing. He doesn't frighten anyone but he doesn't make the place light up with laughter either: he is, after all, the insurance man, whom you can only beat by dying.

That was the other surprise about Malamud. Very little laughter, no display at all of the playfulness that flickered on and off even in those barren, underheated, poorly furnished flats wherein were enacted the needs of his entombed, let alone of the eerie clowning that is the charm of *The Natural*. There were Malamud stories like "Angel Levine"—and later "The Jewbird" and "Talking Horse"—where the joke seemed only an inch away from the art, where the charm of the art was just the way it humorously hovered at the edge of the joke, and yet during all our meetings, over twenty-five years, I remember him telling me two jokes. Jewish dialect jokes, recounted very expertly indeed, but that was it—for twenty-five years two jokes were enough.

There was no need to overdo anything other than the responsibility to his art. Bern didn't exhibit himself and he didn't consider it necessary to exhibit his themes, certainly not casually to a stranger. He couldn't have exhibited himself even if he'd been foolish enough to try, and foolish enough he couldn't have been either—never being foolish was a small part of his larger burden. S. Levin, the Chaplin-esque professor of *A New Life*, teaching his first college class with a wide-open fly, is hilariously foolish time and again, but not Bern. No more could Kafka have become a cockroach than Malamud could have metamorphosed into a Levin, comically outfoxed by an erotic mishap on the dark backroads of mountainous Oregon, and sneaking home-wards, half-naked, at 3 A.M., the Sancho Panza beside him a sexually-disgruntled, bar-room waitress dressed in only one shoe and a bra. Seymour Levin the ex-drunkard and Gregor Samsa the bug ingeniously embody acts of colossal self-travesty, affording both authors a weirdly exhilarating sort of masochistic relief from the weight of sobriety and dignified inhibition that was plainly the cornerstone of their staid com-portment. With Malamud as with many writers, exuberant showman-ship, like searing self-mockery, was to be revealed only through what Heine called *Maskenfreiheit*, the freedom conferred by masks.

The sorrowing chronicler of human need clashing with human need, of need mercilessly resisted and abated glancingly if at all, of block-aded lives racked with need for the light, the life, of a little hope—"A child throwing a ball straight up saw a bit of pale sky"—preferred to present himself as someone whose needs were nobody's business but his own. Yet his was, in fact, a need so harsh that it makes one ache even now to consider the sheer size of it. It was the need to consider long and seriously every last demand of an overtaxed, overtaxing con-science torturously exacerbated by the pathos of human need un-abated. That was a theme of his he couldn't hide entirely from anyone who thought at all about where the man who could have passed himself off as your insurance agent was joined to the ferocious moralist of the claustrophobic stories about "things you can't get past." In *The Assis-tant*, the petty criminal and drifter Frank Alpine, while doing penance behind the counter of a failing grocery store that he'd once helped to rob, has "a terrifying insight" about himself: "that all the while he was acting like he wasn't, he was a man of strong morality." I wonder if early in adult life Bern didn't have an insight no less terrifying about himself—maybe more terrifying—that he was a man of stern morality who could act *only* like what he was.

Cynthia Ozick

Remembrances: Bernard Malamud

*Cynthia Ozick**

In 1976 I answered the telephone and heard privately an instantly recognizable public voice. I knew this voice with the intimacy of passionate reverence. I had listened to it in the auditorium of the 92nd Street
Y reading an as yet unpublished tale called "The Silver Crown," a story
so electrifying that I wished with all my heart it was mine. Since it was
not, I stole it. In my version, I described the author of the stolen story
as "very famous, so famous that it was startling to see he was a real
man. He wore a conventional suit and tie, a conventional haircut and
conventional eyeglasses. His whitening mustache made him look con-
ventionally distinguished. He was not at all as I had expected him to
be—small and astonished, like his heroes."

His voice on the telephone was also not what I had expected. Instead of bawling me out for usurping his story, he was calling with
something else in mind. He had noticed that the dedication to a collection containing the stolen story was to my daughter, who was then
ten years old. "Joy of my life," I had written. "I have to tell you," he
said, "that I understand just how you feel." And he spoke of his own
joy in being the father of his own children—but in such a way that it
was clear he understood love as something both particularized and ca-
pacious, belonging to everyone. The more you have it yourself, the
more you see it everywhere. A magic barrel. When after a while we
hung up, I recognized that I had been visited through this awkward
instrument by an angel. I had been blessed, anointed, by an illumination of generosity fetched up out of the marrow of human continuity.
Malamudian annunciations are not overly fussy, and are sometimes
willing to materialize as birds or talking horses or even on the
telephone.

After that, it became possible to say hello on occasion, face to face.
But I always found this difficult. His largeness afflicted my courage.
This, after all, was the very writer who had brought into being a new
American idiom of his own idiosyncratic invention; this was the writer
who had introduced the idea of blessing—virtue as insight, virtue as

*Reprinted by permission of the author from *Partisan Review* 53, no. 3 (1986):464–
66.

crucible—into the literature of a generation mainly sunk in aestheti-cism or nihilism or solipsism. The last time I saw him on a public platform—he was standing before the historic lectern at Cooper Union—he was reading from a work in progress, and since this was not so long ago, I imagine a grieving table upon which an unfinished chap-ter liturgically murmurs its loss. That meticulous and original hand will not come to it again.

The reading at Cooper Union: a straight back, a straightforward voice, tricky cadences hidden in it, an audience intensely alert to the significance of its own memory, taking in Presence and sending back the hunger of its homage. Afterward, there was, as always, the knot of admirers at his margins. But I fled him, afraid of so much light.

Consequently, I never learned, or dared, to say "Bern." So I settled on "Maestro," and it seemed just right, not merely because it reflected the stories with Italian landscapes but because he is, and always will be, one of our Masters.

Is he an American Master? Of course. He not only wrote in the American language, he augmented it with fresh plasticity, he shaped our English into startling new configurations. Is he a Jewish Master? Of course. Some people appear to be confused by why he resisted being called a Jewish writer. I think I have this figured out, and it may be simple enough. It troubled him, and he was right to be troubled, that the term *Jewish writer* sometimes carries with it the smudge of so-called ethnicity, a cataloguing of traits or vulnerabilities in place of meaning. *Jewish writer* is a usage that often enough smacks of parochi-alism. And when it is put to that purpose it is a plain lie. The Jewish spirit is the opposite of ethnicity or parochialism, and this cry out of Sinai is all over the Maestro's work. It is everywhere.

"The important thing," Morris Bober says to Frank Alpine, "is the Torah. This is the Law—a Jew must believe in the Law. . . . This means to do what is right, to be honest, to be good. This means to other people. Our life is hard enough. Why should we hurt somebody else? For everybody should be the best, not only for you and me. We ain't animals. This is why we need the Law. This is what a Jew be-lieves." Artists are never equivalent to their own characters, this goes without saying; but it is also true that to separate certain charactero-logical strains from the blood and lungs of their maker is to do violence to the force of authorial conscience. Morris Bober is the whole soul of Malamud's sacral knowledge; no one can gainsay that. And in his own language, in the preface of *The Stories of Bernard Malamud*, he wrote: "And let me say this. Literature, since it values man by describing him, tends toward morality in the same way that Robert Frost's poem is 'a momentary stay against confusion.' Art celebrates life and gives us our measure." So if this Maestro of humanity protested the phrase *Jewish writer*, it was the imputation of parochialism he was, with furious justice, repudiating. Whoever thinks of Jewish writers as "ethnic" has long ago lost the origin, intent, and meaning of our civilization; or, worse yet, believes that conscience and mercy are ethnic traits.

I danced with him once. We linked arms—wasn't this in Donald Barthelme's living room in the Village?—and twirled together. It was a wedding party, and the only music available was in the strong throat of the Israeli writer Matti Megged, who sang, in Yiddish, a song about a frolicsome rabbi with certain affinities to Old King Cole. The Rabbi Eli Melech calls for his fiddlers, his drummers, his cymbal-players; his phylacteries fly from him, his robes; he goes rollicking with the sexton, he cavorts, he carouses, he drinks! To this tune the Maestro and I danced, arm in arm, and will do it again, I trust, when the International PEN Congress meets at last in the Garden of Eden, in Paradise.

He wrote about suffering Jews, about poor Jews, about grocers and fixers and birds and horses and angels in Harlem and matchmakers and salesmen and rabbis and landlords and tenants and egg candlers and writers and chimpanzees; he wrote about the plenitude and unity of the world. And that is why, in his memory and for his sake, I want to recite the Shi'ma, which calls us to listen to the indivisible voice of Unity, of Allness—that Unity and Allness in whose image all mankind is made, well-worn words that are found on the living and dying lips of every Jew:

שמע ישראל יי אל׳הינו יי אחד

[Hear, O Israel, the Lord our God, the Lord is one]

—that comprehensive vision of mercy under whose wings we stand.

May the memory of this great and humane Master be blessed and forever green. As it will be, as long as there are readers.

Chronology

1914	Born 26 April at Williamsburg Hospital in Brooklyn, New York, to Max and Bertha Fidelman Malamud.
1928–1932	Student at Erasmus Hall High School, Brooklyn.
1929	Bertha Malamud dies.
1932–1936	Attends City College of New York; receives B.A. in 1936; starts graduate work at Columbia in the fall of 1936.
1934–1936	Forms and helps lead actors' group; works in hotels in the Catskills as waiter and entertainer.
1936–1939	Works in yarn factory and department stores; holds other temporary jobs.
1939–1940	Teacher in training at Lafayette High School in Brooklyn; tutors immigrants.
1940	Clerk for Census Bureau in Washington, D.C.
1940–1948	Teaches high school evening classes at Erasmus Hall High School.
1942	Receives M.A. from Columbia; thesis on Hardy's *The Dynasts*.
1943	First stories published in *Threshold* and *American Preface*.
1945	Marries Ann de Chiara 6 November. Moves to 1 King Street, Greenwich Village.
1947	Son, Paul, born.
1948–1949	Teaches high school evening classes in Harlem.
1949–1961	Teaches at Oregon State College, Corvallis.
1950	Stories appear in *Partisan Review, Harper's Bazaar, Commentary*.
1952	*The Natural*. Daughter, Janna, born.
1956–1957	Receives a *Partisan Review*-Rockefeller grant and a sabbatical leave; travels in Europe, lives in Rome.

Chronology

1957   *The Assistant.*

1958   *The Magic Barrel*; receives Rosenthal Foundation Award of the National Institute of Arts and Letters for *The Assistant.*

1959   *The Magic Barrel* wins the National Book Award; Ford Foundation Fellowship.

1961   *A New Life*; joins Division of Language and Literature, Bennington College, Bennington, Vermont.

1963   *Idiots First*; travels in England and Italy.

1964   Becomes member of American Academy, National Institute of Arts and Letters.

1965   Travels in France, Spain, Soviet Union.

1966   *The Fixer.*

1966–1968   Visiting lecturer at Harvard.

1967   Wins National Book Award and Pulitzer Prize for *The Fixer*; becomes member of the American Academy of Arts and Sciences.

1968   Visits Israel.

1969   *Pictures of Fidelman: An Exhibition.*

1971   *The Tenants.*

1973   *Rembrandt's Hat.*

1979   *Dubin's Lives.*

1979–1981   President, P.E.N.

1980   Becomes member of American Academy-Institute of Arts and Letters.

1982   *God's Grace*; undergoes heart bypass surgery, which precipitates stroke.

1983   *The Stories of Bernard Malamud*; receives American Academy-Institute Gold Medal for Fiction.

1986   Dies 18 March.

Bibliography

Primary Works

Short Story Collections

Idiots First. New York: Farrar, Straus & Giroux, 1963. Includes "Idiots First," "Black Is My Favorite Color," "Still Life," "The Death of Me," "A Choice of Profession," "Life Is Better Than Death," "The Jewbird," "Naked Nude," "The Cost of Living," "The Maid's Shoes," and "The German Refugee." The collection also includes "Suppose a Wedding," a scene from an uncompleted play.

The Magic Barrel. New York: Farrar, Straus & Cudahy, 1958. Includes "The First Seven Years," "The Mourners," "The Girl of My Dreams," "Angel Levine," "Behold the Key," "Take Pity," "The Prison," "The Lady of the Lake," "A Summer's Reading," "The Bill," "The Last Mohican," "The Loan," and "The Magic Barrel."

Pictures of Fidelman: An Exhibition. New York: Farrar, Straus & Giroux, 1969. Includes "The Last Mohican," "Still Life," "Naked Nude," "A Pimp's Revenge," "Pictures of the Artist," and "Glass Blower of Venice."

Rembrandt's Hat. New York: Farrar, Straus & Giroux, 1973. Includes "The Silver Crown," "Man in the Drawer," "The Letter," "In Retirement," "Rembrandt's Hat," "Notes from a Lady at a Dinner Party," "My Son the Murderer," and "Talking Horse."

The Stories of Bernard Malamud. New York: Farrar, Straus & Giroux, 1983. Includes "Take Pity," "The First Seven Years," "The Mourners," "Idiots First," "The Last Mohican," "Black Is My Favorite Color," "My Son the Murderer," "The German Refugee," "The Maid's Shoes," "The Magic Barrel," "The Jewbird," "The Letter," "In Retirement," "The Loan," "The Cost of Living," "Man in the Drawer," "The Death of Me," "The Bill," "God's Wrath," "Rembrandt's Hat," "Angel Levine," "Life Is Better Than Death," "The Model," "The Silver Crown," and "Talking Horse."

Uncollected Stories

"Alma Redeemed—a Story." *Commentary* 78, no. 1 (July 1984):30–34.
"An Apology." *Commentary* 12, no. 5 (November 1951):101–12.
"Benefit Performance." *Threshold* 3, no. 3 (February 1943):20–22.

Bibliography

"An Exorcism." *Harper's* 237, no. 1423 (December 1968):76–79.

"In Kew Gardens." *Partisan Review* no. 4 (1984) and no. 5 (1985):536–40.

"A Long Ticket for Isaac." In *Creative Writing and Rewriting: Contemporary American Novelists at Work*, edited by John Kuehl, 70–86 (even-numbered pages). New York: Meredith Publishing Co., Appleton-Century-Crofts, 1967. Early draft of "Idiots First."

"A Lost Grave." *Esquire* 103 (May 1985):204–5.

"The Place Is Different Now." *American Preface* 8, no. 3 (Spring 1943): 230–42.

"A Wig." *Atlantic* 245, no. 1 (January 1980):33–36.

Novels

The Assistant. New York: Farrar, Straus & Cudahy, 1957

Dubin's Lives. New York: Farrar, Straus & Giroux, 1979.

The Fixer. New York: Farrar, Straus & Giroux, 1966.

God's Grace. New York: Farrar, Straus & Giroux, 1982.

A New Life. New York: Farrar, Straus & Giroux, 1961.

The Natural. New York: Harcourt, Brace, 1952.

Pictures of Fidelman: An Exhibition. New York: Farrar, Straus & Giroux, 1969.

The Tenants. New York: Farrar, Straus, & Giroux, 1971.

Drama

"Suppose a Wedding," a scene from an uncompleted play, is included in *Idiots First.*

Nonfiction

Autobiographical essay in *World Authors, 1950–1970: A Companion Volume to Twentieth-Century Authors*, edited by John Wakeman, 917. New York: H. H. Wilson, 1975.

Letter to Whit Burnet in *This Is My Best in the Third Quarter of the Twentieth Century*, edited by Whit Burnet, 505. Garden City, N.Y.: Doubleday & Company, 1970.

Introduction to *The Short Stories of Bernard Malamud*, vii–xiii. New York: Farrar, Straus & Giroux, 1983.

"Living Is Guessing What Reality Is." *U.S. News and World Report*, 8 October 1979, 57

"Long Work, Short Life." *Michigan Quarterly Review* 26, no. 4 (Fall 1987):601–11

"Theme, Content and the 'New Novel.'" *New York Times Book Review*, 8 October 1967, 2, 29.

"The Writer's Task." In *Writing in America*, edited by John Fischer and Robert B. Silvers, 173. New Brunswick: Rutgers University Press, 1960.

Secondary Works

With its relative thoroughness, good introduction and indexing, and pointed summaries for each of the sources, Joel Salzberg's *Bernard Malamud: A Reference Guide* (Boston: G.K. Hall, 1985) is an invaluable starting point for research on Malamud's fiction. Richard O'Keefe's "Bibliographical Essay: Bernard Malamud" (*Studies in American Jewish Literature* 7, no. 2 [Fall 1988]: 240–50) bridges the bibliographical gap between 1983, Salzberg's terminus, and 1987. Below are listings and brief summaries of sixteen of the many critical efforts that illumine Malamud's short stories. The notes from part 1 also suggest a good many more helpful sources.

Alter, Robert. "Ordinary Anguish." *New York Times Book Review*, October 14, 1983, 1, 35, 36. A characteristically intelligent review of *The Stories*. Interesting arguments as to why Malamud's melancholy vision of existence is better suited for the short story than the novel and the ways in which his gift for fantasy and control of language transfigures the gloomy subjects.

Bilek, Dorothy S. *Immigrant Survivors: Post-Holocaust Consciousness in Recent Jewish-American Fiction*. Middletown, Conn.: Wesleyan University Press, 1981. Helpful background chapters on the most important twentieth-century American fiction that deals with Jewish immigrants. Good chapter on Malamud's use of immigrant situations and speech patterns.

Gealy, Marcia B. "Malamud's Short Stories: A Reshaping of Hasidic Tradition." *Judaism* 28, no. 1 (Winter 1979):51–61. Lucid discussion of Hasidic elements in "The Last Mohican," "The Magic Barrel," "Idiots First," "The Jewbird," and "The Silver Crown."

Hellerstein, Kathryn. "Yiddish Voices in American English." In *The State of the Language*, edited by Leonard Michaels and Christopher Ricks, Berkeley and Los Angeles: University of California Press, 1980. Helpful discussions of the workings and benefits of Yiddish in the works of a number of authors, Malamud among them. Interprets "Talking Horse" as an allegory of the Yiddish language imprisoned in English.

Helterman, Jeffery. *Understanding Bernard Malamud*. Columbia: University of South Carolina Press, 1985. The intelligent chapter on the stories emphasizes the ways in which Malamud's characters are driven by their dominant emotions (or inseparable emotional dualities) and the ways in which characters can only fulfill themselves through interactions with other humans.

Hershinow, Sheldon. *Bernard Malamud.* New York: Frederick Ungar Publishing Co., 1980. The fifteen-page chapter that confronts the short stories offers brief but intelligent comments on Malamud's dominant themes and shifting tones, particularly those that involve fantasy and the fictional achievement of the stories.

Howe, Irving. "The Stories of Bernard Malamud." In *Celebrations and Attacks: Thirty Years of Literary and Cultural Commentary,* New York: Horizon Press, 1979. A response to *The Magic Barrel,* emphasizing Malamud's innovative strategies in his representation of the immigrant world.

Pinsker, Sanford. *The Schlemiel as Metaphor: Studies in the Yiddish and American Jewish Novel.* Carbondale: Southern Illinois University Press, 1971. Although Pinsker's study deals with novels and not stories, he offers a great deal about modes of characterization that can be translated to many of the stories.

Richman, Sidney. *Bernard Malamud.* New York: Twayne Publishers, 1966. More than twenty years after its publication, the chapter on the stories collected in *The Magic Barrel* and *Idiots First* is still perhaps the single most helpful discussion of Malamud's shorter fiction.

Roth, Philip. "Imagining Jews." In *Reading Myself and Others,* 215–46. New York: Farrar, Straus & Giroux, 1976. A fascinating discussion of the image of the Jew in contemporary American fiction and of Malamud's stance toward "the characteristic connection . . . between the Jew and conscience, and the Gentile and appetite." Particularly provocative on *Pictures of Fidelman.*

Rovit, Earl H. "Bernard Malamud and the Jewish Literary Tradition." *Critique* 3, no. 2 (Winter–Spring 1960):3–10. Relatively brief but illuminating discussion of the ways Malamud compares and contrasts with some of the masters of Yiddish fiction.

Shechner, Mark. "Sad Music." *Partisan Review* 5 (1984):451–58. A review of *The Stories* emphasizing the pervasiveness of hopelessness and the number of stories that are "case studies of conscience gone haywire." Good comments on the sources of the appeal these stories have for the reader.

Scholes, Robert. "Portrait of the Artist as 'Escape-Goat.'" *Saturday Review,* 10 May 1969, 32–34. Blends an appreciative interpretation of *Pictures of Fidelman* as the making of an artist of life with a summary of Malamud's career in terms of his master theme of regeneration.

Warburton, Robert F. "Fantasy and the Fiction of Bernard Malamud." In *Imagination and the Spirit,* edited by Charles A. Huttar, Grand Rapids, Mich.: William B. Eerdmans Publishing Company, 1971. An ambitious attempt to lay out a taxonomy of the different kinds of fantasy Malamud employs and to place Malamud among such great fantasists of the past as Sterne and Gogol. Fine discussions of "Take Pity" and "The Jewbird."

Wegelin, Christof. "The American Schlemiel Abroad: Malamud's Italian Stories and the End of American Innocence." *Twentieth Century Literature* 19 (April 1973):77–88. Perceptive discussion of *Pictures* within the larger context of Americans' changing conceptions of their innocence vis-à-vis that of Europeans.

Wisse, Ruth R. *The Schlemiel as Modern Hero*. Chicago: University of Chicago Press, 1971. A fine study of the causes and workings of the schlemiel figure in Yiddish literature, and a discussion of the uses of the schlemiel in contemporary American fiction that includes consideration of *Pictures of Fidelman*.

Index

Index

The Author

Robert Solotaroff was educated at the University of Michigan and the University of Chicago. The author of *Down Mailer's Way* (University of Illinois Press, 1974), he is an associate professor in the Department of English at the University of Minnesota and lives in Minneapolis with his wife and daughter. He is currently at work on a book on the fiction of Robert Stone.

The Editor

General editor Gordon Weaver earned his B.A. in English at the University of Wisconsin-Milwaukee in 1961; his M.A. in English at the University of Illinois, where he studied as a Woodrow Wilson Fellow, in 1962; and his Ph.D. in English and creative writing at the University of Denver in 1970. He is the author of several novels, including *Count a Lonely Cadence, Give Him a Stone, Circling Byzantium*, and most recently *The Eight Corners of the World* (1988). Many of his numerous short stories are collected in *The Entombed Man of Thule, Such Waltzing Was Not Easy, Getting Serious, Morality Play*, and *A World Quite Round*. Recognition of his fiction includes the St. Lawrence Award for Fiction (1973), two National Endowment for the Arts Fellowships (1974, 1989), and the O. Henry First Prize (1979). He edited *The American Short Story, 1945–1980: A Critical History*. He is a professor of English at Oklahoma State University and serves an an adjunct member of the faculty of the Vermont College Master of Fine Arts in Writing Program. Married, and the father of three daughters, he lives in Stillwater, Oklahoma.